Revolutionary Detroit

Portraits in Political and Cultural Change, 1760-1805

Edited by

Denver Brunsman
Wayne State University

Joel Stone
Detroit Historical Society

DETROITHISTORICAL
S O C I E T Y
est. 1921

DETROITHISTORICAL
S O C I E T Y
est. 1921

Revolutionary Detroit: Portraits in Political and Cultural Change, 1760-1805

Published by the Detroit Historical Society, 5401 Woodward Avenue, Detroit, Michigan 48202.

Second printing, 2010.

Design, Cover – Uproar Communications
Compositor – Margaret Lin Chen
Typeface – Sabon and Univers
Printer – Compton Press Industries

ISBN 978-0-615-32114-1

Cataloging Information
Revolutionary Detroit: Portraits in Political and Cultural Change, 1760-1805
Edited by Denver Brunsman and Joel Stone; with a foreword by Brian Leigh Dunnigan.
Detroit, MI : Detroit Historical Society, 2009.
202 p. : ill. ; 21 cm.
Includes bibliographical references.
1. Detroit (Mich.) – History – Siege, 1763. 2. United States – History – Revolution, 1775-1783.
3. Pontiac's Conspiracy, 1763-1765. I. Detroit Historical Society. II. Brunsman, Denver. III.
Stone, Joel. IV. Dunnigan, Brian Leigh.
977.401–ddc22

www.detroithistorical.org

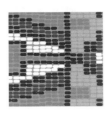

For the people of Detroit, past and present

CONTENTS

List of Illustrations iii
Abbreviations iv
Style v
Acknowledgments vi

Foreword 1
Brian Leigh Dunnigan

Introduction 3
Denver Brunsman

PART ONE
EARLY BRITISH DETROIT: TENUOUS RELATIONS

On Fragile Ground: Donald Campbell and the Question of 25
Amity in Early Detroit
Jeff Beauchamp

The Myth of the Maiden and Pontiac's Real Betrayer 29
Jerold Sommerville

Getting Away with Murder: Elizabeth Fisher, Alexis Cuillerier, 36
and the Cultural Complexities of Early Detroit
Steve Lyskawa

British Métis in Eighteenth-Century Detroit: The Askin and 42
Mitchell Families
Nicole Satrun

Robert and Elizabeth Rogers: The Dissolution of an Early 49
American Marriage
Ann Marie Wambeke

Belle Isle and Grosse Ile: The Islands In-Between 55
Cathryn Eccleston

The Potawatomi Indians of Detroit: Great Lakes Pioneers 59
Susan Ward

PART TWO
REVOLUTIONARY WAR: RAIDS AND COERCION

Liberty Hangs at Detroit: The Trial and Execution of 67
Jean Contencineau
Errin T. Stegich

Clark and Lernoult: Reduction by Expansion 73
Donald Lee

Little Navy on the Great Lakes   78
Stephen Al-Hakim

American Sympathy and Resistance in British Detroit   82
Alexandria Reid

Crawford's Defeat: Raids and Retaliation on the Frontier   86
John Maisner

Unfree Detroit: The Varied Experiences of American Prisoners   93
Caitlyn A.O. Perry

John Leeth: Neutral on the Run   98
Juliegha Norus

Caught in the Revolution: The Moravians in Detroit   102
Melissa R. Luberti

PART THREE
LATE BRITISH TO EARLY AMERICAN DETROIT: GRADUAL TRANSITION

The Courts of Hesse as a Middle Ground   109
Sharon Tevis Finch

Blue Jacket: Pan-Indian Leader, Warrior, and Cultural Mediator   117
Molon Rahman

Safe at Home: The French in Detroit   123
Leslie Riehl

From Detroit to Fort Malden: The Transfer of Sovereignty and Subjects   128
Mark A. Mallia

Meldrum & Park: Commerce, Society, and Loyalty in Frontier Detroit   133
Charles Wilson Goode

"Will Diligently and Faithfully Serve": Mr. Askin's Indentured Servants   141
Kimberly Steele

A Dollar Lost, a Life Taken: The Impact of Great Lakes Shipwrecks on Detroit   147
Jaclyn Kinney

Loyalty for Sale: British Detroiters and the New American Regime   152
Douglas D. Fisher

David Bacon: Detroit Meets America   158
Joshua Shelly

Selected Bibliography   163

ILLUSTRATIONS

Map of the United States and Canadian Provinces, 1783   viii

Plan of the Fort at Detroit, 1760   24

Unveiling the Conspiracy   30

Portraits of Elizabeth Browne Rogers and Robert Rogers   48

Portrait of Henry Hamilton   66

Plan of Detroit, 1796   72

Oliver Spencer Taken Prisoner   92

Assignment of first judges to the District of Hesse, 1788   108

A View of Detroit, 1794   122

Silhouette of John Askin   140

ABBREVIATIONS

BHC   Burton Historical Collection, Detroit Public Library

City of Detroit   Clarence M. Burton, *The City of Detroit, Michigan, 1701-1922*, 5 vols. (Detroit and Chicago: S.J. Clarke, 1922)

CL   William L. Clements Library, University of Michigan, Ann Arbor

Askin Papers   Milo Milton Quaife, ed., *The John Askin Papers*, 2 vols. (Detroit: Detroit Library Commission, 1928-31)

MPHC   *Michigan Pioneer and Historical Collection*, 40 vols. (Lansing: Michigan Historical Commission, 1877-1929)

WHC   *Collections of the State Historical Society of Wisconsin*, 31 vols. (Madison: State Historical Society of Wisconsin, 1854-1931)

STYLE

In most areas, this volume conforms to the *Chicago Manual of Style*. Quotations are rendered as faithfully to the original sources as possible, including capricious spellings and capitalizations. Although occasionally vexing, eighteenth-century language has a spirit and energy distinct from our own. The term *sic* has therefore been avoided. Instead, the editors have inserted brackets when an original term is unclear.

The book uses the terms Indian and Native American interchangeably, recognizing fully the fallacies of both terms. The best solution is to refer to native peoples by their specific tribal or village names, which the authors have tried to do whenever possible. For clarity and consistency, Ojibwa is used for Ojibwe, Ojibway, Chippewa, and Chippeway; Wyandot for Wendat and Huron; and Potawatomi for Pottawatomie and Pottawatomi.

The term slave is used throughout the volume to refer to any human being held as chattel, not a specific ethnic or racial group. Both African peoples and Native Americans, known as Panis (or Panise), were enslaved in early Detroit. Most historical records do not distinguish between the two groups. Small numbers of Africans also lived in the Great Lakes region as servants and free blacks.

Geographical and historic place names in Michigan, Ohio, and Ontario can be confusing. As such, the historical name is used whenever possible with parenthesis identifying its present-day equivalent. When historical and current names coincide, no parenthesis or explanation is given. The names "Mackinac" and "Michilimackinac," referring to the area at the Straits of Mackinac, which connect lakes Huron and Michigan and divide Michigan's upper and lower peninsulas, merit their own explanation. In 1760, the British assumed control, along with Fort Pontchartrain in Detroit, of the mainland French fort and trading post at Michilimackinac (today Mackinaw City, Michigan). The British kept the fort until 1781, when they moved to nearby Mackinac Island. Despite some attempts to call the new site Fort Mackinac, the term "Michilimackinac" persisted well into the American period after 1796. The essays in this volume follow the language of historical contemporaries, and use Michilimackinac to describe the fort and larger area throughout the period between 1760 and 1805. Fort Mackinac is used only in specific cases to refer to the military outpost on Mackinac Island after 1781.

ACKNOWLEDGMENTS

Volumes like this are the result of work by many people, this one perhaps more than most. The project, from conception to publication, took about twelve months. *Revolutionary Detroit* began as a history class at Wayne State University during the winter semester of 2009, developed into a public symposium at the Detroit Historical Museum in April 2009, and is now a book. Those who have been involved in similar efforts will recognize the amount of focus and dedication this represents.

The editors are deeply grateful to the people who have contributed so much to making this book a reality, starting with Community*Engagement*@Wayne, a program of the Irvin D. Reid Honors College at Wayne State University. Dr. Jerry Herron, dean of the college, and Dr. Elizabeth Barton, director of the program, supported and sponsored this project as a class, as a symposium, and finally as a publication. At the Detroit Historical Society, we gratefully acknowledge the Society's president and board chair, Francis W. McMillan II, for his encouragement as we proceeded with this new undertaking. Every department and much of the staff was also involved, first with the symposium and then with the publication effort. We thank, in particular, the Society's executive director, Robert A. Bury; chief operating officer, Michelle Wooddell; director of exhibitions and programs, Tracy Irwin; and director of marketing and sales, Peter Poulos. Their assistance was enthusiastic and professional in every way, and most appreciated. We also thank the Louisa St. Clair Chapter of the Daughters of the American Revolution and the John Paul Jones Society of the Children of the American Revolution for generously supporting the book and symposium. The Michigan Humanities Council, an affiliate of the National Endowment for the Humanities, also helped to make the symposium possible.

Professor Brunsman offers sincere appreciation to the Humanities Center at Wayne State University and the Eisenberg Institute for Historical Studies at the University of Michigan for providing the office and financial support necessary to complete the book. Without the History Department at Wayne State and its chair, Dr. Marc Kruman, this effort would never have been more than an enlightening class. Brian Leigh Dunnigan of the University of Michigan was encouraging from the outset, delivering the symposium's keynote address and giving extensive help with images for this book. His graceful Foreword that follows will help readers to develop a mental image of Detroit during the revolutionary era.

Special thanks to the authors and historians who served as panel chairs at the symposium and provided expertise as final text reviewers. They include

Dr. Charles K. Hyde of Wayne State University, Mike Smith of the Walter P. Reuther Library, Dr. Thomas A. Klug of Marygrove College, and Arthur M. Woodford of the Detroit Historical Society History Advisory Council. David J. Silverman of George Washington University and Kidada Williams and Danielle McGuire of Wayne State University also provided generous help in reviewing selected essays. Any errors that remain are the responsibility of the editors.

Advice and assistance came from many places. Jane Hoehner of Wayne State University Press provided invaluable direction to the project in its early stages. Heather B. Wendt and Margaret F. Booras of Uproar Communications did superb work facilitating the book's production. Dr. Gerald Dreslinski's generous scholarship fund for early American history at Wayne State University benefited several of the authors. Librarians and archivists across Michigan and Ontario were extremely helpful, especially those at the Burton Historical Collection of the Detroit Public Library; William L. Clements Library at the University of Michigan; Purdy/Kresge Library at Wayne State University; Grosse Pointe Historical Society; Grosse Ile Historical Society; Library of Michigan in Lansing; Clarke Historical Library at Central Michigan University; Leddy Library at the University of Windsor; Archives of Ontario in Toronto; Fort Malden National Historic Site of Canada in Amherstburg, Ontario; and Marsh Collection Society, also in Amherstburg. The Circa 1890 Saloon, with its friendly staff, served as the ideal "middle ground" between the university and museum for several editorial meetings.

Recognition is also extended to Professor Brunsman's students who contributed substantially to the overall success of the project. Brandon Davis, Paul Derochie, Dante De Benedictis, Patrick Duckett, Thomas Jankowski, Travis King, Thomas Latouf, Karrine Molek, Angella Smith, Andrew Opalewski, Michael O'Shea, Andrew Terrien, and Emeka Umachi all presented outstanding papers at the symposium. Steve Lyskawa, Susan Ward, Umadevi Ravishankar, Jerold Sommerville, John McKimmy, and particularly Douglas D. Fisher helped behind the scenes as project assistants. Doug was involved with the project from the beginning, and in addition to compiling the world's finest bibliography on Revolutionary Detroit, spent countless hours proofing the text.

Finally, the editors thank their families for their love and good humor. Without you, this book would still be trapped on a cocktail napkin.

FOREWORD

Visitors to Detroit in the years between 1760 and 1805 were invariably struck by the distinctive nature of the settlement. The place was located six hundred miles up the Great Lakes from Montreal and the farms of the St. Lawrence Valley, and even farther from the British seaboard colonies that became the United States in 1776. Other points of European colonial development along this chain of lakes— Oswegatchie, Oswego, Niagara, far-off Michilimackinac, and some smaller forts —were simply military or trading posts or clusters of warehouses to facilitate the movement of furs, goods, and military stores. Detroit was very different. It was a settled agricultural and commercial community with a long-established population and rudimentary public institutions. Detroit was a substantial colonial center that supported the Great Lakes fur trade, produced an agricultural surplus, and grew steadily throughout the period.

The appearance of the settlement, wrote one of its British governors, was "very smiling." As travelers ascended the Detroit River from Lake Erie, they were met with a peaceful scene of farms, agricultural buildings, fruit trees, pastures, and windmills. For a dozen miles below the town, farmhouses lined both banks, with their close spacing on narrow "ribbon" lots giving the visual impression of a "continuous village." The town itself was a large stockaded cluster of about one hundred substantial, wooden houses. Its military garrison occupied an impressive barracks complex and, after 1778, also had the advantage of a respectable fort. The town included a parish church, wharves, stores, warehouses, and even a shipyard. Above the town, the farms resumed and continued up to and along Lake St. Clair.

Detroit was a welcome sight to the traveler accustomed to a wilderness vista of lakes, forest, and the occasional military post or Indian village. Those who lingered discovered a cosmopolitan community composed largely of French-speaking inhabitants with a smattering of British merchants, a military garrison, and large numbers of Native Americans who visited from nearby villages. Detroit was a multi-faceted community that had been growing and changing since its establishment by the French in 1701.

The arrival of British authority in 1760 marks the beginning of the period this volume designates "Revolutionary Detroit," which would continue through the transfer of the place to American sovereignty in 1796, and until the eighteenth-century town was totally consumed by fire in June 1805. Town, fortifications, and agricultural areas were altered continuously throughout this time. Militarily and politically, Detroit was an important position in the British defense of the Great Lakes before and during the American Revolutionary War, and figured as a bulwark of British Canada during the Ohio Indian wars of the 1780s and 1790s.

Considering the rich variety of political, social, and commercial activity in this colonial metropolis set in the wilds of the Great Lakes, it is surprising and disappointing that eighteenth-century Detroit has attracted so little attention from historians. The city is, of course, much better known for its more recent social and industrial history. But the influential, early colonial settlement deep within the interior of the continent needs to be examined as well. It is encouraging that, in the years since the celebration of Detroit's tercentennial in 2001, a number of younger historians have begun to explore parts of the settlement's early history. One hopes that their work will result in some substantial new literature on the topic.

It is doubly encouraging to note the production of this volume of essays by Wayne State University students, who have had the unique opportunity, through an imaginative history course taught by Professor Denver Brunsman, to conduct original research and publicly present the results of their work on the people, issues, and events of Revolutionary Detroit. This was done first in April 2009 at a well-attended symposium at the Detroit Historical Museum that the students organized with curator Joel Stone and other museum staff members. The essays that follow are a selection from those presentations.

The diversity of topics hints at the riches that further study of early Detroit is liable to uncover. Roughly divided between the early British period, the years of the American Revolution, and late British/early American Detroit, the twenty-four essays range in subject matter from military and political history to biography, maritime activities, social history, Native Americans, and more. The enthusiasm of these young scholars for their topics and for their city bodes well for a continuing revival of interest in the study of colonial and early national Detroit.

Brian Leigh Dunnigan
Curator of Maps at the William L. Clements Library, University of Michigan, and author of *Frontier Metropolis: Picturing Early Detroit, 1701-1838*

INTRODUCTION

Denver Brunsman

Like so many things today, even those pertaining to eighteenth-century history, this book began with an email.

In the fall of 2008, Community*Engagement*@Wayne, a program of the Irvin D. Reid Honors College at Wayne State University, announced by email an open faculty competition for service-learning grants. The idea was that faculty members would design a service project for one of their classes in partnership with a local Detroit community organization. By definition, service-learning means more than doing typical community service tasks, such as serving food in a soup kitchen or building houses for the poor, although such activities are certainly a component. Rather, it connects service to rigorous academic study by engaging students in structured projects that benefit their community and produce deeper, longer-lasting comprehension than in usual classes. As someone with a passion for public service and creative forms of teaching, I was taken with the idea. Still, I did the same thing with Community*Engagement's* grant announcement that I do with all emails that seem too good to be true: I deleted it.[1]

The problem was that I was overly enamored by the prospect of a service-learning grant. I worried that my plan to use a grant to build awareness of Detroit's history during the American Revolution was too ambitious. With its founding by the French in 1701, Detroit has a colonial past that is underappreciated even though it rivals cities on America's eastern seaboard such as Boston, Philadelphia, and Charleston. A historian primarily of the eighteenth-century British Atlantic world, I peered like a tourist into Detroit's early history for several years, mainly by encouraging students to undertake various research projects. I knew just enough to realize that Detroit was one of the most fascinating places in North America during the revolutionary period; perhaps more than any other locale, it was where French, British, American, and Native American cultures collided and melded during the second half of the eighteenth century. The question was whether the students in my "Revolutionary America" class and I were up to the task of unraveling such a complex story in just one semester.

Fortunately, we could not have found a more ideal community partner than the Detroit Historical Society and its talented curator Joel Stone. Joel supported my successful grant application, and assured me that, yes, it was possible to develop a project to educate the public about Detroit's role in the American Revolution in a few months. With the guidance of Community*Engagement*, we developed a three-stage process that asked my undergraduate and graduate students to do nothing less than mirror the normal work cycle of professional historians: engage in original research, present their findings publicly, and publish their work for other scholars and the general public.

The first stage began during the cold months of the winter semester of 2009. Students spent several weeks exploring original primary documents from the late 1700s and early 1800s in the Burton Historical Collection of the Detroit Public Library and other regional archives, particularly the William L. Clements Library at the University of Michigan. Joel and I decided that appreciating Detroit's rich history during the Revolution required more than focusing on the strict dates of the war between 1775 and 1783. We defined "Revolutionary Detroit" as the period from 1760, when the British first took control of the Great Lakes region from the French, to 1805, when most of Detroit's original settlement burned and Congress granted Michigan status as a territory—the first step toward statehood. In roughly two generations, the people of Detroit experienced numerous revolutionary changes caused by the transfer of power from the French to the British to the Americans. My students each researched how these changes affected an individual, family, or other group, and, in turn, how Detroit's residents shaped the shifting world around them.

The "portraits" in the pages that follow provide a great service to the historical profession that extends beyond the Detroit community. More than once during this project, we encountered skepticism that the town's history during the late-eighteenth- and early-nineteenth centuries could be written because the 1805 fire destroyed so many records. Clarence Burton's magisterial five-volume *City of Detroit*, written in the 1920s, proved this notion to be false long ago. However, Burton's work, still the most complete history of early Detroit, has no citations. Any scholar interested in researching the revolutionary period has to begin with a limited blueprint of sources. The notes and bibliography in this volume seek to address this void by facilitating future research on early Detroit.[2]

The second stage of the Revolutionary Detroit project was a public symposium held at the Detroit Historical Museum on April 25, 2009. Detroit's free weekly newspaper, the *Metro Times*, unintentionally provided the best evidence of the city's need for the event. The newspaper's bold headline announcing the symposium stated "DETROIT VS. THE REDCOATS." The problem: Detroit was the redcoats! The town remained a loyalist British stronghold during the American Revolution—so loyal that the British kept control of Detroit until 1796, thirteen years after the war ended. The symposium's strong turnout of 124 people demonstrated a hunger to explore and discuss this and other unusual features of Detroit's early history.[3]

The symposium took place amidst historic events in our own time: an economic recession that gripped the nation and devastated Michigan's manufacturing economy. Just days after the symposium, one of Detroit's "Big Three" automakers, Chrysler, declared bankruptcy. Another, General Motors, soon followed. At the time, one might have assumed, based on national media reports, that Detroit's founding coincided with the birth of the Model T in the early twentieth century. The Revolutionary Detroit symposium offered a refuge from the daily onslaught of bad economic news and an opportunity to appreciate the wonder of the city's early history. Engaging presentations by thirty-three Wayne State University students, and spirited discussions led by local history experts, would have given even the most pessimistic critics of Detroit hope for its future.[4]

The essays in this book signify the third and final stage of the Revolutionary Detroit project. Each essay was first presented at the symposium in April 2009, or was written by a graduate assistant to the project. As a group, they employ a cultural historical approach pioneered for the Great Lakes region by scholars such as Richard White, James Axtell, and Susan Sleeper-Smith, but never used so directly for Detroit outside of Gregory Dowd's outstanding work on Pontiac's War. White's concept of the "middle ground" continues to dominate the historical literature on the colonial Great Lakes because no other idea so elegantly captures the constant cultural negotiation and compromise that took place between Europeans, particularly the French, and Native Americans in the region. The research in this book confirms White's findings, that a relatively low European population combined with a collaborative economic enterprise such as the fur trade, produced a colonial environment notable for its extensive cooperation between different cultural groups. Indeed, the essays in *Revolutionary Detroit* make a strong argument for extending the temporal bounds of the Great Lakes middle ground through the British period to 1796.[5]

The portraits also share a transnational perspective. Joel and I urged the authors, as they formulated their topics, to clear any notion of the modern U.S.-Canadian border from their minds. The Detroit River today separates Detroit from Windsor, Ontario, but for early Detroiters, the river was a highway, not a border. As the work of Alan Taylor, John Bukowczyk, and others has demonstrated, economic and cultural developments gave the Great Lakes region coherence independent of borders.[6]

Geography also remained a constant during the political instability of the revolutionary era. In 1701, the French colonial official Antoine Laumet de La Mothe, Sieur de Cadillac, founded Fort Pontchartrain, named for a French minister, on the Detroit River for its prime geographic location. *Le détroit* ("the strait") not only connects lakes Erie and Huron, but it also gave the French a link between the Great Lakes region and its empire to the east, based in the St. Lawrence River Valley. Detroit developed a symbiotic relationship with the French fur-trading post at Michilimackinac (today Mackinaw City, Michigan) and joined a transatlantic commercial network that extended to Montreal, Paris, and, eventually, London.[7]

During the eighteenth century, Detroit expanded into a sprawling, nearly borderless area. In 1760, when the British renamed the post Fort Detroit, it was much more than the original stockaded fort and town. French "ribbon" farms extended into the interior along both sides of the river. In 1749, Petite Côte (today parts of Windsor and LaSalle, Ontario) became the first European settlement on the south shore of the Detroit River—"Detroit's first suburb," in Brian Leigh Dunnigan's words.[8] It was not the last. During the American revolutionary era, "Detroit" referred to a vast area stretching southward to the suburbs of present-day Toledo, Ohio, along the Maumee River, and northward to the Saginaw Bay area. At different times during the period, greater Detroit included settlements at Frenchtown (Monroe, Michigan), Brownstown (at the mouth of the Detroit River), Spring Wells (today the site of Historic Fort Wayne in Detroit), Grosse Pointe (then also known as Grand Marais), the Huron River (the Clinton River), and St. Clair. Until 1796, Detroit also included large portions of what later became the Western District of Upper Canada (today southwestern Ontario), including settlements along the Thames River such as Moraviantown and Chatham. Detroit was a region long before it was a city.[9]

In addition to its vast beauty, visitors to the Detroit River region nearly always commented on its cultural diversity. In 1793, Joseph Moore, a Quaker traveling from Philadelphia, remarked, "The inhabitants of the town are as great a mixture, I think, as ever I knew in any one place. English, Scotch, Irish, Dutch, French, Americans from different states, with black and yellow, and seldom clear of Indians of different tribes in the daytime."[10] Indians were evident only in the daytime because of a curfew that barred them from inside the town's stockade after dark, a policy dating to Pontiac's siege of the fort in 1763.

Through the British period, Native Americans were the largest group in the Detroit area. They lived in villages outside the fort on both sides of the Detroit River. Groups of Wyandot and Ottawa may have occupied the region when Cadillac first arrived. Thousands more Indians from multiple tribes answered his invitation to settle near the fort. Eventually, Wyandots, Ottawas, and Potawatomis became the dominant Indian groups in Detroit, with Ojibwas from the north and Miamis from the south and members of numerous other tribes visiting regularly.[11]

Among Europeans, French *habitants* were the dominant population in Detroit until about 1820. The British takeover of the fort in 1760 left the French, like Native Americans, as a majority population living under an alien minority. Five years later, French settlers still accounted for about eight hundred of Detroit's total European population of approximately nine hundred. British migrants, particularly Scots-Irish (people mostly from what is today Northern Ireland) and Scots, increasingly settled in Detroit during the revolutionary era. By 1773, the area's non-Indian population had swelled to 1,367, including eighty-five slaves, ninety-three servants, and 120 soldiers of the 8th (King's) Regiment of Foot. The census in 1782 recorded the non-Indian population at 2,191, including soldiers, prisoners, and 179 slaves.[12] On July 11, 1796, when the Americans assumed control of Detroit, about five hundred people lived within the town's stockade with approximately 2,100 more on nearby farms; at least thirty-one slaves also lived in the area. The French still comprised about two-thirds of the European population; by this time, many lived in the settlement of Frenchtown along the River Raisin. Groups of Scots, Scots-Irish, English, Irish, German, and Dutch settlers also greeted the Americans in 1796.[13]

Detroit's slave population included both Panis Indians and people of African descent. Although most censuses taken during the revolutionary era included slaves, the numbers did not distinguish between the two groups. The French enslaved both African and Indian peoples at Detroit, but the majority were Indians. The earliest Panis in Detroit likely came from the western side of the Mississippi River; the French acquired them through trade with other Indian groups. "Panis" may have been a phonetic spelling of "Pawnee," a tribe from the west. Over time, the term came to include any Native American enslaved at Detroit, usually after being taken captive on Indian raids.[14]

Whereas enslaved Indians were a minority of the Native American population in early Detroit, enslaved Africans were a majority of the black population. The number of enslaved Africans expanded dramatically in the British period, particularly during the American Revolutionary War. Between 1773 and 1782, the total number of slaves more than doubled, from 85 to 179. The reason was twofold. First, British merchants and military officers flooding into Detroit had prior experience with African slaves and valued them for their labor and as tradable commodities. Second, raids from Detroit into the Ohio River Valley, particularly Kentucky, netted large numbers of African slaves. Without definite numbers, historians have relied on a combination of documentary evidence from raids and records left by slaveholders—including, in some cases, slave names—to determine that African slavery outpaced Indian slavery during the revolutionary era.[15]

American and British Canadian laws only gradually ended slavery in the Detroit River region. The Northwest Ordinance of 1787, which banned slavery in the areas that became the states of Ohio, Michigan, Indiana, Illinois, Wisconsin, and parts of Minnesota, was not initially recognized by the residents of British Detroit. After 1796, Jay's Treaty superseded the ordinance by protecting slavery that already existed in the former British territories handed over to the United States, including Detroit. In October 1807, Michigan Territory Chief Justice Augustus Woodward recognized Jay's Treaty when he ruled that "a right of property in the human species cannot exist in this Territory, excepting as to persons in the actual possession of British settlers within this Territory on the 11th June [July], 1796."[16] In 1793, the Legislative Assembly of Upper Canada passed a law that resembled gradual emancipation statutes in the northern United States. The law banned new cases of slavery, but it did not change the status of persons who were enslaved on or before May 31, 1793; children born to slave women after that date were limited to twenty-five years of enslavement. In practice, these American and British provisions meant that slavery did not fully disappear from the Detroit River region until the second quarter of the nineteenth century.[17]

The diverse people of Detroit lived under a dizzying number of political and administrative changes between 1760 and 1805. To make sense of the changes, we have divided the essays in the book into three parts: Part One: Early British Detroit; Part Two: Revolutionary War; and Part Three: Late British to Early American Detroit.

The essays in Part One explore the tensions created by the British takeover of Detroit in November 1760. Detroit was spared any battles during the French and Indian War (1754-1763), the North American component of the global Seven Years' War (1756-1763). The fort and settlement came under British control following French losses at Quebec City on September 13, 1759, and Montreal on September 8, 1760. After Montreal fell, France capitulated all its territory in the *pays d'en haut* (the "upper country"), land encompassing the present-day provinces of Quebec and Ontario; states of Michigan, Illinois, and Wisconsin; and parts of Ohio, Indiana, Missouri, and Minnesota. France may have lost but "a few acres of snow," as the *philosophe* Voltaire characterized New France, but for French *habitants* and their Native American allies, the transfer to British rule was traumatic. In late 1760, Detroit's native groups reminded their new British rulers that "this country was given by God to the Indians."[18]

Detroit was nominally part of the province of Quebec (today Quebec and Ontario), but the British governed it as an independent military garrison without formal attachment to any colony or civil administration. Jeff Beauchamp's essay shows that British military rule at Detroit began smoothly under the leadership of Captain Donald Campbell between 1760 and 1762. Campbell oversaw the British policy of allowing French settlers to retain possession of their lands and to continue practicing Catholicism in exchange for taking an oath of allegiance to George III. For Indians, he kept trade networks open, and treated native peoples with respect. In August 1762, General Jeffrey Amherst dramatically reversed course in Detroit by demoting Campbell in favor of Major Henry Gladwin, whose views aligned more closely with Amherst's—particularly on the issue of Indian gifts. Amherst viewed giving Native Americans goods, such as rum, metal wares, and textiles, to secure their loyalty and partnership in the fur trade as an insult to British power. What he misunderstood was that gift-giving was a key form of diplomacy and a foundation of the former French-Indian alliance in the Great Lakes region.

In the spring of 1763, the Ottawa leader Pontiac responded to British slights by forging a broad pan-Indian alliance to attack British forts in the northwest. Pontiac's War shocked the British. All thirteen British posts from present-day Wisconsin to New York fell except for Detroit, Pitt (also known from this period as Pittsburgh), and Niagara (today Youngstown, New York). Detroit would have almost certainly fallen if an unknown person had not tipped off Major Gladwin about Pontiac's planned surprise attack on May 7, 1763.[19] The essay by Jerold Sommerville brings together previously scattered evidence that points to the strong possibility that British merchant James Sterling was the informant, or was closely connected to Gladwin's source. The intelligence was crucial, for Pontiac and his allies were forced into a six-month siege of Detroit that ultimately failed and drained momentum from the larger Indian rebellion against British rule on the northwest frontier.

Pontiac's War helped set in motion the major events of the American Revolution. The original rationale for British taxes, such as the Stamp Act, was for American colonists to pay for their own defense against the remaining French and Indian threat after the Seven Years' War. When news of Pontiac's War reached London, it reinforced the British government's decision to leave soldiers stationed at its new western outposts gained from France. The Indian rebellion also expedited the issuing of the Proclamation of 1763, which organized governments in British Canada, Florida, and other conquered territories and barred settlement west of the Appalachian Mountains. The proclamation infuriated southern land speculators and surveyors, including George Washington, as much as the Stamp Act and later measures upset northern colonists.[20]

In Detroit, a period of relative calm followed the conclusion of Pontiac's War in 1765. Pontiac's alliance may have failed in its grandest ambitions, but it succeeded in others. The British reinstituted gift-giving and showed more outward forms of respect to Native Americans—in short, they acted like the French.[21] The contribution by Steve Lyskawa illustrates that the British had no interest in prosecuting crimes from Pontiac's War. In 1767, British authorities let the Frenchman Alexis Cuillerier go free rather than convict him for murdering a young girl during the opening days of Pontiac's siege. Cuillerier came from a prominent Detroit French family and had deep connections with local Indian groups. His case proved that, though defeated, the majority populations still held the balance of power in British Detroit.

Nicole Satrun's essay shows that leading British merchants, including John Askin, also embraced the French custom of marrying and cohabitating with Indian women. The marriages produced a class of métis children that was unusual in other areas of British North America. The British métis helped to mediate and maintain trade relations between Europeans and Indians in the Detroit River region into the nineteenth century. Not all frontier marriages were happy. Ann Marie Wambeke's essay provides a fascinating look into the private lives of Elizabeth and Robert Rogers, the British army officer who accepted control of Detroit from the French in 1760. Elizabeth, a native of New Hampshire, endured long absences and infidelity by her husband before securing a divorce in 1778.

By comparison, Detroit had only mild public controversies in the years before the Revolutionary War. In 1766, the British administration caused a brief firestorm by resurrecting an old French policy that forced residents to provide pickets for the stockade. Detroit's townspeople viewed the measure as a tax on top of their land rents and levies to pay for the garrison, but compromised in 1767 by agreeing to help install three hundred new pickets. Unpopular British policies such as the Stamp Act, Townshend Acts, and Tea Act did not apply to Detroit because of its official status as a military garrison. The Quebec Act of 1774 changed the fort's status by annexing it to the province of Quebec in April 1775. The act was deeply unpopular with American patriots for establishing a policy of toleration for the Catholic faith and recognition of French civil law in Quebec. But most Detroiters, particularly the French majority, welcomed the Quebec Act's forceful reiteration of religious and civil liberties that they had enjoyed since 1760.[22]

The final essays in Part One, by Cathryn Eccleston and Susan Ward, provide broad overviews of the revolutionary changes that shaped Detroit after the British takeover of 1760. Each essay views the transfer from French to British to American control from particular vantages: in Eccleston's case, Belle Isle and Grosse Ile, and in Ward's case, the Potawatomi Indians. Belle Isle and Grosse Ile were microcosms of Detroit. The islands shifted from sites of French imperial ambition to public commons and Indian lands to private ownership by the British merchants and brothers William and Alexander Macomb. The Potawatomi Indians were the last Indian group to hold title to Grosse Ile before selling it to the Macombs on July 6, 1776. The timing proved ironic, for during the American revolutionary era, the Detroit Potawatomis lost most of their land and independence. No group in Detroit faced more daunting challenges after 1760 than its Indian population.

The essays in Part Two demonstrate that during the Revolutionary War, trends in Detroit continued to be the inverse of those on the eastern seaboard. The war left the town more, not less, British. In 1768, Britain redeployed the majority of its troops from western forts to quell resistance in eastern cities, particularly Boston. The move helped to fulfill Benjamin Franklin's famous warning that "they [the British military] will not find a rebellion; they may indeed make one."[23] The army had the opposite affect in Detroit. The fort was one of just three western posts that Britain deemed too valuable to abandon. In addition to fur trade revenues, Detroit's large French and Indian population was still considered too much of a threat to leave unguarded. The British also kept soldiers stationed at Fort Michilimackinac to secure the fur trade and at Fort Niagara because of its strategic importance at the mouth of the Niagara River on Lake Ontario. During the war, Detroit also served as the western headquarters of the British Indian Department. Indian agents helped to keep the region's Native Americans loyal to the British. In tandem, Britain's strong military presence and careful Indian diplomacy helped to prevent a repeat of Pontiac's War or the revolutionary fervor that engulfed the eastern seaboard in the 1770s.[24]

Detroit's greatest civil disturbance during the Revolutionary War did not take place because of its military administration but as a result of its first civil government under the British. The Quebec Act of 1774, in addition to permitting Catholic religion and French law in Quebec, provided for a handful of lieutenant governors, vested with civil authority, to help govern the province's expanded territory in areas such as Detroit.[25] As Errin Stegich vividly describes, Detroit's first lieutenant governor, Henry Hamilton, faced public opposition to his administration of justice. Hamilton allowed Justice of the Peace Philip Dejean to continue exercising the powers of a judge rather than sending court cases to Montreal, as the lieutenant governor had been instructed. Controversy erupted after a trial in the spring of 1776 that convicted a Frenchman, Jean Baptiste Contencineau, and a female slave, Ann Wiley, of larceny. Dejean ordered the pair to be hanged. When he could find no one to carry out the execution, he offered Wiley a bargain: her life in exchange for executing her accomplice. She accepted, prompting a group of Detroit townspeople to protest the harsh justice to Quebec Governor Guy Carleton. A grand jury ultimately issued a nine-page indictment against Hamilton and Dejean, but London officials never pursued the case.

By 1777, Hamilton also became deeply unpopular with Americans. Beginning that year, remembered as the "Bloody Sevens," dozens of joint British and Indian war parties left from Detroit and terrorized American frontier settlements, particularly in Ohio Country and Kentucky. Hamilton developed a reputation as "Hamilton the Hair-Buyer" because it was said that he paid Indian warriors for scalps. No existing evidence supports the charge; Hamilton actually cautioned departing raiders to not hurt women and children. Regardless, United States General George Washington worried enough about the raids to encourage Congress and his officers on repeated occasions to make plans for capturing Detroit. In early 1778, Virginia Governor Patrick Henry came closest to fulfilling the general's wishes by approving a scheme by George Rogers Clark, a colonel in the state's militia, to capture British posts in Illinois Country in preparation for taking Detroit.[26]

Donald Lee's essay explores Clark's enormous influence on Detroit. The colonel's threat from the west, combined with the approach of other American forces from the east, struck fear in the British command. In late 1778 and early 1779, the fort's acting commandant, Captain Richard Lernoult, oversaw a massive operation to relocate the post's main fort from the north shore of the Detroit River to higher ground (the present-day intersection of Fort and Shelby Streets in downtown Detroit). Named Fort Lernoult in honor of the British commandant, it was completed in the spring of 1779. Clark never came. But, as Lee argues, the effort required to build the new fort helped to distract the British from mounting campaigns from Detroit on major American targets, such as Fort Pitt.

The army garrison was not Britain's only military force stationed at Detroit. Scholars have neglected the role played by the British Royal Navy in keeping Detroit and other Great Lakes posts loyal during the Revolution. The essay by Stephen Al-Hakim makes an important contribution by detailing the activities of the navy's Upper Great Lakes Fleet, commanded from Detroit. The fleet established a monopoly over all ships on Lake Erie and the three uppermost Great Lakes. British control of the lakes not only prevented possible American attacks, but also provided the logistical support to help protect Britain's dominance of the fur trade.

The navy also played an important role in suppressing dissent at a time when most people traveled to and from Detroit by boat. Alexandria Reid's essay shows that against steep odds, a small number of American sympathizers inhabited Detroit. She argues convincingly that issues more immediate than republican ideology or American independence united them: opportunism and disgust at the British and Indian frontier alliance. Raids especially offended the sensibilities of American supporters in Detroit. John Maisner profiles one of Detroit's most successful raids, called alternately Crawford's Defeat and the Battle of Sandusky. In June 1782, British Captain William Caldwell led a company of mounted Butler's Rangers and a party of

Indians to intercept American militia near the Sandusky River in Ohio Country. The ensuing battle ended in the brutal mutilation of American Colonel William Crawford. The action cemented Detroit's reputation as the center of savagery on the frontier.

Raids also had a major impact on the size and composition of Detroit's population. As mentioned, they were a major reason that the town's slave population more than doubled during the war. But slaves were not the only people who lived in a condition of bondage in Detroit. Captives taken by British and Indian war parties also swelled the town's prisoner population. The 1779 census counted about five hundred prisoners in Detroit, nearly all captured on raids in the previous two years.[27] In her essay, Caitlyn Perry provides an insightful comparison between Detroit and better known British prison sites. Contrary to protocol elsewhere, Detroit's remote location meant that American prisoners were not regularly exchanged for British combatants in American jails. Instead, the British evaluated prisoners for their potential use to their cause, particularly as traders with Indians. The practice resulted in a system of unequal justice whereby well-known frontiersman such as Daniel Boone and Jean Baptiste Pointe du Sable, today recognized as the founders of Kentucky and Chicago, respectively, received light sentences. Boone spent just ten days in captivity in Detroit, and du Sable was allowed to pursue his normal commercial activities while still technically a prisoner.

Juliegha Norus provides a portrait of a less fortunate prisoner, John Leeth. Leeth attempted to stay neutral during the war, but landed as a prisoner in Detroit in 1776. Lieutenant Governor Hamilton mistreated him before trying to take advantage of Leeth's Indian language skills. With great difficulty, Leeth escaped his bondage in Detroit in 1777. The Moravians, the subject of Melissa Luberti's essay, were also initially captives in Detroit. The British suspected the German Protestant sect of supporting the American cause from their village of Gnadenhütten in Ohio Country (today Gnadenhutten, Ohio). In the spring of 1782, Major Arent De Peyster, commandant of Fort Detroit, ordered Moravian leaders to stand trial. Acquitted, they returned home to Gnadenhütten to discover that ninety-six of their Delaware Indian followers had been massacred by American militiamen from nearby Fort Pitt. Later that summer, the British, still suspicious of the group, ordered the Moravians to return to Detroit. The group built a community on the present-day Clinton River, where they stayed until the spring of 1786. Perhaps the most telling sign of Detroit's British loyalty during the American Revolution was that its strongest concentration of American supporters was its prison population.

The essays in Part Three detail the unusual way that Detroit ended the American revolutionary era. By the Treaty of Paris of 1783, the post should have joined the former American colonies on the eastern seaboard in the United States. The treaty determined that the international border between British Canada and the U.S. would follow the middle of the Great Lakes. All British posts on the lakes, with the exception of Fort Erie, fell on the American side. Wrestling the northwest frontier from the British was a diplomatic coup for the U.S. negotiating team of Benjamin Franklin, John Adams, and John Jay. The treaty did not reflect reality on the ground, for little of present-day Indiana and Illinois and none of Wisconsin and Michigan had been won by the Americans. Ohio Country, as it had been since the French and Indian War, was a contested battleground.[28]

By the end of 1783, British policy was to continue holding the Great Lakes forts, most notably Detroit, Michilimackinac, and Niagara, indefinitely. Britain never claimed outright possession of the posts. After the Treaty of Paris, all maps printed in England and the United States clearly identified Detroit as American real estate (for example, see the 1783 map printed in London at the beginning of this volume). Officially, the British continued to govern the northwest forts because the United States had not upheld its treaty obligation to compensate British loyalists for losses suffered during the war. The British also wanted to keep the posts for economic and geopolitical reasons: The fur trade still produced revenue, and it was always possible that the new American republican experiment would fail. The United States did nothing to discourage British logic. Its national government was too weak to force individual states to pay the loyalists or to expel the British from the northwest.[29]

During this limbo period, the Americans and British both created political jurisdictions that incorporated Detroit. As of 1787, the post fell within the Northwest Territory of the United States, although the town did not play an active role in territorial government until after the American takeover of 1796. For the British, Detroit was still governed as part of Quebec after the American Revolutionary War. The entire Detroit River region became more Anglicized during the 1780s and early 1790s, when thousands of "late loyalists" flooded into British Canada from the United States with promises of free or nearly free land and low taxes. Detroit's loyalist population could not help but expand during the migration.[30]

In 1788, Quebec Governor Guy Carleton (also known as Lord Dorchester after 1786) created four new administrative districts stretching across what is now Ontario. Detroit belonged to the largest, Hesse, which included lands beyond the uppermost Great Lakes. As the district's only population center, Detroit received a Court of Common Pleas—its first formal court in nearly three decades under British rule. The British were careful, however, to place the court on the south shore of the Detroit River in what became Sandwich (today Windsor, Ontario).[31]

More changes soon followed. The Constitutional Act of 1791 (also known as the Canada Act) created Upper Canada (today Ontario) and Lower Canada (today

Quebec) out of the former province of Quebec. Detroit fell under the jurisdiction of Upper Canada. The next year, the old districts were renamed, and Hesse became the Western District. Upper Canada also divided into nineteen counties. Geographically, Detroit was connected to Essex County, but for election purposes it was considered part of Kent. In 1792, longtime Detroit area residents William Macomb and Francois Baby were elected from Kent in Upper Canada's first parliamentary election.[32]

Sharon Tevis Finch's essay on the courts of Hesse puts a human face on these British institutions and helps to explain why Detroiters embraced British rule after 1783. In a word, it worked. Using White's concept of the middle ground, Finch demonstrates, through well-chosen case studies, that the courts of the District of Hesse not only brought civil legal order to Detroit and Michilimackinac, but also provided for surprisingly equal justice under the law for Native Americans and Europeans. Molon Rahman's portrait of the Shawnee leader Blue Jacket further shows how the British maintained an alliance with Indian groups after the Revolutionary War. Detroit remained the western base of the British Indian Department and outfitted Indians with guns and supplies, with which they wreaked havoc on American settlements on the Ohio frontier. With British support, leaders such as Blue Jacket and the Miami chief Little Turtle forged a pan-Indian alliance in the tradition of Pontiac. The confederated Indians of the Great Lakes region and Ohio River Valley scored stunning victories over the U.S. military in 1790 and 1791.

The battles were part of a larger conflict that historians now refer to as the Northwest Indian War or Ohio War. Following the 1791 defeat, President George Washington put General "Mad" Anthony Wayne, his trusted friend and fellow officer from the Revolutionary War, in charge of training and commanding the American army for a final showdown with the confederated Indians. After nearly two years of preparing and drilling his legion of more than two thousand men, Wayne defeated the Indians in about an hour at the Battle of Fallen Timbers on August 20, 1794. Rather than fight the superior force, most Indian warriors sought refuge with the British at nearby Fort Miami (today Maumee, Ohio). The British, trying to avoid a direct engagement with American forces, locked the fort's gates. Without British support, Native Americans had little choice but to surrender nearly all their land in Ohio Country to the United States in the Treaty of Greenville in 1795.[33]

The United States also tried to resolve a host of outstanding commercial and boundary disputes through diplomacy with Britain. In London, news of Wayne's victory gave U.S. diplomat John Jay the leverage he needed to convince the British to evacuate America's Great Lakes posts. Jay's Treaty, as it became known, was signed in November 1794 and ratified by the Senate in the summer of 1795. The treaty led directly to the British handover of Detroit to the U.S. Army on July 11, 1796.

However, the legacy of a combined ninety-five years of first French and then British rule did not disappear quickly. Upon the American arrival, the Detroit area still had a sizeable French majority and an influential British minority. By Article II of Jay's Treaty, inhabitants of Detroit who wished to remain British subjects could make a formal declaration of their intentions within a year after the fort's transfer, and stay in the United States indefinitely. More than one hundred residents declared for Britain. Most prominently, Commodore Alexander Grant commanded the Royal Navy's fleet on the upper Great Lakes from his home in Grosse Pointe—on American soil—until his death in 1813. In Detroit's first years under U.S. control, the group most conspicuously absent in any large numbers was American citizens.[34]

The trio of essays by Leslie Riehl, Mark Mallia, and Charles Goode examine the influence of the 1796 transfer on migration patterns in the Detroit River region. The strait that had always linked land and people now separated the area for the first time. Riehl focuses on Detroit's French majority, a group difficult to study because of few surviving original sources. She shrewdly compensates by using census records and town plots in Detroit and the newly named community of Sandwich on the south shore to discern that, more than any other group, the French stayed at home. Only thirty joined the list to be British subjects. The inhabitants on the north side of the river remained relatively fixed. French residents who lived on the south side also stayed, giving early Sandwich and the community of Petite Côte an unmistakable French character.

Mallia profiles the initial migration from Detroit to Fort Malden and the community of Amherstburg at the mouth of the Detroit River in 1796. He finds that the new British settlement attempted, in essence, to recreate Detroit's function as a site for monitoring shipping on Lake Erie and the upper Great Lakes, for conducting trade with Indians, and for garrisoning soldiers in the Detroit River region. Most early migrants to Malden and Amherstburg had some connection to one of these three pursuits. Goode's essay illustrates the impact of the new border on Meldrum & Park, one of Detroit's most successful trading firms. Its proprietors, George Meldrum and William Park, each chose initially to remain British subjects, but they ultimately went separate ways: Park moved across the Detroit River to Petite Côte in the spring of 1798, and Meldrum, who never left the United States, died an American citizen in 1817.

The essays by Kimberly Steele and Jaclyn Kinney highlight two features of daily life in late British and early American Detroit: indentured servitude and shipwrecks, respectively. Steele's group portrait of John Askin's indentured servants suggests that the institution on the frontier, at least as practiced by Askin, more closely resembled today's internships than a precursor to slavery as it was in the early American colonies. Askin needed assistance with his sprawling business affairs, and his servants enjoyed the freedom to engage in private land speculation and other ventures while they lived under his control. Kinney's essay also features Askin in its larger survey of Great Lakes shipwrecks during and after the American Revolution. Far from an aberration, shipwrecks were a frequent occurrence that influenced economic decisions and caused great personal tragedy in the Great Lakes region. In 1798 alone, Askin lost two of his three ships.

Detroit's American administration evolved slowly. In 1796, following the transfer of authority, Wayne County was carved out of the Northwest Territory. The county included the lower peninsula of present-day Michigan, part of the upper peninsula, and parts of present-day Ohio, Wisconsin, Illinois, and Indiana. Detroit received its first American courts and government officials within the county's jurisdiction. In 1802, Detroit was incorporated as a town that was governed by a local board of trustees. Two of the first trustees elected were British subjects, including John Askin. That year, a loyalty oath administered by the newly organized town finally forced out Askin and several other British loyalists, but not many French residents Taking loyalty oaths had become routine for Detroit's French population by this time. In 1803, Detroit became part of Indiana Territory after Ohio was admitted as a state to the Union. In the fall of 1804, Detroiters petitioned Congress to form another separate territory out of Wayne County. The petition was successful, and on July 1, 1805, Indiana Territory was divided into the territories of Indiana and Michigan.[35]

The final essays in the volume, by Douglas Fisher and Joshua Shelly, give a flavor for early American Detroit. Fisher explores why so many declared British subjects, including much of Detroit's merchant class, never left the United States. In a trenchant analysis, which echoes Alexandria Reid's findings, he concludes that political values had little to do with decisions of national loyalty on the frontier. "Land-jobbers," as speculators were known, cared most about getting ahead. In Fisher's words, their loyalty was "for sale." Shelly's essay depicts a similar lack of conviction in early national Detroit. He examines religion through the eyes of the Connecticut Congregationalist missionary David Bacon. Between 1800 and 1802, Bacon established missions in Detroit and on Mackinac Island. After much optimism and some early success, Bacon became frustrated with the region's multiple Indian dialects and disillusioned with its residual Catholicism and religious indifference. His experiences showed that by the early nineteenth century, Detroit may have been under American control, but it was unlike anywhere else in the United States. Detroit was still a middle ground.

If frontier Detroit had many differences with nineteenth-century America, it feels remarkably current in the twenty-first century. The remote outpost was an early globalized society. Revolutionary Detroit was a place where everyday financial transactions took place in French, British, and American currencies, family members wrote to one another separately in English and French, and trials produced court documents in the language most relevant for particular cases. It was where Indians mixed with Europeans, the French mixed with the British, and they all mixed with the Americans. It was where a French majority lived under British and American rule, Britons lived as British subjects on U.S. soil, and Americans were enormously outnumbered. It was where indentured servants ran up enormous bar tabs, Protestant missionaries ran away in horror, and the Protestant British government subsidized an Irish-born Catholic priest to tend to the region's faithful and—just as often—faithless. Finally, it was where an American administration felt compelled to institute a loyalty oath more than a quarter-century after the *Declaration of Independence.*

As community service-learning, this volume aspires to advance Detroit's future by sharing the experiences of its improbable revolutionary past. The essays that follow were written during some of the worst economic conditions imaginable; at publication time, Detroit's official unemployment rate hovered near 30 percent. The past cannot provide exact solutions to the city's entrenched problems. Detroit will not reverse its fortunes by returning to the fur trade, after all. But history can give the perspective and confidence to imagine different and better outcomes for the city. The portraits here remind us that centuries ago, competing powers prized Detroit for its strategic alliances and natural features. Impressive resources still grace the Detroit River region. Most important, the following pages introduce us to the people of Revolutionary Detroit, who continually responded to the crisis and uncertainty of their times by making a virtue of cultural difference. We live in the world that they created.

NOTES

1 For service-learning, see Timothy K. Stanton, "Service-Learning: Groping Toward a Definition," in *Combining Service and Learning: A Resource Book for Community and Public Service*, ed. Jane C. Kendall et al., 3 vols. (Raleigh: National Society for Internships and Experiential Education, 1990-2000), 1:65-68; The National Service-Learning Clearinghouse, *Defining Service-Learning* (Scotts Valley, CA: NSLC, 1994); Timothy K. Stanton, Dwight E. Giles Jr., and Nadinne I. Cruz, *Service-Learning: A Movement's Pioneers Reflect on its Origins, Practice, and Future* (San Francisco: Jossey-Bass, 1999); Anne Colby et al., *Educating Citizens: Preparing America's Undergraduates for Lives of Moral and Civic Responsibility* (San Francisco: Jossey-Bass, 2003); and the articles in the *Michigan Journal of Community Service Learning*. For history and service-learning, see Ira Harkavy and Bill M. Donovan, eds., *Connecting Past and Present: Concepts and Models for Service-Learning in History* (Washington: American Association for Higher Education, 2000). See also Ken Bain, *What the Best College Teachers Do* (Cambridge: Harvard University Press, 2004), for the benefits of goal-oriented projects in the college classroom.

2 Although no work matches the detail of *City of Detroit*, several studies have made important contributions to understanding Detroit's history during the revolutionary era. Philip P. Mason, *Detroit, Fort Lernoult, and the American Revolution* (Detroit: Wayne State University Press, 1964), has long been the leading scholarly work on the subject. Brian Leigh Dunnigan, *Frontier Metropolis: Picturing Early Detroit, 1701-1838* (Detroit: Wayne State University Press, 2001), is an incomparable visual history of early Detroit with equally enlightening text and citations. Two other monographs published for Detroit's tercentennial anniversary are also useful resources: Arthur M. Woodford, *This is Detroit, 1701-2001* (Detroit: Wayne State University Press, 2001), and David Lee Poremba, ed., *Detroit in its World Setting: A Three-Hundred Year Chronology, 1701-2001* (Detroit: Wayne State University Press, 2001). Several other recent works make reference to Detroit within larger histories of the frontier during the American Revolution, including Colin G. Calloway, *The American Revolution in Indian Country: Crisis and Diversity in Native American Communities* (New York: Cambridge University Press, 1995); Patrick Griffin, *American Leviathan: Empire, Nation, and Revolutionary Frontier* (New York: Hill and Wang, 2007); and Walter Scott Dunn, *Choosing Sides on the Frontier in the American Revolution* (Westport, CT: Praeger, 2007). For Detroit's transition to American control, Frederick Clever Bald, *Detroit's First American Decade, 1796-1805* (Ann Arbor: University of Michigan Press, 1948), remains the strongest study. The printed primary documents in *MPHC*, *Askin Papers*, and Ernest J. Lajeunesse, ed. *The Windsor Border Region, Canada's Southernmost Frontier; a Collection of Documents* (Toronto: Champlain Society, 1960), are also indispensable for understanding British and early American Detroit.

3 Megan O'Neil, ed., "Night and Day," *Metro Times* (Detroit), April 22, 2009, 113.

4 For Detroit's social climate in the period surrounding the symposium, see Mitch Albom, "The Courage of Detroit," *Sports Illustrated*, January 12, 2009, 56-62; Paul Clemens, "Lean Tuesday," *New York Times Magazine*, March 29, 2009, 62; and Rochelle Riley, "To Detroit: Never, Never Give Up!," *Detroit Free Press*, April 28, 2009, A2. For an overview of the historical literature on Detroit's longer decline, see Kevin Boyle, "The Ruins of Detroit: Exploring the Urban Crisis in the Motor City," *Michigan Historical Review* 27 (2001): 109-27.

5 Richard White, *The Middle Ground: Indians, Empires, and Republics in the Great Lakes Region, 1650-1815* (New York: Cambridge University Press, 1991); James Axtell, *The Invasion Within: The Contest of Cultures in Colonial North America* (New York: Oxford University Press, 1985); Susan Sleeper-Smith, *Indian Women and French Men: Rethinking Cultural Encounter in the Western Great Lakes* (Amherst: University of Massachusetts Press, 2001); Gregory Evans Dowd, *War under Heaven: Pontiac, the Indian Nations, and the British Empire* (Baltimore: Johns Hopkins University Press, 2002). For analysis of the impact of White's *Middle Ground* upon the twenty-fifth anniversary of its release, see Susan Sleeper-Smith, ed., "Forum: The Middle Ground Revisited," *William and Mary Quarterly* 63 (2006): 3-96.

6 Alan Taylor, *The Divided Ground: Indians, Settlers and the Northern Borderland of the American Revolution* (New York: Alfred A. Knopf, 2006); John J. Bukowczyk et al., *Permeable Border: The Great Lakes Basin as Transnational Region, 1650-1990* (Pittsburgh: University of Pittsburgh Press, 2005); Jeremy Adelman and Stephen Aron, "From Borderlands to Borders: Empires, Nation-States and the Peoples in Between in North American History," *American Historical Review* 104 (1999): 814-41. See also the articles in Nora Faires, ed., "Emerging Borderlands," special issue of the *Michigan Historical Review* (Spring 2008): vii-117.

7 For the early goals and geographical placement of Fort Pontchartrain, see Dunnigan, *Frontier Metropolis*, 18-19, and William J. Eccles, *The French in North America*, 3rd rev. ed. (East Lansing: Michigan State University Press, 1998), 114-15. In the 1670s, French Jesuits founded missions at the Straits of Mackinac. By the early 1690s, France established the first military garrison at Michilimackinac, before abandoning it in 1697 and later building Fort Michilimackinac in 1715. During the eighteen-year hiatus, the area remained an unofficial site of trading activity. See Brian Leigh Dunnigan, *A Picturesque Situation: Mackinac before Photography, 1615-1860* (Detroit: Wayne State University Press, 2008).

8 Dunnigan, *Frontier Metropolis*, 43.

9 Dunnigan, *Frontier Metropolis*; R. Alan Douglas, *Uppermost Canada: The Western District and the Detroit Frontier, 1800-1850* (Detroit: Wayne State University Press, 2001), 1-2; Bert Hudgins, "Evolution of Metropolitan Detroit," *Economic Geography* 21 (1945): 206-20. I am also indebted to Douglas D. Fisher for generously offering me a geography lesson on early Detroit.

10 Moore quoted in Bald, 28.

11 Dowd, *War under Heaven*, 28; Dunnigan, *Frontier Metropolis*, 20-21, 34-35, 48-49, 71, 102. For background to Native Americans in the Great Lakes region, see also Helen Hornbeck Tanner et al., eds., *Atlas of Great Lakes Indian History* (Norman: University of Oklahoma Press, 1986).

12 Reginald Horsman, *Frontier Detroit: 1760-1812* (Detroit: Michigan in Perspective Conference, 1964); Dunnigan, *Frontier Metropolis*, 50, 70-72; "A General Return of All the Inhabitants of Detroit, September 22, 1773," in *MPHC*, 9:649; "A Survey of the Settlement of Detroit Made by Order of Major De Peyster the 16 Day of July 1782," in *MPHC*, 10:601-10.

13 Poremba, ed., 67; "The 1796 Census of Wayne County," in *Michigan Censuses, 1710-1830, under the French, British, and Americans*, ed. Donna Valley Russell (Detroit: Detroit Society for Genealogical Research, 1982), 59-74. African slaves were likely undercounted in the 1796 census. They were not included in the returns for each community in the Detroit area, and sixteen African American children were not designated as free or enslaved.

14 Dowd, *War under Heaven*, 65; Bald, 40; *Askin Papers*, 1:95 n53. See also Brett Rushforth, "'A Little Flesh We Offer You': The Origins of Indian Slavery in New France," *William and Mary Quarterly* 60 (2003): 777-808.

15 "A General Return of All the Inhabitants of Detroit, September 22, 1773"; "A Survey of the Settlement of Detroit Made by Order of Major De Peyster the 16 Day of July 1782"; Dunnigan, *Frontier Metropolis*, 72; Norman McRae, "Early Blacks in Michigan, 1743-1800," *Detroit in Perspective: A Journal of Regional History* 2 (1976): 159-75.

16 August B. Woodward, "Opinion, Supreme Court, 23d Oct. 1807," in *MPHC*, 12:521. See also "Opinions of Judge Woodward Relative to the Subject of Slavery," in *MPHC*, 12:511-18; Frank B. Woodford, *Mr. Jefferson's Disciple: A Life of Justice Woodward* (East Lansing: Michigan State College Press, 1953), 84-91; and Bald, 40, 40 n9. For the origins of the ban on slavery in the Northwest Ordinance of 1787, see Staughton Lynd, "The Compromise of 1787," *Political Science Quarterly* 81 (1966): 225-50.

17 "Legislative Proceedings at Niagara" (D.W. Smith to John Askin, Niagara, June 25, 1793), in *Askin Papers*, 1:476-77; *Askin Papers*, 2:772 n47; McRae; Bald, 40 n9; Douglas, 16-17.

18 Voltaire, *Candide: Or Optimism*, trans. John Butt (New York: Penguin, 1947), 110; Detroit Indians quoted in White, 260. For the Seven Years' War, see Fred Anderson, *The Crucible of War: The Seven Years' War and the Fate of Empire in British North America, 1754-1766* (New York: Alfred A. Knopf, 2000).

19 The literature on Pontiac's War is vast. For recent treatments, see Dowd, *War under Heaven*; David Dixon, *Never Come to Peace Again: Pontiac's Uprising and the Fate of the British Empire in North America* (Norman: University of Oklahoma Press, 2005); and Richard Middleton, *Pontiac's War: Its Causes, Course, and Consequences* (New York: Routledge, 2007).

20 Peter D.G. Thomas, *British Politics and the Stamp Act Crisis: The First Phase of the American Revolution, 1763-1767* (New York: Oxford University Press, 1975), 42-43; John Shy, *Toward Lexington: The Role of the British Army in the Coming of the American Revolution* (Princeton: Princeton University Press, 1965), 111-25; Colin G. Calloway, *The Scratch of a Pen: 1763 and the Transformation of North America* (New York: Oxford University Press, 2006); Woody Holton, *Forced Founders: Indians, Debtors, Slaves, and the Making of the American Revolution in Virginia* (Chapel Hill: University of North Carolina Press, 1999), 3-38.

21 White, 269-314.

22 Dunnigan, *Frontier Metropolis*, 49-50; Horsman, 4, 8; Douglas, 2-3. For controversy over the Quebec Act in the American colonies and in England, see Pauline Maier, *From Resistance to Revolution: Colonial Radicals and the Development of American Opposition to Britain, 1765-1776* (New York: Norton, 1972), 225, 238, 248.

23 Franklin quoted in "The Role of Benjamin Franklin," February 13, 1766, in *Prologue to Revolution: Sources and Documents on the Stamp Act Crisis, 1764-1766*, ed. Edmund S. Morgan (Chapel Hill: University of North Carolina Press, 1959), 144. For the crises precipitated by the British military occupation of Boston, see Hiller B. Zobel, *The Boston Massacre* (New York: Norton, 1970); Robert A. Gross, *The Minutemen and Their World* (New York: Hill and Wang, 1976); and David Hackett Fischer, *Paul Revere's Ride* (New York: Oxford University Press, 1994).

24 Shy, 271; Mason. Detroit was not alone in staying loyal to Britain during the American Revolution. For the spectrum of choices made by British colonial territories, see Andrew Jackson O'Shaughnessy, *An Empire Divided: The American Revolution and the British Caribbean* (Philadelphia: University of Pennsylvania Press, 2000); Eliga H. Gould and Peter S. Onuf, eds., *Empire and Nation: The American Revolution in the Atlantic World* (Baltimore: Johns Hopkins University Press, 2005); and Maya Jasanoff, "The Other Side of Revolution: Loyalists in the British Empire," *William and Mary Quarterly* 65 (2008): 205-33.

25 Dunnigan, *Frontier Metropolis*, 70; Mason, 1-2; Horsman, 8.

26 Woodford, 30-31; Mason, 3-4; *City of Detroit*, 2:905-23.

27 Dunnigan, *Frontier Metropolis*, 71-72; "Survey of the Settlement of Detroit Taken 31st March 1779," in *MPHC*, 10:311-27.

28 Dunnigan, *Frontier Metropolis*, 72, 91; Mason, 13; Calloway, 272-91; Gregory Evans Dowd, *A Spirited Resistance: The North American Indian Struggle for Unity, 1745-1815* (Baltimore: Johns Hopkins University Press, 1992), 93-94; *City of Detroit*, 1:137-50.

29 Mason, 13; Douglas, 3; Dunnigan, *Frontier Metropolis*, 72; Woodford, 33; Robert F. Berkhofer Jr., "Barrier to Settlement: British Indian Policy in the Old Northwest, 1783-1794," in *The Frontier in American Development: Essays in Honor of Paul Wallace Gates*, ed. David M. Ellis et al. (Ithaca: Cornell University Press, 1969), 249-76.

30 Horsman, 4-5; Bukowczyk et al., 21, 26. For the late loyalists, see Alan Taylor, "The Late Loyalists: Northern Reflections of the Early American Republic," *Journal of the Early Republic* 27 (2007): 1-34; Gerald M. Craig, *Upper Canada: The Formative Years, 1784-1841* (New York: Oxford University Press, 1963); and Marion C. Keffer, *Migrations to/from Canada* (Ann Arbor: Genealogical Society of Washtenaw County, 1982).

31 Douglas, 4; Poremba, ed., 59. See also William Renwick Riddell, *Michigan under British Rule: Law and Law Courts, 1760-1796* (Lansing: Michigan Historical Commission, 1926).

32 Douglas, 5-8; Horsman, 11-12; *City of Detroit*, 1:212-16.

33 Dowd, *Spirited Resistance*, 111-15. For Wayne, see Glenn Tucker, *Mad Anthony Wayne and the New Nation: The Story of Washington's Front-Line General* (Harrisburg: Stackpole, 1973); Wiley Sword, *President Washington's Indian War: The Struggle for the Old Northwest, 1790-1795* (Norman: University of Oklahoma Press, 1985); and Alan D. Gaff, *Bayonets in the Wilderness: Anthony Wayne's Legion in the Old Northwest* (Norman: University of Oklahoma Press, 2004). For the Treaty of Greenville, see Andrew R.L. Cayton, "'Noble Actors' upon 'the Theatre of Honour': Power and Civility in the Treaty of Greenville," in *Contact Points: American Frontiers from the Mohawk Valley to the Mississippi, 1750-1830*, ed. Cayton and Fredrika J. Teute (Chapel Hill: University of North Carolina Press, 1998), 235-69.

34 Bald, 9, 32, 56; Poremba, ed., 66; Horsman, 13; Douglas, 9; *City of Detroit*, 1:238, 242-53, 275-76.

35 Woodford, 36-37; Dunnigan, *Frontier Metropolis*, 102-3; Horsman, 14-15; *City of Detroit*, 1:154-56, 268-74; Bald, 207-49.

PART ONE

EARLY BRITISH DETROIT: TENUOUS RELATIONS

Representatives of the French crown enjoyed more than six decades of congenial trade with trappers, natives, and settlers throughout the upper Great Lakes before the British army arrived. When the Union Jack flew over Detroit for the first time on November 29, 1760, it signified impending victory in the conflict known variously as the Seven Years' War, the French and Indian War, and the War for Empire.

The British gained a diverse frontier community composed of multiple European and Native American groups. Detroit's non-Indian population in 1760 was about five hundred, including military personnel. There were several hundred more settlers on farms along the area's lakes and rivers. The vast majority of residents were of French descent. Accompanying the British administration was a retinue of Scots-Irish, Scottish, English, German, and Dutch settlers.

Ottawa, Potawatomi, and Wyandot Indians also inhabited thriving villages in the Detroit area. The size of the native population varied based on the season or military activities, but it surpassed the rest of the population well into the American revolutionary era. Both the French and British depended on native warriors to supplement their garrisons, and shifting loyalties among Indian groups played an important role in the politics of the region. Pontiac's Rebellion between 1763 and 1765, though unsuccessful, demonstrated the collective strength of native peoples.

In this milieu, a succession of British commanders attempted to maintain a delicate equilibrium, influenced by the fluid situation in Detroit, as well as directives coming from both Montreal and London. Throughout the period, the cross-currents remained volatile, and tenuous frontier relations set the tone.

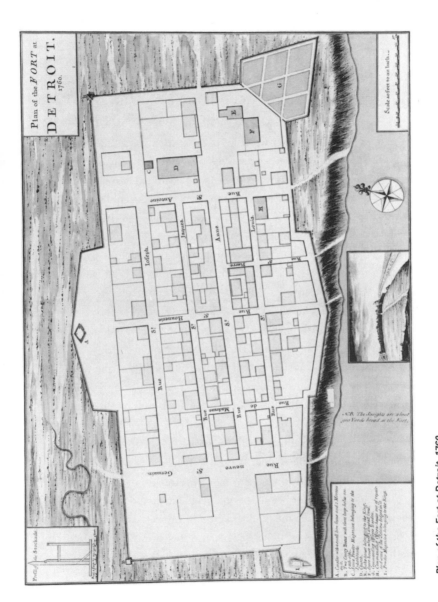

Plan of the Fort at Detroit, 1760

Drawn by Lieutenant Diedrich Brehm (1761). Pen, ink, watercolor on paper. Courtesy of the Burton Historical Collection, Detroit Public Library.

On Fragile Ground: Donald Campbell and the Question of Amity in Early Detroit

Jeff Beauchamp

As Detroit transitioned from French to British control in 1760, British administrators slowly began to implement reforms to the economic structure imposed on Indians and French *habitants*. Caught in the middle of these reforms was Donald Campbell, a British army captain of Scottish descent, who embodied the cultural sensitivity needed to build prosperous relations with the French and local Native American groups. Campbell was the first British commandant of Fort Detroit between 1760 and 1762. His cruel murder in 1763 by the Indians he helped forge alliances with reveals just how poorly Campbell's superiors managed Indian relations in the Great Lakes region. The bigoted and tyrannical policies of General Jeffrey Amherst quickly unraveled Campbell's accomplishments at the fort, ripening Detroit for the insurrection that took Campbell's life. Had he stayed commandant of Fort Detroit and survived Pontiac's Rebellion, Campbell's diplomatic approach may have sustained peace with Detroit's Indian population.[1]

In November 1760, the British flag rose majestically over Fort Pontchartrain as weary French soldiers looked on. Donald Campbell, captain of the Royal Americans, presented a reluctant Captain François-Marie Picoté de Belestre with an official copy of the Capitulation of Montreal, thus ending France's territorial rule. Assuming full command of Fort Detroit a month after his arrival, Campbell, joined by Major Robert Rogers and Captain George Croghan, met with deputies of the Iroquois Confederacy and leaders of the Ojibwas, Potawatomis, and Wyandots. During the three-day council, the Indians expressed the need for fixed prices on goods and the creation of a thriving trade. Agreeing to these terms, the British also promised the crown's protection if the Indians willingly returned prisoners. With agreements reached on both sides, an alliance was made and all parties decided to meet again in the spring. The British were given a chance to prove themselves.[2]

The transition to British rule went well despite depleted stores of food and ammunition at the renamed Fort Detroit. The shortage was aggravated by Britain's decision to assume France's former obligation to provision French settlers.

"The Inhabitants seem very happy at the change of government," Campbell declared in a letter, "but they are in great want of everything."[3] In early December 1760, Campbell also agreed to continue the French practice of giving the Indians access to a doctor and blacksmith in the fort. In welcoming traders from Fort Pitt, Campbell solved the shortage crisis by the spring, and his concessions helped to enhance the new regime's popularity in Detroit's outlying Indian villages. By March 1761, many of the region's inhabitants admitted how the alteration of power was more favorable than first imagined. Lieutenant James McDonald observed, "The Inhabitants here seem very well pleased with their change . . . They are very well satisfied with Capt. Campbell."[4]

During his short career as commandant of Fort Detroit, Campbell was held in high regard amongst his own men as well as the area's settlers. Lieutenant James McDonald said of Campbell: "I never had, nor shall ever have, a Friend or Acquaintance that I valued more than him."[5] Though a far distance from Britain, Campbell made the best of his situation. It was not uncommon for a gathering of French, Indian, and British inhabitants to stay up playing cards until midnight in the commandant's quarters. Campbell developed an "impressive sensitivity" for culture and a deep appreciation for Detroit and its people. "A most beautiful country," is how he described the area upon first arriving. The townswomen also surpassed his expectations. This ease and relaxation of tensions helped other groups—namely the Irish, German, and British soldiers—to integrate peacefully with French and Indian company.[6]

No doubt fearing the severity of an Indian insurrection, Campbell was receptive to the needs of the local Native Americans, which earned their trust. The removal of French competition in the fur trade caused much discontent among the native trappers who began to view the British as domineering. Captain Campbell, on his own volition, supplied the local Indians with whatever ammunition and presents he could obtain. In June 1761, when plans for an Indian attack on forts Pitt and Niagara became evident, the Detroit Indians did not ally themselves with the eastern tribes and refused to attend the council called by the Six Nations; they refused to reply unless Campbell was present. Despite growing regional tensions, Campbell remained an admired leader by Indians and Europeans alike.

In August 1762, Campbell was demoted to second-in-command of Fort Detroit by the order of General Jeffrey Amherst, commander-in-chief of British forces. Major Henry Gladwin, who better represented Amherst's ambitions and sheer hatred of the Indians, took the place of Campbell, whom they believed had become too cautious. During the calamitous events of Pontiac's Rebellion in May 1763, Campbell ventured into an Ojibwa camp along with Lieutenant James McDougal and various French men from Fort Detroit. Campbell's greatest quality, and his greatest flaw, was that he was "a character which desired only unity and concord," according to the anonymous author of the "Journal of a Conspiracy." Believing that his mere presence at the Indian camp would be enough to quell unrest and bring about peace, he approached the camp exuding the same vigor, optimism, and bravery he displayed in past situations. Consequently, Campbell and McDougal were deceitfully taken hostage by Pontiac in an attempt to force the British to meet his demands over the next month. Believing that an escape at night would be difficult due to his impaired vision, Campbell declined to flee with Lieutenant McDougal. Campbell's decision proved to be fatal; he was handed over to the Ojibwa Chief Wasson and executed in retaliation for the killing and scalping of Wasson's nephew a day earlier. According to the various gruesome accounts, most notably in London's *Gentlemen's Magazine*, Donald Campbell was dismembered and cannibalized; the rest of his remains were thrown into the Detroit River. His brutal execution took place two days after McDougal and others escaped safely back to Fort Detroit.[7]

Beginning in 1763, the British crown implemented many changes to manage its expanded North American territory. Amherst's imperialistic policies, driven by an ideology that treated Indians as conquered subjects, abolished the peace which Campbell helped to forge while in command. Aid to the Indians was eliminated, blacksmith privileges removed, ammunition withheld, and gift-giving—a practice held in especially high regard by the Indians—was prohibited as Amherst contrived policies that rewarded or punished Indians based on their behavior. The historian Richard White surmises, "The politics of villages no longer mattered. Only politics of empire counted."[8]

Nearly two years of building trust, calming agitation, and peacefully integrating with the Indians quickly dissolved when Major Gladwin relieved Campbell as commandant. If Campbell represented progressive change for the British Empire, Major Gladwin signified the opposite. Gladwin's brutal tactics erupted into a violent climax early in his command when he hanged a Panis (Indian slave) woman in 1763, clearly demonstrating to natives where they fit into the new order. While Campbell held the Indians in high regard, Gladwin referred to them as "dogs," and Detroit as a "scoundrel country, among savages."[9] The harsh change in attitude fueled discontent between Detroit's Native Americans and the British. Campbell's death during Pontiac's Rebellion signified all that had gone wrong in early British-Indian relations. Aspirations of cultural negotiation and compromise dissolved with each group attempting to drive out the other at all costs.[10]

The situation did not improve until Pontiac's War ended in 1765. Soon thereafter, the British restored traditional French policies such as gift-giving, not out of amity but to avoid another Indian rebellion. Campbell's approach to colonial governance proved to be the successful model adopted by British officials up to the American takeover of Detroit in 1796. He demonstrated that cooperative and peaceful coexistence was possible between the British and most Indian groups. Sadly, in the initial uncertainty of Britain's imperial regime, Campbell stood on fragile ground. The policies of his superior, an aggressive ideologue, cost him his life.[11]

NOTES

1 This is the first study exclusively on Donald Campbell and his policies. For background to European and Indian relations in the Great Lakes region, see Richard White, *The Middle Ground: Indians, Empires, and Republics in the Great Lakes Region, 1650-1815* (New York: Cambridge University Press, 1991). For excellent introductions to Campbell, see *City of Detroit*, 1:118-19, and Gregory Evans Dowd, *War under Heaven: Pontiac, the Indian Nations, and the British Empire* (Baltimore: Johns Hopkins University Press, 2002), 59-66, 75-77, 82, 103, 120.

2 Dowd, 59.

3 Donald Campbell to Henry Bouquet, December 2, 1760, in *MPHC*, 19:45.

4 James McDonald to Henry Bouquet, March 10, 1761, in *MPHC*, 19:64.

5 James McDonald to Henry Bouquet, July 12, 1763, in *MPHC*, 19:218.

6 Dowd, 62; Donald Campbell to Henry Bouquet, December 11, 1760, in *MPHC*, 19:48; McDonald to Bouquet, March 10, 1761, 19:63-64.

7 M. Agnes Burton, ed., *Journal of Pontiac's Conspiracy, 1763* (Detroit: Clarence M. Burton and the Michigan Society of Colonial Wars, 1912), 72 (quote), 190, 208-10; Dowd, 64. See *City of Detroit*, 2:899, for the description from *The Gentleman's Magazine*.

8 White, 256.

9 Henry Gladwin to Henry Bouquet, November 1, 1763 ("dogs"), and Gladwin to Thomas Gage, January 9, 1764 ("scoundrel country"), quoted in Dowd, 65.

10 David Dixon, *Never Come to Peace Again: Pontiac's Uprising and the Fate of the British Empire in North America* (Norman: University of Oklahoma Press, 2005), xiii.

11 Daniel K. Richter, *Facing East from Indian Country: A Native History of Early America* (Cambridge: Harvard University Press, 2001), 190-91; White, 315-65.

The Myth of the Maiden and Pontiac's Real Betrayer

Jerold Sommerville

The Ottawa leader Pontiac's attempt to capture the British garrisoned at Fort Detroit on May 7, 1763, failed because a person or persons revealed his plan to Major Henry Gladwin. Gladwin, the British commandant at Detroit, never disclosed his source in any document, leading to much speculation about the responsible party. The most often repeated theory is that a Native American woman betrayed Pontiac; she appears in countless reports and has as many identities. This person is most often referred to as Catherine and identified as Gladwin's lover. A less common version cites a Native American warrior named Mahigan, Mahigama, or Mohican, as the betrayer. Another account maintains that one or more of Detroit's French inhabitants claimed responsibility.[1]

As with most myths, these stories lack credence. In the shadow of France's defeat in the Seven Years' War, Pontiac and his pan-Indian alliance targeted British soldiers and settlers in western forts with the goal of reestablishing French control. It would have made little sense for an Indian—man or woman—to save the very people who were destroying their way of life and had broken promises to limit expansion. The same was true for French residents of Detroit. They had little to gain by aiding the British after France's ignominious defeat in 1760. Instead, the former British soldier and loyalist James Sterling, who had the means, motive, and opportunity to alert Gladwin to save the fort, the garrison, and his own life, was the real betrayer of Pontiac's plan.[2]

Despite evidence pointing to Sterling, three factors helped to create and sustain the theory blaming Native Americans for the betrayal: the warriors' actions later that same May afternoon, preconceived notions based on earlier accounts of Indian betrayal, and an account reportedly written during the time. Six warriors confronted Gladwin that afternoon accompanied by a woman they suspected as the betrayer. Gladwin denied this, but acknowledged that the betrayer was an Indian, whom he refused to identify. The "Journal of a Conspiracy," an anonymous contemporary work, followed this line and favored a warrior over a woman as the betrayer.

Unveiling the Conspiracy
Painted by John Mix Stanley (c. 1840). Oil on Canvas. Courtesy of the Burton Historical Collection, Detroit Public Library.

Myths linking indigenous peoples with betrayal reached back to the very beginnings of European settlements in the Americas and had at least two earlier precedents at Detroit. Given this history, it was not surprising that Pontiac's informant quickly became identified as an Indian.[3]

Subsequent accounts reinforced the Catherine myth. John Porteous, a trader in Detroit during Pontiac's Rebellion, named her as the betrayer without substantiating Catherine's identity beyond calling her an "old Popish squaw." Later, influential early Michigan residents Henry Conner, Thomas McKinney, Henry Schoolcraft, Charles Lanman, and Lewis Cass perpetuated the theory. Charles Trowbridge compiled the accounts of five French families in 1824 in the "Conspiracy of Pontiac," and became one of the first to offer alternatives to the Catherine story without dismissing her entirely. His version cited three people that named Catherine as the betrayer and two that claimed French responsibility. Francis Parkman, with access to all the information for and against Catherine, chose her as the betrayer and heavily influenced later authors.[4]

If the Indian woman, warrior, and French settler theories are discounted for lack of evidence, then few plausible suspects remain. The informant had to be someone who spoke multiple languages, moved freely within the Indian, French, and British communities and, above all else, enjoyed the trust of all three groups. James Sterling was able to cross these multicultural, multiethnic, and multilingual barriers with apparent ease. Sterling's diverse background provided an invaluable source of intelligence for Gladwin.

Sterling's time in the Detroit area is something of an enigma, and it is easy to see why others have failed to follow his story or accept him as Pontiac's betrayer. The majority of records list him as a merchant or fur trader. Detroit's 1762 census established that he was a merchant living within the fort. Although the 1765 and 1768 censuses provided no listing for him, Father Christian Denissen, in his extensive genealogical research of early Detroit, listed Sterling's marriage to Angelique Cuillerier dit Beaubien and the births of his three children in Detroit as late as 1775. Correspondence between British officers and other documents place Sterling as an interpreter for Major Henry Bassett in 1773, leaving Detroit in 1777, appearing in Quebec in 1778, and finally moving to London by 1779, where he continued his business ventures until about 1783. After that, details concerning Sterling's location, time, and place of death have been lost to posterity.[5]

Although Sterling's business activities gave him the most contact with Indian groups, his connections to Pontiac came through his personal life. Sterling was courting Angelique Cuillerier at the time of Pontiac's War and later married her. Angelique was the daughter of Antoine Cuillerier dit Beaubien, the half brother to the last French commander at Fort Ponchartrain, François-Marie Picoté de Belestre. Antoine Cuillerier became the leader of the French community when Belestre departed with French military forces in 1760. Pontiac knew Antoine well and looked to him as his "father come to life." If his rebellion succeeded, Pontiac planned to place him in charge of the fort until Belestre returned.[6] Antoine also knew of Pontiac's plan for the British garrison, and remarked that he "would be sorry only for Campbell and Sterling" if the plan worked. At least one council took place at the Cuillerier home before the rebellion, indicating connections among Pontiac, Antoine, and Sterling, but sources do not reveal exactly how Sterling learned of the plot.[7]

Sterling moved about the three factions with relative ease as a merchant and well-respected member of the community. He spoke English, French, and Indian languages, and Major Henry Bassett referred to him as the most "influential man in Detroit," someone who "conferred with the French and Indians" and was a "prudent counselor." The major also told General Frederick Haldimand that the "Indians can't well begin without his [Sterling] well having information of their designs."[8] Sterling could have pieced together Pontiac's plans for Detroit and surrounding areas just as easily as other British friends of the Great Lakes Indian community, such as Indian agent Sir William Johnson, who warned General Jeffrey Amherst of the impending danger to all British positions in the summer of 1762. Sterling received a large Indian order for gunpowder and "all the Scalping knives" he could get during that summer, a warning that trouble was brewing. He likely did not fill the request, particularly for the gunpowder, which would have violated Amherst's directive in August 1761 to limit Indian access to powder.[9]

Sterling could have heard of Pontiac's plan in a variety of ways, but the most verifiable one was through his fiancé, Angelique Cuillerier. She probably heard of the plan during one of the councils held at her home between her father and Pontiac. Cuillerier may have told Gladwin herself, but, fearing for her lover's life, she probably relayed the information directly to Sterling, and he informed Gladwin. In August 1773, Bassett recorded this chain of events in a letter to Haldimand: "I recommend James Sterling, who is the first merchant at this place and a gentleman of good character, during the late war, through a Lady, that he then courted, from whom he had the best information, was in part the means to save the garrison." Clarence Burton came to the same conclusions in his research of the failed attack, but the story remained untold in favor of the more romanticized versions of Parkman and others. Whoever informed Gladwin likely did so for a price. A large sum of money passed between the British officer and a Caesar Cormick or McCormick on May 13, 1763, just a week after Pontiac's War began. In his research, Howard Peckham discovered this bill record from Gladwin: "To paid a Person for privet Intelligence £617-6."

Cormick reportedly paid the informant and was reimbursed by Gladwin, suggesting that the information had value. It would have been unusual to pay such a sizeable amount in hard currency to either an Indian or a French settler.[10]

Sterling was loyal to the crown. Once Pontiac's surprise attack failed, the fort was besieged by an alliance of Ottawa, Wyandot, Potawatomi, and Ojibwa Indians. Sterling responded by organizing a volunteer civilian militia to fight alongside British soldiers against Pontiac's alliance. At the end of July 1763, Captain James Dalyell led an expedition to break the siege. Dalyell's efforts failed when a Native American force overwhelmed his column. When the stragglers returned to the fort to report on the action, many feared that the French settlers had alerted the Indians. Sterling claimed to "know enough to hang a dozen of them" and that "all the rest . . . merit at least transportation." He showed a readiness to punish the French even though he was supposedly their friend and consul.[11]

If Sterling could betray his French allies, what would have prevented him from betraying Pontiac? The only thing Sterling would have feared was identification as the informant in the event of a British loss. The expected treatment from the French or Indians would have been brutal. His best bet was to remain anonymous and aid the British to victory. If the British won, his standing within the French community would remain intact, along with his life and business. Any rifts between Sterling and Detroit's Indian community could have been overcome eventually through his position as a leading merchant.

By chance or design, James Sterling made himself into an ideal informant in the multicultural Great Lakes region. Because he lived in Detroit as a British soldier, settler, and then merchant, he interacted with the French and Indians. He showed respect for both groups and gained their trust while meeting their needs as a merchant. Sterling was privy to information that was unattainable for the average British settler. He was the most likely informant who had the means, motive, and opportunity to learn of Pontiac's plot and relay it in time, according to Gladwin's timeline, to save the garrison and himself. All that was required was anonymity, which has been maintained in popular lore to this day. Pass the word: Sterling did it.

NOTES

1 Numerous works exist on each of the three main informants. For theories on Catherine, see Francis Parkman, *The Conspiracy of Pontiac and the Indian War after the Conquest of Canada*, 2 vols. (Boston: Little Brown, 1903), 1:227-28; Charles Trowbridge, "The Conspiracy of Pontiac," in *MPHC*, 8:340-44, 357-64; Fred Anderson, *The Crucible of War: The Seven Years' War and the Fate of Empire in British North America, 1754-1766* (New York: Alfred A. Knopf, 2000), 538; and David Lee Poremba, *Detroit: A Motor City History* (Charleston, SC: Arcadia, 2001), 31. For Mahigan, see "The Pontiac Manuscript," in *MPHC*, 8:266-339; Helen F. Humphreys, "Identity of Gladwin's Informant," *Mississippi Valley Historical Review* 21 (1934): 147-62; and Richard Middleton, *Pontiac's War: Its Causes, Course, and Consequences* (New York: Routledge, 2007), 68-69. For French inhabitants, see George B. Catlin, *The Story of Detroit* (Detroit: The Detroit News, 1923), 41-44, and Trowbridge, 8:344-57. For a nearly complete list of major informants suspected of betraying Pontiac, including Sterling, see Howard Peckham, *Pontiac and the Indian Uprising* (1947; reprint, Detroit: Wayne State University Press, 1994), 125-26. See Wilbur R. Jacobs, *Dispossessing the American Indian: Indians and Whites on the Colonial Frontier* (New York: Scribner, 1972), 92-93, for Parkman's use of the Catherine theory.

2 For speculation that Sterling was the informant, see "Lewis Bond Papers," in *MPHC*, 37:423, and Henry Bassett to Frederick Haldimand, August 29, 1773, in *MPHC*, 19:310-11. Peckham, 125-26, and Poremba, 31, also both mention Sterling as a possible suspect.

3 James McDonald to Henry Bouquet, Detroit, July 12, 1763, "Bouquet Papers 1759-1765," in *MPHC*: 19:212-13; Gregory Evans Dowd, *War under Heaven: Pontiac, the Indian Nations, and the British Empire* (Baltimore: Johns Hopkins University Press, 2002), 119-20; "Pontiac Manuscript," 8:266-339. The "Pontiac Manuscript" is more commonly known as the "Journal of a Conspiracy." For the source's authorship and authenticity, see Milo Milton Quaife, ed., *The Siege of Detroit in 1763: The Journal of Pontiac's Conspiracy, and John Rutherford's Narrative of a Captivity* (Chicago: R.R. Donnelley, 1958), xlvii, and Dowd, 6. For earlier accusations against Detroit Indians, see Common Council of the City of Detroit, *The Bi-Centenary of the Founding of City of Detroit 1701-1901* (Detroit: C.M. Rousseau, 1902), 158, and Sieur Du Buisson to Marquis de Vaudreuil, Detroit, June 15, 1712, Glen A. Black Laboratory of Archaeology, Indiana University, www.gbl.indiana.edu (accessed June 18, 2009).

4 Porteous quoted in Dowd, 119-20. Porteous came to Detroit in 1762 and became a partner of Duncan and Sterling in 1765. He kept a diary during part of the siege and maintained contact with Sterling even after both men returned to Britain (Porteous to Scotland and Sterling to England). See note 1 for the other theories.

5 Donna Valley Russell, ed., *Michigan Censuses, 1710-1830, under the French, British, and Americans* (Detroit: Society for Genealogical Research, 1982), 23, 29-33, 35-37; Christian Denissen, *Genealogy of the French Families of the Detroit River Region 1701-1936*, ed. Harold F. Powell, 2 vols. (1976; reprint, Detroit: Detroit Society for Genealogical Research, 1987), 1:53; 2:978, 1150. Sterling's marriage is listed as being performed by the fort's commandant and not taking place in the church. This ceremony was highly unusual for a French Catholic (Cuillerier) but a great honor for a former soldier (Sterling). For Sterling's life, see "Lewis Bond Papers," 37:423, and "James Sterling," Dictionary of Canadian Biography Online, University of Toronto, www.biographi.ca (accessed June 8, 2009).

6 Pontiac quoted in "Proceedings of a Court of Inquiry Held by Order of Major Henry Gladwin Commanding at Detroit 9th August 1763," in *MPHC*, 27:641. These court proceedings provide crucial links between Pontiac, Antoine Cuillerier, and Sterling and show that Cuillerier liked and respected Sterling. For connections between Belestre and Cuillerier, see Denissen, 1:53; 2:978, 1204-5, and Peckham, 125. For more on Angelique Cuillerier's influence in British Detroit, see the essay in this volume by Steve Lyskawa.

7 Cuillerier quoted in "Proceedings of a Court of Inquiry," 27:641. The Campbell mentioned here is Captain Donald Campbell, who had attempted to limit or ban the trade in rum between Indians and the British. See Dowd, 103, and the essay in this volume by Jeff Beauchamp.

8 Bassett to Haldimand, August 29, 1773, 19:310-11.

9 Jon W. Parmenter, "Pontiac's War: Forging New Links in the Anglo-Iroquois Covenant Chain 1758-1766," *Ethnohistory* 44 (1997): 626. For Amherst's intention to keep the region's Indians deprived of gunpowder, see Dowd, 86-7, 112; Donald Campbell to Henry Bouquet, Detroit, August 17, 1761, "Bouquet Papers 1759-1765," 19:103-5; Richard Middleton, "Pontiac: Local Warrior or Pan-Indian Leader?," *Michigan Historical Review* 32 (2006): 7-8; and Richard White, *The Middle Ground: Indians, Empires and Republics in the Great Lakes Region, 1650-1815* (New York: Cambridge University Press, 1991), 274.

10 Bassett to Haldimand, August 29, 1773, 19:310-11; Peckham, 124. For Burton, see "Lewis Bond Papers," 37:423.

11 Dowd, 70-71, 136 (quote); "Lewis Bond Papers," 37:423; "James Sterling."

Getting Away with Murder: Elizabeth Fisher, Alexis Cuillerier, and the Cultural Complexities of Early Detroit

Steve Lyskawa

One of the few criminal acts investigated by the British at the close of the Seven Years' War was the murder of Elizabeth Fisher. In one of the opening raids of Pontiac's War, a group of Indians attacked the family of former British military officer James Fisher. During the assault, the adults of the family were killed and Elizabeth— and possibly a sibling—was taken captive. While in captivity, Elizabeth was drowned. In the summer of 1767, the French trader Jean Maiet accused fellow Frenchman Alexis Cuillerier of the crime.[1]

Although the murder of Elizabeth Fisher was tragic, the death of a young girl in the harsh North American borderlands hardly seems significant. The event, however, provides an opportunity to appreciate the political and economic intricacies of a diverse frontier community. In 1763, Detroit was three years into British rule and inhabited by a non-Indian population of about nine hundred. The majority of European inhabitants were French or métis and resided outside of the fort famously besieged by Ottawa, Potawatomi, Wyandot, and Ojibwa Indians between May and October of that year. The number of Indians living in and around the fort was difficult to estimate, but surpassed the European population. In addition to the French, British, and Indians residing in the area, there were other European immigrants hoping to take advantage of favorable trade conditions; métis who, in most instances, represented the union of French traders and Indian women; and a handful of African and Indian slaves owned by wealthy members of the European community.[2]

Detroit's heterogeneity challenges those attempting to apply monocultural attributes to the region. The French fort-community handed over to Major Robert Rogers in 1760 epitomized the "middle ground" so well defined by Richard White. On the eve of Pontiac's War, by contrast, Detroit was defined by difference. It was a region in transition, with a population difficult to characterize. Analyzing specific events in and around the fort presents the best opportunity to uncover Detroit's layers of cultural complexity. The Cuillerier murder case is such an example.[3]

The attack at the Fisher home on Hog Island (today Belle Isle) was not an isolated incident. Indian violence on May 9, 1763, was part of a coordinated effort to strike fear into the hearts of the British and hasten the return of the Indians' "French Father." As one of the few British families living outside of the fort, the Fisher family was particularly vulnerable. For more than a decade, Detroit, and the surrounding *pays d'en haut* (the "upper country"), had been a front in the global conflict between the French and British empires. Native Americans who made their homes within disputed North American territories played a key role in negotiating and, in some cases, escalating this conflict.[4]

The Indians who attacked the Fisher family on May 9 had no interest in negotiation. Pontiac's failure to take Fort Detroit by surprise two days earlier set in motion a series of events that ended in Elizabeth Fisher's death. Prior to the planned attack on the fort, its commandant, Major Henry Gladwin, learned of the uprising and thwarted the effort by arming the garrison with 130 soldiers at the ready. Recognizing the precariousness of the situation, Pontiac did not signal his warriors to arms. The Indians left frustrated by the strategic defeat and returned to camp intent on punishing the traitor they believed to be among them. After publicly flogging an elderly woman thought guilty of the betrayal, several groups of Indians sought revenge against British settlers outside of the fort.[5]

Living on Hog Island, James Fisher shared the atoll with one other family, a number of servants, and crown-owned cattle.[6] When the Indians attacked, all was lost. All, that is, except those taken captive.[7] After the attack, the Ottawa forced Elizabeth to camp at a winter retreat on the Maumee River. While there, she met her demise. According to witnesses, Pontiac, while under the influence of alcohol, ordered Elizabeth's drowning. The people ordered to commit the heinous crime were Jean Maiet and Alexis Cuillerier. Maiet later testified that he refused to harm the girl and Cuillerier acted alone. According to Jehu Hay, the British officer serving as justice for the trial, Maiet's account was "clear and point blank."[8]

Based largely upon Maiet's testimony of August 4, 1767, Cuillerier was arrested and placed in the fort's stockade. By August 17, Cuillerier had "escaped." Hay was angered by this turn of events and believed that the guards did not do their duty in keeping Cuillerier secure. Hay had reason to believe that the negligence was intentional. The crime was first reported in 1765, by Maiet to Lieutenant George McDougall that spring, and not prosecuted for two years, which raises the question of preferential treatment. The possible reasons for Cuillerier's "escape" provide insight into the cultural complexity of Detroit's frontier community.[9]

There are many reasons that Cuillerier gained his freedom. The first is based on rumor, and debated to this day. Alexis Cuillerier was the brother of Angelique

Cuillerier, a woman believed by some to be Henry Gladwin's informant prior to the outbreak of Pontiac's siege. Adherents to this theory contend that Angelique overheard a conversation between Pontiac and her father, Antoine Cuillerier, that took place at the Cuilleriers' home days before the attack on the fort. An influential French family, the Cuilleriers had long been allied with the Indian tribes residing in the area. Angelique, however, was also the fiancée of prominent British trader James Sterling, a resident of the fort. As Jerold Sommerville's essay in this volume shows, she could have told Sterling, or Gladwin, of Pontiac's plan. In either case, Angelique Cuillerier is not easily removed from the chain of events that foiled Pontiac's surprise attack.[10]

Further evidence that the Frenchwoman was held in high regard by the British military can be found in a diary entry of the commander of Indian Affairs, Sir William Johnson. Upon arriving in Detroit in 1761, Johnson was greeted with a celebration. Of the event, he wrote, "I opened the ball with Mademoiselle Curie [Cuillerier]—a fine girl. We danced until five o'clock next morning." Later, after another ball, Johnson recorded, "Promised to write Mademoiselle Curie as soon as possible my sentiments; there never was so brilliant an assembly here before."[11] Cuillerier seemed to think highly of the encounters as well. After her marriage to Sterling, she instructed Captain Donald Campbell to "present . . . her best compliments" to Johnson. Sterling later requested employment from Johnson, referencing his wife when doing so. While exchanged pleasantries do not prove that Anglique was Gladwin's informant, interactions such as these indicate that she had influence among the British. The question is whether Anglique's influence had something to do with the lax treatment of her brother, Alexis.

Alexis's treatment may also have been a simple matter of class. He was not only a member of an influential trading family, but also the nephew of the former French commander of the fort, François-Marie Picoté de Belestre. The commandant was highly regarded by the surrounding Indian communities. These circumstances made Cuillerier a valuable asset to the British, who were continually attempting to develop trade relations and stave off conflict with Indians.

With the sentence of banishment levied against Cuillerier in 1765, it became obvious that the British were unwilling to punish a wealthy, politically connected Frenchman. It was only upon returning to Detroit in 1767 that Cuillerier was imprisoned. As the historian Jan Grabowski makes clear, banishment was a punishment traditionally used by the French. The British were more likely to have the accused stand trial, either in a military court setting or in a civil court in Montreal. Clarence Burton argued that Cuillerier's family status allowed for English clemency, evidenced by the sentence of banishment. The judicial leniency in the Cuillerier case may have been due to political motivation or class distinction. Whatever the reason, the accused escaped justice—not once, but twice.[12]

Cuillerier's freedom may also have been due to the emerging influence of Native Americans with the British after Pontiac's War. By the time of his trial in 1767, an uneasy truce between the two groups had been established. The British believed that Pontiac was responsible for maintaining this accord. When the investigation of Cuillerier began, several people—including French trader Maiet and Pontiac's "Brother in Law," Oskkigoisin—testified that Pontiac ordered the murder of Elizabeth Fisher. If the British thought Pontiac was culpable, they did not act on this belief. The historian Gregory Dowd attributes British judicial inaction in part to the questionable legal status of Indians. Unlike the French, who, with their defeat in the Seven Years' War, swore allegiance to the British, Indians remained outside of the legal limits of the crown. To pursue legal action against an Indian was an act of aggression, and British command had no interest in prosecuting Pontiac or his allies at the risk of inciting further Indian attacks.[13]

While Pontiac provided a beneficial legal escape for Cuillerier, it was not the only one. His accuser, Jean Maiet, offered another diversion when several witnesses testified "concerning the infamous character of that perjured villain, Jn. Myer [Maiet], who has since given himself a very glaring and but too strong proof of said testimony by premeditated murdering James Hill Clark, trader at the Maumee River."[14] Such accusations brought Maiet's testimony into question and plunged the Cuillerier case into doubt. Proceedings were further complicated when interpreter Elleopolle Chêsne, who initially testified that Pontiac confessed to ordering Cuillerier to drown Elizabeth Fisher, later contradicted his story and abandoned the fort after the trial to winter with Pontiac at the Maumee River. Jehu Hay declared him a deserter and the case against Cuillerier rapidly derailed.[15]

The murder of Elizabeth Fisher, and the trial that followed, offers insight into the frontier community in and around Fort Detroit. The crime would not have taken place but for the anger of the Indian population, fueled by the cultural affronts of the British. Disdain for the tribes living in the area was grounded in British perceptions of Indians not only as savages but allied with the French. The cultural interplay of Detroit's diverse community created the conditions that led to the Fishers' tragic deaths.

The case further showed that, even in defeat, Native American groups held the balance of power in Detroit. Indians attacked the Fisher farm and, if witnesses are to be believed, Pontiac ordered the death of Elizabeth from his winter camp. The British did not press the case against Pontiac, and possibly Cuillerier, due to the tenuous peace that had been established between the British and tribal communities by 1765.

The fact that Indians inhabited a legal no man's land, being neither British subjects nor enemy combatants, allowed for a surprising amount of Indian autonomy in the region that had, but a few years earlier, witnessed the failure of Pontiac's Rebellion.

The influence of women in frontier Detroit was also critical to the Fisher case. That the victim of the crime was female suggests a compromised status for women, both child and adult, on the borderlands of empires. Yet Angelique Cuillerier's contribution to the case also demonstrates the role of women as cultural mediators and powerbrokers. Alexis's relation to Angelique evidently had a great deal to do with his freedom. She had achieved high status among the British military elite. And although her status may have been due to the romantic feelings of a single officer, or the political accomplishments of family members, Angelique likely played a pivotal role in saving Fort Detroit. A French woman who moved freely among Indian and European groups, she had become a powerful figure in early British Detroit.

The murder of Elizabeth Fisher may have been an historical footnote, but much can be learned about the complexities of a community that struggled for survival on the North American frontier. After the Seven Years' War, Detroit was composed of multiple European and Indian groups. Individuals, however, were defined by their political and cultural connections as much as their gender or ethnicity. As evidenced by Angelique Cuillerier, traditional social categories were fluid. Alexis Cuillerier was the heir to an influential French family who, along with all French inhabitants at the end of the war, became at once a subject and a suspect of British authority. When charged with murder, this French outlaw was granted freedom. Cuillerier's liberty resulted from the restored status of Indians and French setters—the two groups recently defeated by the British—by the mid-1760s. He showed that, with the right connections, one could get away with murder in frontier Detroit.

NOTES

1 Limited details of the Cuillerier murder case are in *City of Detroit*, 1:174-75, and Gregory Evans Dowd, *War under Heaven: Pontiac, the Indian Nations, and the British Empire* (Baltimore: Johns Hopkins University Press, 2002), 254-58. Burton states that Elizabeth Fisher was killed during the initial attack on the Fisher home, but Dowd argues that the murder took place months later. For documents related to the trial, see Milton W. Hamilton et al., eds., *The Papers of Sir William Johnson*, 14 vols. (Albany: The University of the State of New York, 1921-65), 5:644, 652-653, 723, and the Thomas Gage Papers, American Series, CL.

2 Brian Leigh Dunnigan, *Frontier Metropolis: Picturing Early Detroit, 1701-1838* (Detroit: Wayne State University Press, 2001), 36, 50. The census of 1750 counted 483 non-Indians, and in 1765 French inhabitants numbered 801. Dunnigan estimates the Indian population at more than two thousand by 1756. The British had a garrison of at least 130 soldiers during the raid on the fort in spring of 1763. M. Agnes Burton, ed., *Journal of Pontiac's Conspiracy, 1763* (Detroit: Clarence M. Burton and the Michigan Society of Colonial Wars, 1912), 54.

3 Richard White, *The Middle Ground: Indians, Empires, and Republics in the Great Lakes Region, 1650-1815* (New York: Cambridge University Press, 1991), and Greg Dening, "In Search of a Metaphor," in *Through a Glass Darkly: Reflections on Personal Identity in Early America*, ed. Ronald Hoffman, Mechal Sobel, and Fredrika J. Teute (Chapel Hill: University of North Carolina Press, 1997), 1-6, have provided useful models for interpreting the interplay of culture and events in frontier Detroit. For cultural interaction in the Great Lakes region, see also Susan Sleeper-Smith, *Indian Women and French Men: Rethinking Cultural Encounter in the Western Great Lakes* (Amherst: University of Massachusetts Press, 2001), and the essay in this volume by Nicole Satrun.

4 Dowd, 63-65. For the role of Detroit and the western frontier in the Seven Years' War, see Fred Anderson, *The Crucible of War: The Seven Years' War and the Fate of Empire in British North America, 1754-1766* (New York: Alfred. A. Knopf, 2000), 469-71, 535-50.

5 Burton, ed., 54. For theories on Pontiac's betrayer, see Helen F. Humphrey, "The Identity of Gladwin's Informant," *Mississippi Valley Historical Review* 21 (1934): 147-162; Howard Peckham, *Pontiac and the Indian Uprising* (1947; reprint, Detroit: Wayne State University Press, 1994), 125-26; and Jerold Sommerville's essay in this volume.

6 Some accounts of the Fisher family indicate that four soldiers and a servant were also living on Hog Island. Burton, ed., 57. For historical background on the island, see the essay in this volume by Cathryn Eccleston.

7 One account notes that Mr. and Mrs. Fisher were buried in the same grave. On the day following the burial, the hand of Mr. Fisher was seen sticking up from the grave. Days later, the hand was again seen protruding from the grave. A priest was called and re-interred the hand. At that point it remained buried. Burton, ed., 57.

8 Hay quoted in Dowd, 255.

9 Dowd, 256.

10 For speculation of Angelique Cuillerier's and James Sterling's involvement in informing Gladwin, see Henry Bassett to Frederick Haldimand, August 29, 1773, in *MPHC*, 19:310-11.

11 Johnson quoted in Humphrey, 154.

12 Jan Grabowski, "Criminal Justice and Indians in Montreal 1670-1760," *Ethnohistory* 43 (1996): 419; *City of Detroit*, 1:174.

13 Dowd, 256.

14 Burton offers this account of the accusations made against Maiet as the rationale for Cuillerier's recall from banishment on June 4, 1769. *City of Detroit*, 1:174.

15 *City of Detroit*, 1:174; Dowd, 258.

British Métis in Eighteenth-Century Detroit:
The Askin and Mitchell Families
Nicole Satrun

The métis of eighteenth-century Detroit were the offspring of French or British men and Indian women. French cohabitation with Native Americans was common, and métis history in the colonial period has largely been written from this perspective. This study looks into lesser known cases of British métis in Detroit and Michilimackinac.[1]

British cohabitation and intermarriage occurred less frequently and at later dates than similar French relationships. But in the mid-to-late eighteenth century, British military officers and fur traders such as John Askin and David Mitchell had relations with native women. Their children shared cultural identities neither wholly British nor Indian, but a mixture of both. British métis used their ethnicities to advance trade and to support Britain in wartime. In the competition for the resources of Detroit and the northwest frontier, these British-Indian offspring had cultural identities that helped Britain to maintain crucial trade and military relationships with various Native American groups.[2]

The métis in North America today are a distinct cultural group. In September 2002, the Métis National Council estimated Canada's métis population at 350,000 to 400,000, with additional numbers in the Great Lakes region and northern plains of the United States. The origin of métis peoples in the Great Lakes extends from the era of first contact. In Detroit, Frenchmen married native women before Antoine Laumet de La Mothe, Sieur de Cadillac, commissioned Fort Ponchartrain. Métis births and settlements occurred most often at trading areas along waterways where interaction between Europeans and Indians was frequent, such as at Grosse Pointe, Fort Gratiot, Amherstburg, River Rouge, River Raisin, and in clusters around Michilimackinac. Of 351 recorded births in the register at Michilimackinac from 1698 to 1765, métis formed the greatest number at 136 or 38.75 percent. Many métis children were the offspring of French voyageurs involved heavily in the fur trade and had an advantage in their cultural duality. They used their kinship ties to mediate between French and Indians in trade, diplomacy, and other social interactions.[3]

The official French position on intermarriage was uneasy. Early officials accepted intermarriage upon grounds of religious assimilation as a way to solidify the French population in the new world. As Indians migrated near European posts for trade, Detroit's primarily male population took advantage of ready contact with indigenous women by establishing relationships in and out of wedlock. The historian Richard White suggests that as underlying European social attitudes about racial mixing came to the surface, Jesuits and colonial officials considered marriage the lesser of two evils: "Such marriages were undesirable, they admitted, but the alternative was *métis bâtards* [bastards] among all the tribes. They explained to the court that *métis legitimes* [legitimates] invariably became French in outlook, culture, and loyalty . . . *Métis bâtards* however, were invariably Indian, remaining among their mothers' people." The importance of métis developing a French cultural identity was strategic and political: It helped to exclude the British from the fur trade.[4]

For decades, kinship roots between French and Indians grew in the interior of the Great Lakes region, and métis played a vital role in keeping the French dominant in the fur trade. French advantage through kinship was centuries in the making. After the British conquest of New France in 1760, British traders found it difficult to squeeze into the already established networks of trade beyond official colonial trading posts. Officially, the British were even less enthusiastic about using intermarriage and sexual relations with native peoples to access the fur trade. The existence of such relationships, however, was undeniable. In 1772, the missionary David McClure wrote, "The greater part of the Indian traders keep a squaw . . . they allege the good policy of it, as necessary to a successful trade."[5] At Detroit, those who did gain trade networks in the interiors of Indian country did so through intermarriage and kinship. Before the American Revolution, these relationships were not as multitudinous as the French; nonetheless, they occurred and created métis who provided support for the British through the War of 1812.

A notable example was John Askin, who fathered three métis children. Askin was Scots-Irish and arrived in America with the British army in 1758. He became a prominent fur trader, landowner, speculator, farmer, merchant, justice of the peace, commandant of militias, and supplier of goods to British army posts. Stationed at Michilimackinac, Askin's three eldest children (of twelve) were métis: John Jr., Catherine, and Madelaine all had the reputation of being born to an Ottawa mother. Official records do not suggest marriage, but Askin built his home on the site of an old Ottawa farm and manumitted a slave woman named Manette or Monette at Detroit on September 9, 1766. The timing of the births and manumission suggest she was likely their mother. Later, Askin had nine other children with his legal wife, Marie Archange Barthe, a member of a prominent French family in Detroit.[6]

Askin treated his métis children as his own. They held the same family status as his other children and enjoyed the privileges of education and honorable marriage contracts. Catherine married Captain Samuel Robertson. The couple became the first European settlers in present-day Cheboygan, Michigan, setting up trade with Indians there for maize and furs. After Samuel's death, Catherine married Robert Hamilton, founder of Hamilton, Ontario. Madelaine married a Scottish surgeon named Robert Richardson, one of the Queen's Rangers. They eventually settled in Amherstburg and had a son, John, who volunteered for military service with the British, fighting with Indian warriors against the Americans in the War of 1812 and later against Napoleon's last army. He wrote several novels, including *Wacaosta; or, the prophecy*, published in 1832, a historical novel set in Detroit during the siege of Pontiac. John Askin Jr., the eldest of the Askin children, was an interpreter for the British Indian Department stationed at St. Joseph's Island at the outbreak of the War of 1812. He helped lead a group of Ojibwa and Ottawa against the Americans on Mackinac Island in July 1812. According to Milo Quaife, Askin Jr. fathered a son, named Jean B., with a "woman living in the Indian country." The child was raised mostly by his grandfather, John Askin Sr. Therese Askin, the eldest non-métis child, married Thomas McKee, son of Alexander McKee of the British Indian Department. Thomas was the culturally mixed product of a relationship between his father and a white Shawnee captive considered by the Shawnee to be "one of thiere Nation," according to Scots-Irish trader George Croghan. Only one of John Askin Sr.'s children married an American of European ancestry.[7]

On the surface, it would seem that the Askin children grew up and followed European custom. Yet in many ways they show that contrary to the dominant model of assimilation, in which mixed children identified wholly with European culture, British métis grew up with a distinct identity relating to both cultures. Catherine married a British man as her Indian mother had. Then, like her father, she and her husband settled in a frontier area (Cheboygan) where her métis kinship status helped to ensure vibrant trade in furs. Madelaine also married a British man, and her son showed perhaps the most insight into his own mixed culture in his voluntary service and novel writing. Even Therese married within métis culture. Finally, John Askin Jr.'s actions as a British Indian agent showed his devotion to both heritages.

John Askin was not the only British trader at Michilimackinac to have a native woman for his mate. David Mitchell of Edinburgh came first to New York as a common sailor. He studied medicine with his uncle, a medical officer on the British army staff. As a surgeon's mate in the King's 8th regiment, David was transferred to Michilimackinac in 1774. There he married an Ottawa métis, Elizabeth Bertrand, in 1776. In 1779, Mitchell replaced John Askin as deputy commissioner of

Michilimackinac. When word circulated that his regiment might be transferred, David, devoted to his wife, put in his resignation, which took effect in 1783. Upon the implementation of Jay's Treaty in 1796, he chose to remain in American-held Mackinac with his wife and children rather than relocate to the new British post on St. Joseph Island. Elizabeth's métis connections helped David establish a prestigious and successful trading business. Their children were educated in European fashion: the sons in Montreal and the daughters in Europe. Two of their daughters married British army officers. One son joined the British navy, another studied medicine in England, and another gained a local reputation as a talented mathematician. A daughter, Jessie, married trader Lewis Crawford, who recruited Indians for the British cause during the War of 1812. The children appeared to follow the European models of marriage and education more so than the Askins, yet in their involvement with trade and Indian military ventures, they acknowledged both cultures.[8]

Elizabeth, Mitchell's métis wife, was a strong symbol of her mixed heritage. Like the Indian women of her ancestry, she was involved in the public trading of goods and became quite wealthy doing so. During the War of 1812, her husband rejoined the British army as a doctor. During his absence, Elizabeth was so active in using her métis kinship influence for Indian recruitment that she later drew negative attention from the United States Indian Department and fled before being captured and sent to Detroit for trial. After the Treaty of Ghent in 1815, her husband could not bear to return to an American Mackinac Island. He relocated to Drummond Island, then still a British possession, while Elizabeth stayed to manage the family's vast business holdings with her sons. She displayed an extraordinary amount of independence for a woman on the frontier, due at least in part to her métis heritage.[9]

Outside of the Great Lakes, British métis were most strongly connected with the Hudson Bay Company. Originally incorporated in 1670, the company was granted an English trade monopoly along all waterways flowing into Hudson Bay, an area designated as Rupert's Land. The company's employees were largely indigenous people and French and British métis. The company sold Rupert's Land to the newly formed Canadian government in 1869, but not before a group of Red River métis, led by Louis Riel, a French métis, rebelled to secure their survival as a distinctive francophone, Catholic community. Today's border between Minnesota and North Dakota, the Red River, was a route used by fur traders, especially métis, to expand trade farther northwest. The Red River Colony developed north of the U.S.-Canadian border as a concentration of métis and Indian traders.[10]

Over time, British métis became absorbed into this greater métis population. By the early nineteenth century, Canadian government officials referred to métis as "half-breeds." This term distinguished them from Indians, but took away any trace of their British identity. Fellow Canadian settlers responded to Riel's petition by calling the métis the "Half-breed" inhabitants of Rupert's Land. The Manitoba Act of 1870 addressed "half-breeds" directly and attempted to answer some of the grievances of the petition. A distinctly British métis identity never took hold; therefore, many joined the larger métis movement and were recognized as a distinct product of North American cultural mixture.[11]

By contrast, some British métis families in eighteenth-century Detroit were social elites who maintained close ties to both their European and Indian roots. The Askins and Mitchells used their British métis cultural identity to access British traditions and opportunities for wealth, yet each also embraced forms of Indian kinship. The Askin and Mitchell children were a product of America, both British and Indian. Though it was difficult for the British to take root in the fur trade through intermarriage as deeply as the French had, the British métis formed a group of influential cultural mediators. Detroit's British métis remained separate from larger métis populations connected to the Hudson's Bay Company and Red River Colony, but they left their own impressive legacy of cultural genesis and interaction.

NOTES

1 See Susan Sleeper-Smith, *Indian Women and French Men: Rethinking Cultural Encounter in the Western Great Lakes* (Amherst: University of Massachusetts Press, 2001), for the French métis experience in the Great Lakes region. For the Red River métis, see Jacqueline Peterson and Jennifer S.H. Brown, eds., *The New Peoples: Being and Becoming Métis in North America* (Winnipeg: University of Manitoba Press, 1985). See also James Axtell, *The European and the Indian: Essays in the Ethnohistory of Colonial North America* (New York: Oxford University Press, 1981).

2 For further study of the British métis in Detroit and the Askin and Mitchell families, see the following collections in BHC: Canadian Archives, Christian Denissen Papers, Detroit Notarial Records, and Harrow Family Papers.

3 "Who Are the Métis?," Métis National Council, www.metisnation.ca (accessed May 5, 2009). In 1984, the council declared, "Written with a small 'm,' metis is a racial term for anyone of mixed Indian and European ancestry. Written with a capital 'M,' Metis is a socio-cultural or political term for those originally of mixed ancestry who evolved into a distinct indigenous people during a certain historical period in a certain region in Canada." Peterson and Brown, eds., 6 (quote), 44, 50-53. For the purposes of this essay, métis is used in lower-case.

4 Richard White, *The Middle Ground: Indians, Empires, and Republics in the Great Lakes Region, 1650-1815* (New York: Cambridge University Press, 1991), 214; Olivia Patricia Dickison, "A Look at the Emergence of the Métis," in Peterson and Brown, eds., 21.

5 White, 318-19; 324 (quote). McClure observed British relationships with Algonquian women at Fort Pitt.

6 Agnes Haigh Widder, "The John Askin Family Library: a Fur-Trading Family's Books," *Michigan Historical Review* 33 (2007): 27-31; *Askin Papers*, 1:12-13; "John Richardson," Dictionary of Canadian Biography Online, University of Toronto, www.biographi.ca (accessed May 5, 2009). The children wrote to their mother in French and their father in English.

7 *Askin Papers*, 1:12-15, 68-89; 1:69 n7 (quote); Croghan quoted in White, 324; "Spies Heritage Hall," Historical Society of Cheboygan County, http://cheboyganmuseum.com (accessed May 5, 2009); M. Agnes Burton, ed., *Manuscripts from the Burton Historical Collection*, 8 vols. (Detroit: Clarence M. Burton, 1916-18), 1:7. For the business partnership between John Askin Sr. and John Askin Jr., see the essay in this volume by Douglas D. Fisher.

8 Edwin O. Wood, *Historic Mackinac*, 2 vols. (New York: Macmillan, 1918), 2:123. Presumably Elizabeth Mitchell was the product of a French intermarriage because it was said that she could not speak English, and mixed French with her native Algonquian language. "David Mitchell," Dictionary of Canadian Biography Online, University of Toronto, www.biographi.ca (accessed May 5, 2009).

9 "David Mitchell."

10 Thomas Flanagan, *Riel and the Rebellion: 1885 Reconsidered*, 2nd ed. (Toronto: University of Toronto Press, 2000), 3-10. See also Gerhard J. Ens, *Homeland to Hinterland: The Changing Worlds of the Red River Métis in the Nineteenth Century* (Toronto: University of Toronto Press, 1996).

11 Joseph Hume, *A Few Words on the Hudson's Bay Company* (London: Montgomery, 1846), 4; Flanagan, 3-10.

Elizabeth Browne Rogers
Painted by Joseph Blackburn (1761). Oil on canvas.
Courtesy of the Reynolda House Museum of
American Art, Winston-Salem, North Carolina.

Major Robert Rogers
Engraved by Martin Will (n.d.). Print. Courtesy of the
Reynolda House Museum of American Art,
Winston-Salem, North Carolina.

Robert and Elizabeth Rogers: The Dissolution of an Early American Marriage

Ann Marie Wambeke

In eighteenth-century colonial America, ideas about marriage were changing. As the century began, marriage was considered a contract between unequal parties that legalized a highly patriarchal relationship in which the husband had complete control over the marriage and his wife. His only obligation was financial support, and his wife was bound to serve him without question. In the increasingly enlightened latter half of the century, some colonists began to embrace a model of marriage that was less patriarchal and more companionate. Marriage became less hierarchical as women expected their spouses to be faithful companions and partners. Despite the introduction of a companionate marriage model, remnants of the old hierarchy remained; women continued to be economically and legally dependent upon men. Husbands and, increasingly, wives pursued divorce when the realities of marriage failed to meet these changing expectations.[1]

In 1778, Elizabeth Rogers, a New Hampshire native, divorced her husband of seventeen years. Robert Rogers was the British army officer who had accepted the surrender of Fort Pontchartrain at Detroit from the vanquished French military in 1760 and later commanded Fort Michilimackinac. Robert's correspondence with Elizabeth during their marriage, as well as her petition for divorce and the divorce decree, revealed common marital strains in early America that were exacerbated by the special challenges of war, revolution, and a frontier environment. Moreover, their divorce illustrated the complications and gradual changes that were taking place in the nature of the marriage relationship by the time of the American Revolution.[2]

In June 1761, twenty-year-old Elizabeth "Betsey" Browne, the daughter of a prominent preacher in Portsmouth, New Hampshire, married Robert Rogers, a twenty-nine-year-old native of Massachusetts. Major Rogers was a famous and respected Indian fighter in the British army who implemented warfare tactics to successfully lead his group of "Rangers" against the French and Indians in the Seven Years' War. After he married Elizabeth, Major Rogers continued to travel extensively in service of the crown, which meant that he spent more time away from his wife than with her. Moreover, his early military successes did not provide him with long-term economic stability or job security. If he was not fighting Indians, he was arguing with the British government over back pay, expense reimbursement, and future employment. Thus, the Rogers' marriage was marked by long absences and financial hardship.[3]

The absences began almost immediately. Robert left Elizabeth in Portsmouth just six days after they were married. He traveled to South Carolina to lead his Rangers in skirmishes with the Cherokee Indians and did not return to Elizabeth for seventeen months. In these early years of the marriage, he recognized the emotional hardships imposed by his absence and tried to find ways to be with Elizabeth. He wrote of how much he missed her: "I must tell you that I long to see you greatly you are every moment in my mind I am often with you in Imaginations, I pray god to grant me the happiness of being with my wife." He asked her to come stay with him in South Carolina for the winter, promising that she could return home in the spring.[4] Robert also recognized his financial responsibilities to his wife. Shortly after he left, he sought credit for her in an amount "not exceeding one hundred pound sterling" from Portsmouth shopkeeper Henry Apthorp.[5]

Around the end of 1762, Robert returned home from South Carolina and spent five months with Elizabeth before he left for one year to help quell Pontiac's uprising in Detroit. Despite his military successes, however, Robert subsequently found that he was both destitute and without an ongoing military position. In 1765, he traveled to London to seek payment for his efforts and to offer his services again to the crown. While in Britain, Robert was eventually able to secure a commission as commandant of Fort Michilimackinac, and after he reunited with Elizabeth, they moved to the remote outpost in August 1766.[6]

In December 1767, the British government arrested Robert and charged him with insubordination and treason. He was accused of abusing British subjects, encouraging Indian agitation against the crown, and planning to "Desert to the French." British leaders also alleged that Robert spent too much money on the Indians and on an unsuccessful attempt to locate a waterway that would connect the Atlantic and Pacific oceans. In the spring of 1768, Robert was transported from Fort Michilimackinac to Detroit. After a temporary stop at Niagara, he was incarcerated in Montreal while he waited for trial.[7] In August 1768, he wrote a letter to Elizabeth from Montreal. She was back in Portsmouth and pregnant.[8] A court martial hearing was held on October 20, 1768, and, although acquitted, Robert was not allowed to leave Montreal until June 1769. In December 1768, he reassured Elizabeth that she had made the right choice when she left him in Montreal and returned to Portsmouth.[9]

Once he was able to leave Montreal, Robert decided that he needed to return to London to seek a pension and a new commission. He remained in London for six years, during which time his letters to Elizabeth indicated that she was becoming increasingly angry about his absence. In February 1770, he wrote "I am distrut [distraught] that I have had only two letters from you since I left America – why don't you write me oftener it would be pleasing to hear you was well."[10] The tensions between them seemed to accelerate. On March 8, 1770, he tried to explain that he needed to stay in London to complete his business because their financial security and "futur happiness depends on it."[11] By July 1770, Robert was defending himself against Elizabeth's allegations that he was living extravagantly in London, which suggested that she may have had financial problems at home. He wrote:

> this letter . . . I hope will . . . show you how Villenous those persons are that has set you on your High Hors about my Extrovigant living in London–but as it is fal[se] and a Villinous report I shall not trouble my Selfe any further about the matter than to assur you that It was impossible for any man on Earth to be more [Industrious?] than I have been since I arrived in London.[12]

While in London, Robert spent some time in debtors' prison, but he eventually convinced the crown to release his back pay. He finally returned to Elizabeth in 1775 after a six-year absence. A year later, once again without a commission, Robert offered his military expertise to the Continental Congress, but his services were rejected and he was arrested due to suspicions that he was a British spy. He escaped, joined the loyalists around New York City, and formed the Queen's American Rangers. His last military effort on behalf of the crown was unsuccessful. Ironically, the British army, in which he had served for many years, replaced him in 1777 because of, among other factors, its disdain for loyalists. In February 1778, Elizabeth filed for divorce. Thus Robert was literally and figuratively without a home during the American Revolution.[13]

Elizabeth's allegations in her divorce petition suggested that her marriage satisfied neither the patriarchal nor the companionate marriage model. She understood that, as a woman, she was, to some extent, defined by relationships to the men in her life. In her petition she alleged that she was, in fact, a dutiful daughter and wife. Elizabeth asserted that she married Robert, who was at that time a man "of some Character and distinction," at the behest of her parents and friends. Thus, she did not marry him for love. Yet she recognized that she had assumed certain obligations when she married Robert. She shifted from obedient daughter to loyal wife when she accompanied him to Fort Michilimackinac. She was "desirous of doing her duty, and in hopes of wining him by gentleness and condescension," despite the admonitions of her friends. Thus, her expectation was that she should be gentle and deferential to him, and she believed that she had satisfied her obligations. In turn, Elizabeth expected certain things from Robert. She was angered by his failure to support her and their son, forcing her to turn to her father for financial assistance. Robert had failed to live up to his patriarchal duty to support his family, despite Elizabeth's testimony that she had deferred to and obeyed him. She suggested that she would be better able to fend for herself without the burdensome legal constraints of patriarchy imposed by her marriage.[14]

Elizabeth's petition for divorce indicated that she was also angered that their marriage was not companionate. She was disturbed by Robert's extended absences. He traveled British North America fighting Indians in the service of George III, seeking compensation and reimbursement for amounts that he either earned or expended in such service, or in defending himself against charges of ineptitude and treason by British officials. Elizabeth, on the other hand, made her life in Portsmouth, where she had the emotional and financial support of her family. When Robert joined the loyalists, it became clear that he could never return to her.[15]

Perhaps Robert's absences served to shelter Elizabeth from his behavior because her greatest grievance seemed to be the way that he treated her at Fort Michilimackinac. In her petition, Elizabeth asserted that while with him at the frontier outpost she "underwent every hardship, and endured every species of ill-treatment which infidelity uncleaness & drunken barbarity could inflict from one bound by the tenderest & most sacred ties to succour, protect and comfort her." She suggested that he treated her so badly that she would have been embarrassed and the judges would have been offended by her description of their life together. Thus, according to Elizabeth, Robert did not fulfill his obligations to her as a partner and companion. He chose to spend most of his time away from her and when they were together, he not only failed to take care of her, but was unfaithful and otherwise abusive.[16]

Even if Robert had opposed Elizabeth's request for a divorce, the New Hampshire legislature chose to believe Elizabeth's allegations. The lawmakers granted her petition for divorce in March 1778 on numerous grounds, highlighting in particular that Robert had been unfaithful. The decree stated that Robert had failed to support Elizabeth financially, and "in the most flagrant manner, in a variety of ways, violated the marriage contract—but especially by *Infidelity to her Bed*." Just as Elizabeth had argued, then, the legislature found Robert wanting as both a patriarch and a companion.[17]

The marriage and divorce of Elizabeth and Robert Rogers illustrated that the transition from the patriarchal to companionate marriage model was slow and that, during the revolutionary era, ideas about marriage sometimes merged into an amalgam of the two models. Their strained relationship further showed the special difficulties of fulfilling the ideals of either marital model during wartime or in a frontier environment such as the Great Lakes. Elizabeth, however, successfully invoked both models to argue that Robert was an inadequate husband. The New Hampshire Council and House of Representatives agreed with her. As a result, Elizabeth was permitted to dissolve her marriage and to continue her life without Robert. After they were divorced, Elizabeth married sea merchant John Roche; she died in the United States in December 1813. Robert returned to England, drank heavily, spent time in debtors' prisons, and died in relative obscurity and poverty in 1795.[18]

NOTES

1 For the changing models of marriage in the eighteenth century, see Nancy Cott, "Divorce and the Changing Status of Women in Eighteenth-Century Massachusetts," *William and Mary Quarterly* 33 (1976): 611-14, and Merril D. Smith, *Breaking the Bonds: Marital Discord in Pennsylvania, 1730-1830* (New York: New York University Press, 1991), 6, 179-80. There have been many studies of divorce in colonial America, but they tend to focus upon particular geographic regions. For example, Cott examines divorce records in eighteenth-century Massachusetts, and Smith studies divorce proceedings in Pennsylvania from 1730 to 1830. For an examination of the impact of a marital breakdown on a single family, see Alison Duncan Hirsch, "The Thrall Divorce Case: A Family Crisis in Eighteenth-Century Connecticut," in *Women, Family, and Community in Colonial America: Two Perspectives*, ed. Linda E. Speth and Alison Duncan Hirsch (New York: Haworth, 1983), 43-75. For more general histories of marriage and divorce in America, see Norma Basch, *Framing American Divorce: From the Revolutionary Generation to the Victorians* (Berkeley: University of California Press, 1999), and Glenda Riley, *Divorce: An American Tradition* (New York: Oxford University Press, 1991). For a broader examination of women in revolutionary America, the best studies remain Mary Beth Norton, *Liberty's Daughters: The Revolutionary Experience of American Women, 1750-1800* (Ithaca: Cornell University Press, 1980), and Linda K. Kerber, *Women of the Republic: Intellect and Ideology in Revolutionary America* (Chapel Hill: University of North Carolina Press, 1980).

2 Brian Leigh Dunnigan, *Frontier Metropolis: Picturing Early Detroit, 1701-1838* (Detroit: Wayne State University Press, 2001), 48-49, 53. For Robert Rogers, see John F. Ross, *War on the Run: The Epic Story of Robert Rogers and the Conquest of America's First Frontier* (New York: Bantam, 2009); Walter Borneman, *The French and Indian War: Deciding the Fate of North America* (New York: HarperCollins, 2006); and John R. Cuneo, *Robert Rogers of the Rangers* (Ticonderoga, NY: Fort Ticonderoga Museum, 1988). For cultural depictions of Robert Rogers, see Kenneth Roberts, *Northwest Passage* (Camden, ME: Down East Books, 2001) (novel); *Northwest Passage*, directed by King Vidor, Metro-Goldwyn Mayer, 1940 (movie); and *Northwest Passage*, 1951 (television series). Similar histories have not been written about Elizabeth Rogers.

3 *New Hampshire Gazette*, July 3, 1761. The marriage announcement indicated that Rogers had "eminently distinguished himself in the Service of his King and Country."

4 Robert Rogers to Elizabeth Rogers, May 4, 1762, Rogers-Roche Papers, CL. In the same letter, Robert also wrote, "my Dear I have a fine house there and a very pretty orange garden in which I should be very glad to have some agreeable walks with Betsy, my dearest Betsy will you come to me as soon as the scorching heat of summer is over."

5 Robert Rogers to Henry Apthorp, July 19, 1761, Rogers-Roche Papers; *New Hampshire Gazette*, April 13, 1759.

6 Robert Rogers, *Journals of Major Robert Rogers*, with an introduction by Howard H. Peckham (1765; reprint, New York: Corinth, 1961), v-viii.

7 David A. Armour, ed., *Treason? at Michilimackinac: The Proceedings of a General Court Martial Held at Montreal in October 1768 for the Trial of Major Robert Rogers* (Mackinac Island: Mackinac Island State Park Commission, 1967), 1-5, 9-10, 59-65.

8 Robert Rogers to Elizabeth Rogers, August 25, 1768, Rogers-Roche Papers. Rogers wrote, "I could most heartily wish it was in my power to be with you to attend you I[n] your present condition, but my Dearest that cannot be at least for some months – but I don['t] doubt you will have a good time, and I hop[e] a Son – that he may Inherent your Fortun[e] – and be a comfort to you in after times."

9 Armour, ed., 99. Robert Rogers to Elizabeth Rogers, December 24, 1768, Rogers-Roche Papers. Robert tried to console Elizabeth when he wrote, "I am sorry you give your Selfe the Least uneaseyness about your not comming with me to this place and am convinced that you have done everything for me, and much more than you could had you have come to this place."

10 Robert Rogers to Elizabeth Rogers, February 20, 1770, Rogers-Roche Papers.

11 Robert Rogers to Elizabeth Rogers, March 8, 1770, Rogers-Roche Papers.

12 Robert Rogers to Elizabeth Rogers, July 26, 1770, Rogers-Roche Papers.

13 Armour, ed., 101; Petition for Divorce, Rogers-Roche Papers.

14 Petition for Divorce, Rogers-Roche Papers. Elizabeth asserted that she was forced to support herself and her son by herself and "under all the disadvantages that arise from this ungrateful Connection."

15 Petition for Divorce, Rogers-Roche Papers.

16 Petition for Divorce, Rogers-Roche Papers.

17 "Act to dissolve the marriage of Robert Rogers and Elizabeth his wife, passed March 4th, 1778," in *Provincial and State Papers of New Hampshire*, 40 vols. (Concord: State of New Hampshire, 1867-1943), 8:776.

18 Armour, ed., 101.

Belle Isle and Grosse Ile: The Islands In-Between

Cathryn Eccleston

The Detroit River of the American revolutionary era was not the territorial boundary that it represents today, but the main street of the town and a thoroughfare that included no less than twenty-two islands. By the end of the period, many of these islands found themselves in the hands of two brothers: Detroit merchants William and Alexander Macomb. Like mainland Detroit, the islands exchanged hands many times and were sites of continually shifting identities.[1]

Any one of the islands the Macomb brothers owned could be singled out for scholarship. Two of the best known are Grosse Ile,[2] the largest island in the river, and Hog Island (today Belle Isle), the largest island upstream of Detroit. While the islands ended up in the same hands, their history prior to the arrival of the Macombs was radically different.[3] Grosse Ile almost became the location of the French fort along the river. When Antoine Laumet de La Mothe, Sieur de Cadillac, arrived on the Detroit River in 1701 looking for a location for a new French settlement, Grosse Ile was his first choice. Cadillac later decided that the isolated island would eventually run out of natural resources, and was therefore not suitable for a fort. He then focused on Detroit's current location, and eventually gifted the land south of Detroit— including all of the river's islands—to his daughter. Unfortunately for her, Cadillac did not have the right to give away the land grant, and when he was removed from Detroit in 1710 his daughter lost her claim as well. The islands upriver from Detroit— including Belle Isle—were reserved for the common usage of the residents of Detroit.[4]

After Cadillac's departure, the two islands followed very different paths. As Grosse Ile was far south of the fort, Belle Isle was referenced more often in early records. During Pontiac's siege of Detroit in 1763, Indian warriors killed several members of the family of James Fisher, a former British army officer who tended the fort's garden on the island. The warriors also slaughtered the island's cattle to help feed Pontiac's many followers.[5]

After the siege, the British made a point of improving relations with Native Americans on Belle Isle. George III granted the island to Lieutenant George

McDougall in 1768, but only on the condition that McDougall gain the consent of its Indian inhabitants. No mention was made, however, of the long established use of the island as a public commons by Detroit's residents, and that led to an intense debate. McDougall eventually gained control of the island and, after he died, his family sold the land to William Macomb. The Macomb family took over Belle Isle on November 11, 1793.[6]

At the other end of the river, the ownership of Grosse Ile was considerably more straightforward. The island was largely ignored after Cadillac's departure until 1740, when a group of Wyandot formed a new settlement on the island. Local native groups may have used the island before this for food collection or temporary shelter, but the fact that a new settlement was formed suggests that there was not a permanent village on the island before this time.[7]

It was not for another twenty-six years that control of the island passed to Europeans. On July 6, 1776, the Macombs obtained a deed to the island from Potawatomi Indians, who lived nearby the Wyandots. The deed survives and promises the brothers the right to "peaceably and quietly, have, hold, occupy, posses, and enjoy the said Island." They also had the right to lease land to tenants.[8]

William Macomb lived on Grosse Ile occasionally, but land on both islands was used primarily by an eclectic mix of tenants. The Macomb family was English, but not all of their tenants were. There is a record of a Pierre Chêne, from one of the early French families, paying for a year's rent for land on Belle Isle. Other island residents, such as John Weigeli and Leonhard Kratz, were German. There is even record of slaves living on Grosse Ile. A woman named Charlotte, owned by the Macomb family, was left in charge of their island home when the family was not in residence.[9]

Charlotte, though, was not the only person to move to the islands in an unfree condition. Some settlers of European descent also had no choice in their lodging. When loyalists from farther east were captured by Indians, they were brought to Detroit to be ransomed. The Macombs, in several instances, paid that ransom. The captives repaid the debt by becoming tenant farmers on either Belle Isle or Grosse Ile. The Mallot family was brought to Grosse Ile in this manner from their home in Maryland. Kratz was also a captive, taken as a Hessian prisoner of war from the battle of Saratoga.[10]

Diverse visitors came to the islands as well. Moravian missionaries from the southeastern shore were in contact with island residents, although they regretted the lack of religious devotion displayed by island residents. The islanders were apparently receptive to religious services when available. When a group of Quakers stopped at Grosse Ile on their way to Detroit, they conducted a meeting and more than fifty people joined them.[11]

One of the more significant figures attached to both islands, and in turn the Macombs, was a Scottish resident named Angus Mackintosh. Mackintosh assumed management of William Macomb's accounts and lands following his death in 1796, and after the rest of the family had moved away from Michigan. His name appears on receipts and leases, and he reported to Macomb's widow through regular letters.[12]

It is through these letters that the split personality of the islands becomes clear. They were territories caught between two large mainland bodies that, as the eighteenth century faded into the nineteenth, became two separate countries. In 1800, writing from Sandwich (today Windsor, Ontario), Mackintosh informed Macomb that a resident of Grosse Ile had been imprisoned for indebtedness on "the American side." Meanwhile, Mackintosh sued two island residents who were imprisoned for unpaid rent. The fact that he does not specify that they were imprisoned in American territory suggests that they were likely taken to the same side of the river Mackintosh was on—the British.[13]

The territorial status of the islands was not addressed in Jay's Treaty. It was settled in 1822, when a joint commission, acting as a result of the Treaty of Ghent, awarded both islands to the United States. Until that time, residents were subjected to governmental supervision from both shores. When William Macomb was a candidate for the Legislative Assembly of Upper Canada in the 1790s, for example, the residents of Grosse Ile were able to vote for him. This was a time of transition in the region; on the river, that transition was magnified.[14]

The heirs of William Macomb held Belle Isle until 1817, when they sold it for $5,000. Although the Macomb family held the original Potawatomi deed to Grosse Ile until 1953, tenant farmers had become private land owners well before the deed was relinquished. The Macomb name lived on only in memory as Detroit gradually transitioned away from a British cultural identity.[15]

The arrival of the Macombs to Grosse Ile and Belle Isle signified a new individualistic character to the islands that had long been common areas for both Indian and European groups. The islands had changed hands before, but usually in concert with shifting European imperial powers in Detroit. The Macombs held the titles to Grosse Ile and Belle Isle even as individual residents on the islands determined their own loyalties and political ties. The island communities were diverse, and not populated solely by friends and countrymen of their landlords. In this respect, they were both microcosms of Detroit itself.

NOTES

1 Previous works have dealt with both Grosse Ile and Belle Isle, but most look at one or the other and do not study them in tandem. See Isabella E. Swan, *The Deep Roots: A History of Grosse Ile, Michigan to July 6, 1876* (Grosse Ile: Swan, 1977); *City of Detroit*, 1:123-24; and Silas Farmer, *The History of Detroit and Michigan: Or the Metropolis Illustrated* (Detroit: S. Farmer, 1884), 78-79.

2 References to Grosse Ile often include the smaller islands immediately off shore as part of the larger one. Accordingly, here "Grosse Ile" is used as a blanket name for all the islands in the immediate vicinity.

3 Grosse Ile and Belle Isle each went by different names in the past. For the sake of clarity, this essay will use the modern names. At different times, Belle Isle was known as Mah-nah-be-zee, Isle St. Claire, and Isle au Cochons (Hog Island). Grosse Ile was known as both Kitche-minishen and Grand Island.

4 For Grosse Ile's early history, see the essays and documents in *MPHC*, 35:553-604.

5 For the Fisher family massacre, see Gregory Evans Dowd, *War under Heaven: Pontiac, the Indian Nations, and the British Empire* (Baltimore: Johns Hopkins University Press, 2002), 254-58, and the essay in this volume by Steve Lyskawa.

6 Farmer, 78; "Paragraph of General Gage's Letter to Capt. Turnbull 29th August 1768. Relating to Hogg Island Given to Mr. McDougal by His Majesty & Council," in *MPHC*, 10:234; *City of Detroit*, 1:123.

7 Richard White, *The Middle Ground: Indians, Empires, and Republics in the Great Lakes Region, 1650-1815* (New York: Cambridge University Press, 1991), 195; Swan, 2. According to Swan, there is some evidence (but not conclusive proof) that a village might have been located on the island in 1654, and that it was visited by French explorers at that time.

8 "Old Deed—1776—To Grosse Ile," in *MPHC*, 35:580-82; 35:581 (quote). For Potawatomi land dealings, see the essay in this volume by Susan Ward.

9 Receipt to Gabriel and Toussaint Chêne, July 20, 1798, Chêne Family Papers, BHC.

10 Swan, 39, 42.

11 Swan, 62-63.

12 See, for example, "Debts of Francis Vigo" (John Askin, Angus Mackintosh, William Park, and James Abbott to William Mackintosh, November 1, 1805), in *Askin Papers*, 2:489-90.

13 Letter Book Vol. 1, October 20, 1800, Mackintosh Family Papers, BHC. The resident imprisoned on the American side was Tom Williams. Jacob Iler and Johnstone (no first name given) were the ones Mackintosh sued. While Johnstone died in prison, Iler agreed to pay his rent and was released. In a rather sarcastic aside, Mackintosh concludes his description of his legal trouble with the remark, "Iler since is a good boy."

14 Swan, 62.

15 Farmer, 78; Swan, 399. The original deed is now in the Macomb Family Papers, July 6, 1776, BHC.

The Potawatomi Indians of Detroit: Great Lakes Pioneers

Susan Ward

None of Detroit's cultural and ethnic groups experienced more tumultuous changes during the revolutionary era than its Indian population. Whereas the French and British had to negotiate formal and informal settlement terms with one another after 1760, and both had to adapt to the American takeover of 1796, Detroit's three main Indian groups—the Ottawa, Wyandot, and Potawatomi—had to endure three different imperial regimes within two generations. This essay explores how one of these groups, the Potawatomi, responded to Detroit's many political and cultural changes in the second half of the eighteenth century. The Potawatomis did everything possible to adapt and survive, even leaving their homes to become pioneers of new lands.[1]

Before European contact, the Potawatomis were part of an alliance with Ojibwas and Ottawas known as the "People of the Three Fires." Their legend holds that the tribes originated on the Atlantic Ocean, migrated west to escape death and disease, and stopped once reaching the upper Great Lakes region. According to anthropologist James Clifton, the first "unmistakable evidence of the existence of the Potawatomi dates to 1634 but was not recorded until six years later."[2] In 1640, the Jesuit priest Father Le Jeune wrote about French explorer Jean Nicolet and his encounter with Potawatomis during his travels on the Great Lakes from Sault Ste. Marie to Green Bay. It is still not clear whether they originally lived on the east or west coast of Lake Michigan. One thing that has remained constant throughout the tribe's recorded history is its name, under various spellings. The earliest references to the Potawatomis indicate that they viewed themselves as one people, in various geographical locations. Clifton and others suggest that the Potawatomis made decisions that affected more than one village as a larger unified group, not as separate communities.[3]

European colonialism fractured this cultural and political unity. The Potawatomis became French allies, active traders, and warriors of the *pays d'en haut* (the "upper country") from the early days of New France. They fought alongside the French throughout the colonial era until the end of the Seven Years' War. Their reputation as the "most favored tribe" of the French automatically put them at odds with the British, but it also allowed them to play the European powers off each other to sweeten trading and diplomatic terms. The Potawatomi people spread across the western reaches of New France, an area now represented by Michigan, Wisconsin, and Illinois. By the American revolutionary era, Potawatomis identified themselves more closely with their immediate village than with the larger Potawatomi "nation." Their interests, economies, and alliances were intertwined with European society—a major cultural shift for a group that once had such a close and interdependent society.[4]

The Potawatomis helped to develop Detroit. In 1701, the French colonial official Antoine Laumet de La Mothe, Sieur de Cadillac, built a new fort along the Detroit River. His original expedition from Montreal included Frenchmen and Native Americans. Although their tribal identity is unknown, the Indians were probably from the Montreal area. Through correspondence with Jesuit missionaries at Michilimackinac, Cadillac also invited multiple Indian groups to settle at Fort Pontchartrain. Within several years, Potawatomis joined thousands of other Indians in the Detroit area. [5]

Living just south of the fort, the Potawatomis became essential allies in making Detroit a center of the Great Lakes fur trade. The historian John Bowes identifies the Potawatomis and other Indian groups in the Old Northwest as both "exiles" and "pioneers." They served as frontiersmen in their own right and paved the way for white settlers in uncharted western territories in the nineteenth century. Yet this role as pioneers began almost a century earlier in the Potawatomis' move south to Detroit. They helped to make the area a desirable colonial territory.[6]

As French allies, the Potawatomis lamented Britain's victory in the Seven Years' War. In 1763, therefore, they eagerly joined Pontiac's pan-Indian alliance to remove the British from former French forts, including Detroit. Although the rebellion failed, there were positive consequences for Native Americans. The British realized that regional Indian groups were worthy opponents and that they were better off keeping the peace. Detroit's British administration resumed the custom of gift-giving that was so prevalent under the French, and increasingly monitored local fur traders to ensure fairness and integrity. Additionally, the Proclamation of 1763 established a boundary to protect Indian territory and keep American colonists from expanding farther west.[7]

As Great Lakes Indians grew accustomed to their new alliance with the British, the American Revolutionary War began, and the larger Potawatomi community fractured again. Potawatomis split their support for Britain and the United States according to existing geographical divisions. The Detroit Potawatomi supported Britain throughout the war, while other groups from Illinois and Wisconsin sided with the Americans. Potawatomis at St. Joseph on southern Lake Michigan were pulled in both directions before ultimately joining British attempts to curb American expansion. The impact of European war and geopolitics had once again reached the Indian village level.[8]

Like the majority of Detroit's inhabitants, the Potawatomis remained loyal to the British even after America achieved its independence. Most Indian groups strongly opposed American western encroachment, and the Potawatomis did not resign themselves to U.S. sovereignty until after General Anthony Wayne's victory at Fallen Timbers in 1794 and the subsequent Treaty of Greenville in 1795. The battle came after nearly ten years of fighting between Americans and Native Americans, backed by the British, for control of Ohio Country and the upper Great Lakes region. Unlike previous encounters, Indians were greatly outnumbered by American forces at Fallen Timbers, and sought refuge from the British at nearby Fort Miami (today Maumee, Ohio). The British locked the fort's gates to avoid a larger conflict with the Americans, thereby diminishing their long period of influence with local Native Americans.[9]

During this time, many Potawatomis had already left Detroit, and others were in the process of transferring their land holdings along the Detroit River and Lake Erie to private investors. One such investor was Robert Navarre, the royal notary in Detroit under the French who held similar positions with the British and early American governments. He established and maintained good relations with local Indians; the Potawatomis sold him a parcel of land along the river in 1771. They stipulated that the land be for personal use and that Navarre or his sons could build a house and farm the land. The Potawatomis also expected that Navarre maintain their burial ground, which was located on the property. The deed was signed by several Potawatomis using totems as their signatures. The exact number of Potawatomis in British Detroit was not known, but a rash of similar land sales beginning in the 1770s decreased their population even before Fallen Timbers.[10]

The Potawatomis left by a combination of compulsion and their own volition, as both exiles and pioneers. Increased numbers of white settlers at Detroit pushed the Potawatomis off their land while also giving them a financial opportunity. In 1757, several hundred Europeans lived in and around the fort at Detroit. By 1780, there were roughly 2,100 settlers. And by 1796, there were about 2,600 Europeans of various backgrounds living in the Detroit area. Of this population, a growing number were farmers, and the gradual expansion gave the Potawatomis a market for their land. They took advantage of the situation, and moved farther west to keep distance from the settlers.[11]

The Potawatomis lost the rest of their land in the Detroit area through deceitful land dealings and treaties. The United States competed with avaricious British and American land speculators for prime tracts in the Old Northwest. In September 1795, General Wayne described the treaty negotiations at Greenville and complained that speculators had kept Indians in the "Vicinity of Detroit and Raisin River," including the Potawatomis, "in a state of intoxication for many weeks whilst purchasing their lands for the most trifling Consideration."[12] Wayne and other U.S. representatives were frustrated because they wanted the same land for their new government. Eventually, they succeeded. Between the Treaty of Greenville in 1795 and the 1807 Treaty of Detroit, the Potawatomis, Ottawas, and Wyandots ceded all their remaining land in the lower peninsula of Michigan to the United States.[13]

Political changes in the Great Lakes region in the latter half of the eighteenth century had a disastrous effect on Detroit's Native American population. In the case of the Potawatomis and other Indian groups, there was little chance to eliminate British and, later, American influence after Pontiac's defeat in 1765. The Potawatomis adapted creatively to their situation, however, by selling land and moving west as white settlers increasingly migrated to the Detroit area. The Indians showed determination to choose where they lived, before wars and treaties forced their hand. Decades before the Indian Removal Act of 1830, most Detroit Potawatomis had already been pushed toward Lake Michigan. Ultimately, they were relocated west of the Mississippi River. These early inhabitants of Detroit remained pioneers, venturing west toward another new home.[14]

NOTES

1 Studies on the Potawatomis at Detroit are limited. Most works focus on them after they moved to Illinois, Kansas, and eventually Oklahoma. For the Potawatomis in Michigan, see James A. Clifton, George L. Cornell, and James M. McClurken, *People of the Three Fires: The Ottawa, Potawatomi and Ojibway of Michigan* (Grand Rapids: The Michigan Indian Press, 1986). For general overviews of the Potawatomis, see James A. Clifton, *The Prairie People: Continuity and Change in Potawatomi Indian Culture, 1665-1965* (Lawrence: Regents Press of Kansas, 1977), and R. David Edmunds, *The Potawatomis: Keepers of the Fire* (Norman: University of Oklahoma Press, 1978). See Richard White, *The Middle Ground: Indians Empires, and Republics in the Great Lakes Region, 1650-1815* (New York: Cambridge University Press, 1991), for relationships between Europeans and Indians in the Great Lakes region.

2 Clifton, *Prairie People*, 11.

3 Clifton, Cornell, and McClurken, v, 50; Edmunds, 58; White, 101; William Warren, *History of the Ojibway People* (St. Paul: Minnesota Historical Society, 1984), 80-82.

4 Clifton, Cornell, and McClurken, 51.

5 *City of Detroit*, 1:84; Clifton, Cornell, and McClurken, 16; Clifton, *Prairie People*, 86. For Cadillac's correspondence with the Jesuits and early descriptions of Detroit, see *MPHC*, 33:107-51.

6 John Bowes, *Exiles and Pioneers: Eastern Indians in the Trans-Mississippi West* (New York: Cambridge University Press, 2007). Bowes also cites the Shawnees, Delawares, and Wyandots as unintentional trailblazers in the western expansion of the United States.

7 Gregory Evans Dowd, *War under Heaven: Pontiac, the Indian Nations, and the British Empire* (Baltimore: Johns Hopkins University Press, 2002), 177-80; White, 308; Clifton, Cornell, and McClurken, 54.

8 Colin G. Calloway, *The American Revolution in Indian Country: Crisis and Diversity in Native American Communities* (New York: Cambridge University Press, 1995), 41.

9 Clifton, Cornell, and McClurken, 55; Edmunds, 130-32. See also the letters from Anthony Wayne to Henry Knox and Timothy Pickering, in *Anthony Wayne, a Name in Arms: Soldier, Diplomat, Defender of Expansion Westward of a Nation*, ed. Richard C. Knopf (Westport, CT: Greenwood, 1960), 352, 379, 384, 389, 427, 461.

10 Deed signed by thirteen Potawatomi Indians on May 26, 1771, Robert Navarre Papers, BHC. For additional land sales by the Potawatomis before 1795, see the following deeds in BHC: Deed signed by eighteen Potawatomi chiefs on July 6, 1776, giving Alexander and William Macomb Grosse Ile, Macomb Family Papers; Deed signed January 6, 1777, Chêne Family Papers; Deed signed July 26, 1780, Harold E. Stoll Papers; Deed signed July 28, 1780, John Askin Papers; and Deed signed July 8, 1785, Campau Family Papers. For the sale of Grosse Ile, see also the essay in this volume by Cathryn Eccleston.

11 Donna Valley Russell, ed., *Michigan Censuses 1710-1830, under the French, British, and Americans* (Detroit: Detroit Society for Genealogical Research, 1982), 19-74; David Poremba, ed., *Detroit in its World Setting: A Three Hundred Year Chronology, 1701-2001* (Detroit: Wayne State University Press, 2001), 38; Anthony Wayne to Timothy Pickering, September 20, 1795, in Knopf, ed., 461.

12 Anthony Wayne to Timothy Pickering, September 20, 1795, in Knopf, ed., 461.

13 "Treaty of Greenville 1795," The Avalon Project: Documents in Law, History and Diplomacy, Yale Law School, http://avalon.law.yale.edu (accessed July 22, 2009); George E. Fay, ed., *Treaties, Land Cessions, and Other U.S. Congressional Documents Relative to American Indians Tribes* (Greeley: University of Northern Colorado, 1971), 22. The 1807 Treaty of Detroit was formally known as the "Treaty with the Ottawa, etc." and was written and agreed upon on November 17, 1807, and proclaimed on January 27, 1808. For additional cases of land speculation, see the essays in this volume by Alexandria Reid, Kimberly Steele, and Douglas D. Fisher.

14 Potawatomi Indians today live primarily in Oklahoma and Kansas. For Oklahoma, see Citizen Potawatomi Nation, www.potawatomi.org (accessed July 22, 2009). For Kansas, see Prairie Band Potawatomi Nation, www.pbpindiantribe.com (accessed July 22, 2009). There are also still Potawatomis living in Michigan. According to a report in 2000, the Huron Potawatomi Reservation had only eleven registered members, but the Pokagon Band of Potawatomi Reservation, which borders Michigan and Indiana, had 35,415 residents. See "Population of Indian Reservations, Trust Lands and Tribal Statistical Areas in Michigan, 2000," www.michigan.gov/documents/indiancountry_31994_7.pdf (accessed July 22, 2009).

PART TWO

REVOLUTIONARY WAR: RAIDS AND COERCION

As relations between Britain and its American colonies fractured during the 1770s, military administrators in British North America grew painfully aware of their tenuous hold on the western territory. With a small number of regular soldiers at their disposal, they governed a vast area inhabited by a diverse population whose loyalties varied from strong to antagonistic.

The war shaped every aspect of Detroit society. Strategically, the town became the staging ground for an aggressive rear guard action against American settlements in Ohio Country and Kentucky. Indian warriors, aggressively courted with gifts and promises, provided the military strength for these raids. Detroit, in turn, served as the main northern incarceration point for American prisoners taken during the war.

The fort remained the center of trade activity on the upper lakes, but the trade had distinctly military priorities. The British, in critical circumstances, employed politically coercive tactics on all local inhabitants with varying degrees of legality and severity. The population's commitment wavered at times, but Detroit remained solidly loyalist throughout the Revolution.

Lt. Governor Henry Hamilton
Artist unknown (n.d.). Oil on ivory. Courtesy of the Houghton Library, Harvard University.
Gift of Mrs. Caroline Isabella Hamilton Rice, 1902. MS Eng 508.2.

Liberty Hangs at Detroit: The Trial and Execution of Jean Contencineau

Errin T. Stegich

After the Seven Years' War, the transition to British rule was met by remarkably little resistance from French *habitants* in Detroit, even amidst the disturbance of Pontiac's siege of the settlement's fort in 1763. The calm contrasted markedly with the American resistance movements against British imperial policies that took place along the eastern seaboard during the 1760s and 1770s. In Detroit, French, British, and other Europeans continued to coexist quietly under British administration until the appointment of Lieutenant Governor Henry Hamilton, also superintendent of Indian affairs, in November 1775. Hamilton served as lieutenant governor for only four years (1775-1779), but his actions fostered the first extended example of public dissent by European colonists in Detroit. The trial and execution of Jean Baptiste Contencineau in the spring of 1776 epitomized the unpopular authoritative control exercised by Hamilton.[1]

The circumstances of Contencineau's trial dated to the summer of 1774, when a number of petty burglaries disturbed Detroit's residents. On the night of June 24, the fur store of Abbott & Finchley was robbed of several furs, knives, and guns. The culprits were discovered shortly after the incident: Jean Baptiste Contencineau, an employee at the store, and Ann Wiley, a slave belonging to James Abbott, one of the store's owners. Contencineau and Wiley were charged with petty larceny and publicly whipped. A few days after their punishment, the pair set fire to the same fur warehouse and were apprehended for arson. Philip Dejean, justice of the peace at Fort Detroit, called a hearing and took testimony from town residents. Contencineau and Wiley were subsequently imprisoned and waited for trial until the spring of 1776.[2]

In April 1775, the same month as the battles of Lexington and Concord, Detroit was annexed to the Quebec province. Until this point, no civilian governor had exercised full authority over Detroit, and as a result, the fort's commandant acted as the chief civil magistrate and head military official. When news of the war on the east coast reached Quebec Governor Guy Carleton, he declared martial law for the Great Lakes region. Against this backdrop, Henry Hamilton took control at Fort

Detroit. During the Seven Years' War, Hamilton had served as a captain in the 15th Regiment of Foot and participated in Britain's victories at Louisburg and Quebec. His peers regarded him as a man with the ability "to shine in a higher sphere of life." In 1775, he sold his commission in the British army to pursue a political career, which led to his appointment at Fort Detroit.[3]

Hamilton brought a military sensibility to his position as lieutenant governor and expected total subordination by Detroit's population. By the end of 1776, the British realized that the war to maintain control of the northwest could not be fought without the heavy assistance of Native Americans. Hamilton received orders from Governor Carleton to keep "the Indians in readiness for, and a disposition to act as circumstances require." The lieutenant governor gained the reputation as the "Hair-Buyer General" because it was suspected that he financed the killing and scalping of American settlers throughout the Great Lakes region and Ohio River Valley.[4] Whether true or not, Hamilton believed in subduing American advances in western lands at almost any cost. In June 1777, he attempted to strengthen Detroit as a British loyalist center by guaranteeing two hundred acres of land to anyone who would "withdraw themselves from the Tyranny and oppression of the rebels committees and take refuge in [Detroit] or any of the Posts commanded by his Majesty's Officers."[5]

Hamilton's decision to allow Philip Dejean to continue his post as justice of the peace helped to define his tenure as lieutenant governor. Dejean had a notorious reputation. On one occasion, he tried three cases in front of the same jury, and all the offenders were sentenced and hanged. He proved to be just as committed to maintaining order in the case of Contencineau and Wiley. In the spring of 1776, a jury of six British and six French men was called to decide on the charges of arson and petty larceny. The jury acquitted Contencineau and Wiley on the charge of arson, but convicted them of larceny. Dejean ordered the pair to be "hanged, hanged, hanged, and strangled until dead" on March 25 at the public common. The execution order angered the European colonists in Detroit, and on the day of the execution, no one could be found to perform the hanging. Dejean offered Wiley a bargain: her life in return for the execution of Contencineau. Wiley consented, and on execution day a crowd watched the slave woman execute the Frenchman.[6]

After the hanging, a group of four Detroit settlers wrote to Governor Carleton about Hamilton's improprieties. On September 7, 1778, a grand jury issued a nine-page indictment against Hamilton and Dejean, for neither had the provincial authority to issue the death penalty; they should have sent Contencineau and Wiley to stand trial in Montreal. Fearing possible arrest, Hamilton and Dejean left Detroit in October along with several garrison troops and Indians to retake Fort Sackville at Vincennes.

Hamilton had been planning an attack on Fort Sackville for several months. The combination of the indictment and United States Colonel George Rogers Clark's departure from Vincennes gave the British at Detroit an ideal opportunity to attack the small garrison left behind.[7]

In December 1778, Hamilton recaptured Vincennes, but the victory was fleeting. Clark returned in February, and his American forces outnumbered the British by almost 2-to-1. Hamilton surrendered and later wrote, "The mortification, disappointment and indignation I felt, may possibly be conceived if all the considerations are taken together . . . Our views of prosecuting any design against the enemy totally overturned."[8] Detroit's former leader was jailed in Williamsburg, Virginia, until 1781 for supporting frontier Indian raids against American settlements. Hamilton then received parole on the condition that he sail immediately to London, which he did. In 1782, he returned to North America to serve as deputy lieutenant governor of Quebec. Hamilton later held the title of governor of both Bermuda and Dominica before dying in Antigua in 1796—the year his former post at Detroit passed to the Americans.[9]

Dejean fared worse. After being captured in the Vincennes expedition, he spent four months in a Williamsburg prison. Dejean's parole in late 1779 began an itinerant lifestyle that lasted until his death. Although his family was not permitted to leave Detroit, he could not return immediately for fear of being prosecuted. He instead went to Vincennes before returning safely to Detroit sometime in late 1780. By 1783, Dejean was destitute and sought assistance from General Charles Cornwallis, who was then stationed in New York. Dejean asked for £150 for his annual pay as notary and judge, as well as a per diem for his services as pay master and agent for the Detroit district for the time he spent in prison.[10] In 1789, he left Detroit and remained away without disclosing his location; James May, his brother-in-law, assumed control of his estate. Historical records last place Dejean with his family in Vincennes until he died around 1809.[11]

Ann Wiley's role in the Contencineau affair also exposed the significance of slavery in frontier Detroit. Wiley's crimes against her master, if true, fit a larger pattern of slave resistance in North America. Contencineau and Wiley likely acted against James Abbott and his store for deep injustices in the way servile and enslaved workers were treated in frontier Detroit. Larceny and arson were among the most common tactics of slave resistance, as evidenced by the "New York Slave Conspiracy of 1741."[12]

Existing records yield very little information about Wiley except that she belonged to Abbott. She was part of a significant enslaved labor force in Detroit. A census taken in September 1773 indicated that 1,277 people lived in the immediate vicinity of Fort Detroit; eighty-five persons, or 7 percent of the population, were identified as slaves. By April 1778, of the 2,144 inhabitants living at or near the fort, 127 were considered slaves, or 6 percent of the population.[13] The figures did not distinguish between African and Indian slaves, although both groups were in Detroit. The historian Norman McRae has argued that the number of black slaves increased in Detroit during the 1770s (even if the overall percentage fell slightly), due to the influx of British officers and merchants who transferred to the area. The slaves, as McRae posits, "were not only a source of necessary cheap labor but also a capital investment that could be liquidated whenever one chose."[14]

The Contencineau case exposed unrest among both Detroit's free and enslaved populations in the mid-1770s. The excessive punishment against Contencineau and humiliating treatment of Wiley provided the most visible evidence of Hamilton's authoritarian rule. The lieutenant governor was not shy about his approach to governing Detroit. Shortly before leaving the fort for Vincennes, he wrote, "The disposition of the people at this place requires something more than the shadow of authority to keep them in the Bounds of Duty."[15] Hamilton also promised his superiors in Montreal that he would "watch and seize . . . who shall dare make a parade of his disloyalty."[16] If anything, Hamilton's actions as lieutenant governor inspired the very disloyalty that he sought to prohibit. Until his tenure, public dissent among Europeans was virtually non-existent in Detroit. The trial of Contencineau and Wiley and its aftermath signified the most effective challenge to British rule before the American takeover of 1796. At the same time, the affair reminds us that, however egregious, Hamilton's impact on Detroit's European population was temporary; the condition of Ann Wiley and Detroit's other slaves was in most cases permanent.

NOTES

1 For studies on Hamilton's tenure at Fort Detroit, see John D. Barnhart, ed., *Henry Hamilton and George Rogers Clark in the American Revolution: With the Unpublished Journal of Lieut. Gov. Henry Hamilton* (Crawfordsville, IN: R.E. Banta, 1951), 180-85; *City of Detroit*, 2:913-18; Clarence M. Burton, "Henry ('Hair-Buyer') Hamilton," *Magazine of History with Notes and Queries* 1 (1905): 176-81; Silas Farmer, *History of Detroit and Wayne County and Early Michigan: A Chronological Cyclopedia of the Past & Present* (Lansing: S. Farmer, 1890), 242-60; Paul Leake, *History of Detroit: A Chronicle of Its Progress, Its Industries, Its Institutions, and the People of the Fair City of the Straits* (Chicago: Lewis, 1912), 57-60; William R. Nester, *The Frontier War for American Independence* (Mechanicsburg, PA: Stackpole, 2004), 81-84; and Nelson Vance Russell, *The British Régime in Michigan and the Old Northwest, 1760-1796* (Northfield, MN: Carleton College, 1939).

2 David Lee Poremba, ed., *Detroit in Its World Setting: A Three-Hundred Year Chronology, 1701-2001* (Detroit: Wayne State University Press, 2001), 50; John Bell Moran, *The Moran Family: 200 Years in Detroit* (Detroit: Alved, 1949), 27. Ann is referred to as Nancy in some historical records.

3 Earl of Harcourt to Earl of Dartmouth, March 15, 1775, William Legge Dartmouth Papers, BHC (quote); William Hey to Earl of Dartmouth, February 1775, Dartmouth Papers; Major Thomas Mant to Earl of Dartmouth, April 1766, Dartmouth Papers.

4 Guy Carleton to Henry Hamilton, October 6, 1776, in *MPHC*, 9:344. Historians debate whether or not Hamilton actually paid Indians for scalps. See Barnhart, ed., *Henry Hamilton*, 35-36, 219; George E. Greene, *History of Old Vincennes and Knox County, Indiana* (Detroit and Chicago: S.J. Clarke, 1911), 182-85; Daniel S. Murphree, "Redcoats, Regulators, and the Rattletrap: The Back Country Experience," in *American Revolution: People and Perspectives*, ed. Andrew K. Frank and Peter C. Mancall (Santa Barbara: ABC-CLIO, 2007), 97-98; and Bernard W. Sheehan, "'The Famous Hair Buyer General': Henry Hamilton, George Rogers Clark, and the American Indian," *Indiana Magazine of History* 69 (March 1983): 1-28.

5 Henry Hamilton, "Proclamation inciting loyalists, 24 June 1777," Henry Hamilton Papers, BHC.

6 Dejean quoted in Moran, 28; Clarence M. Burton, "23 vol. 1 Detroit History," Clarence M. Burton Papers, BHC. Dejean's conduct had already been called into question a few years earlier in 1768, but the result of the investigation was inconclusive and he returned to his position as notary of Detroit under the command of Captain George Turnbull. See William Renwick Riddell, *The First Judge at Detroit and His Court* (Lansing: Michigan State Bar Association, 1915), 9.

7 Burton, "23 vol. 1 Detroit History", *City of Detroit*, 2:910-19. For Hamilton's limited authority to execute criminals, see Guy Carleton to Henry Hamilton, February 2, 1777, in *MPHC*, 9:346. Historians often overlook the connection between the indictment and Hamilton's attempt to retake Vincennes. For Hamilton's expedition, see John D. Barnhart, "A New Evaluation of Henry Hamilton and George Rogers Clark," *Mississippi Valley Historical Review* 37 (1951): 643-52; John Spencer Bassett, *A Short History of the United States* (New York: Macmillan, 1913), 203-4; Milo M. Quaife, ed., *The Capture of Old Vincennes: The Original Narratives of George Rogers Clark and of His Opponent, Gov. Henry Hamilton* (Indianapolis: Bobbs-Merrill, 1927); and the essay in this volume by Donald Lee. For British court reform in the Detroit River region following the Hamilton/Dejean judicial indiscretions, see the essay in this volume by Sharon Tevis Finch.

8 Henry Hamilton, "Journal entry dated 23 February 1779," in Barnhart, ed., *Henry Hamilton*, 185.

9 For Hamilton's sentencing and imprisonment in Virginia, see the essay in this volume by Caitlyn A.O. Perry.

10 Philip Dejean to Charles Cornwallis, July 22, 1783, Philip Dejean Papers, BHC. It is not clear if Dejean ever received the back pay that he sought.

11 William Renwick Riddell, *The Bar and the Courts of the Province of Upper Canada, or Ontario* (Toronto: Macmillan, 1928), 68; "Phillippe Dejean," Dictionary of Canadian Biography Online, University of Toronto, www.biographi.ca (accessed May 5, 2009).

12 Jill Lepore, *New York Burning: Liberty, Slavery, and Conspiracy in Eighteenth-Century Manhattan* (New York: Knopf, 2005); Peter Charles Hoffer, *The Great New York Conspiracy of 1741: Slavery, Crime, and Colonial Law* (Lawrence: University Press of Kansas, 2003).

13 "A General Return of All the Inhabitants of Detroit, September 22, 1773," in *MPHC*, 9:649; "The state of the settlements taken by order of the Lieutenant Governor, Detroit, April 28, 1778," in *MPHC*, 9:469.

14 Norman McRae, "Early Blacks in Michigan, 1743-1800," *Detroit in Perspective: A Journal of Regional History* 2 (1976): 165.

15 Henry Hamilton to Lieutenant Governor Cramahé, August 12, 1778, in *MPHC*, 9:462.

16 Henry Hamilton to Lieutenant Governor Cramahé, August 17, 1778, in *MPHC*, 9:463.

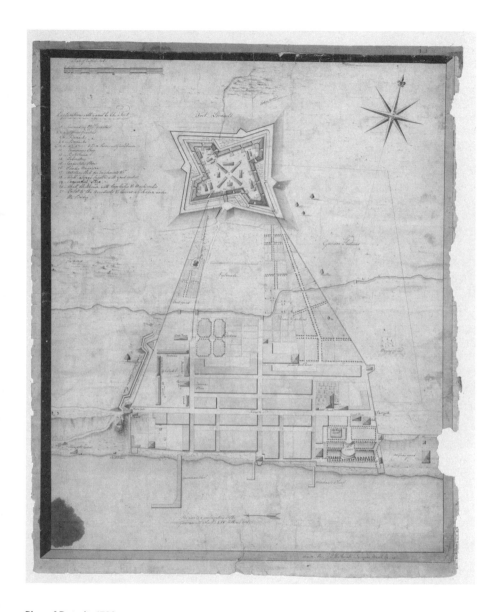

Plan of Detroit, 1796
Drawn by Major John Jacob Ulrich Rivardi (1799). Pencil, pen, ink, watercolor on paper.
Courtesy of the William L. Clements Library, University of Michigan.

Clark and Lernoult: Reduction by Expansion

Donald Lee

I learn by your letter to Governor Hamilton that you were very busy making new works, I am glad to hear it, as it saves the Americans some expences in building[.] my Compliments to the Gentlemen of your Garrison[.]

Colonel George Rogers Clark to Captain Richard Lernoult,

March 16, 1779

The loss of this Post [Vincennes] opens a new road for the Virginians to this place by the Miamis River, I hope strong reinforcement will be sent here from Niagara . . . as the new work is not yet defensible . . . I beg leave to repeat to you the necessity of reinforcement being sent, as the consequences may be fatal . . . All the [French] Canadians are Rebels, to a man. I shall await your orders with great impatience[.]

Captain Richard Lernoult to Lieutenant Colonel Mason Bolton,

March 26, 1779[1]

The excerpts above reveal the differences in the personalities of the two people most responsible for the construction of Fort Lernoult, the new bastion erected on higher ground to the north of the existing Fort Detroit during the American Revolutionary War: the man the fort was named after, Richard Lernoult, and the man that drove him to build it, George Rogers Clark. Biographies and commentaries on Clark are plentiful, and most depict his conquest and capture of Lieutenant Governor Henry Hamilton at Vincennes in February 1779 as heroic. Historical works generally neglect Lernoult; indeed, the majority of information about his tenure as commander of Fort Detroit comes from his correspondence. Lernoult's letters reveal how Clark's bravado enabled him to shake the uncertain British captain. Without ever approaching the fort, Clark managed to influence Detroit's physical growth and neutralize the threat of British forces from the northwest, a case of reduction by expansion.[2]

Lernoult first arrived in Detroit in 1773, and remained at the fort until he was reassigned to Fort Niagara in 1776. In December 1777, he returned to command the military garrison at Detroit, where conditions between Hamilton and his commanding officers had deteriorated greatly. Lernoult was given the task of ending the quarrel and restoring calm to one of Britain's most crucial northwestern outposts.[3]

The fort underwent changes in 1764, shortly after the end of Pontiac's siege, to address its shortcomings. At the time, soldiers lived in empty houses among Detroit's residents. Lessons from the siege shaped the transformation. The British needed a defensible location for barracks and a proper facility to load and unload ships. In August, therefore, Captain John Montresor designed a fortified area within the walls that would later be known as the Citadel, as well as a pier adjoining the fort. The work continued for quite some time, and local residents were required to help. The townspeople's effort was a prelude to a similar situation during the Revolutionary War, when an enemy force again shaped the construction of defenses at Detroit.[4]

Until 1776, the British made additional small improvements to the fort to prepare for another Indian attack. In September 1776, Hamilton wrote to William Legge, the earl of Dartmouth, secretary of state for the American colonies, to describe repairs that provided adequate defense against "Savages, or an Enemy unprovided with cannon."[5] Physically, the fort was a simple stockade made of upright cedar logs fifteen feet high. The repairs included building new blockhouses and batteries to replace those that had rotted. There was a ditch along two sides of the Citadel, but Hamilton did not have the men to defend the fort against a large siege. In an addendum, he stated that news had reached Detroit that an agent for the Virginia assembly was recruiting western Indians to attend a council at Fort Pitt. The agent carried a copy of the *Pennsylvania Gazette* from July "containing a declaration of Colonies, by which they entirely throw off all Dependence on the Mother Country." The war was coming to Detroit.[6]

The fort had significance for both sides in the Revolutionary War. For the British, it provided an ideal staging ground for raids on western American settlements. For the Americans, Detroit was essential to dislodging the upper Great Lakes region from the British. The closest analogy on the American side was Fort Pitt; both forts Pitt and Detroit were vital to the western theater and vulnerable to attack. By December 1777, when Lernoult returned to Detroit, Hamilton was seeking permission to lead a joint British-Indian force against Fort Pitt. The lieutenant governor gathered multiple intelligence reports, and spent the remainder of the winter preparing for a spring offensive. A change of command in Quebec from Guy Carleton to Frederick Haldimand, however, delayed Hamilton's planned assault and eventually denied him the chance altogether.[7]

The Americans did not sit idly waiting for the British to make a move. They first made plans to attack Detroit as early as 1775. In 1777, Clark included Detroit in his larger design to take the western frontier from the British; he planned to begin with posts in Illinois Country and move eastward. The Virginia militia officer was motivated by fears that the British and their Indian allies in Detroit would expand their attacks on western settlements to his native state. Opening another front in the war from the west would distract the United States from defeating the main British army. Clark reasoned that low costs and a high likelihood of success made Detroit a favorable target.[8]

Virginia Governor Patrick Henry approved Clark's plan. In January 1778, Henry sent secret orders to Clark to begin by seizing Kaskaskia in present-day southern Illinois. The Virginians aspired to use guns plundered from there to build an American fort at the mouth of the Ohio River (today Cairo, Illinois). By the summer, Kaskaskia, Cahokia, and Vincennes—all small forts in the region—had fallen to the Americans with minimal resistance from the mostly French inhabitants. The threat to Detroit was growing.[9]

In August 1778, Hamilton wrote to Governor Haldimand detailing the danger of Clark's actions and was rewarded with permission to retake Vincennes. Hamilton's departure in October left Lernoult in command of Detroit. Though widely respected, he never became fully comfortable in his role as commander of Detroit. Lernoult feared attacks by Clark from the west and by Americans at Fort Pitt from the east. Soon after taking command, he determined that the only solution was to build a new fort at Detroit on higher ground north of the original French fort. Lernoult placed his second-in-command, Captain Henry Bird, in charge of the project, and work began in earnest during the winter of 1778-1779. The British command forced settlers, even merchants, to work on the new fort. In February 1779, Lernoult wrote to Hamilton, who was wintering in Vincennes (before his capture), and shared his anxieties about Detroit's security. In addition to the fort's lack of reinforcements, Lernoult expressed concern about his ignorance in handling Indian affairs. For the first time since Pontiac's War, the British military had serious doubts about the survival of its post at Detroit.[10]

Lernoult's insecurities fully surfaced when news of Hamilton's capture reached Detroit in March 1779. He redoubled efforts to complete the new fort. Lernoult also sent a desperate letter to Lieutenant Colonel Mason Bolton, commander of Fort Niagara, pleading for more troops to counter Clark and complaining about the lack of help from Detroit's French inhabitants in building the fort.[11] His frustrations notwithstanding, the structure was ready for action in April. Named Fort Lernoult in honor of the commander, it markedly improved Britain's defenses in the upper Great Lakes region. Detroit was now too secure to be taken by anything short of a major assault. Clark made repeated requests for the men to make such an attack, claiming that just five hundred more would "enable me to do something clever." Despite an impressive record of cleverness, Clark never received his desired reinforcements. The attack on Detroit so long anticipated by all sides in the war never materialized.[12]

Without ever setting foot in the upper Great Lakes, Clark's victories in Illinois Country put British forces on the defensive. They were occupied building Fort Lernoult at a crucial juncture in the war. The British still sponsored Indian raids from Detroit for the remainder of the revolution, but never seriously threatened Fort Pitt or the original thirteen states. The new fort at Detroit became a legacy of Lernoult's command that persisted into the American era as Fort Shelby. In its origin, however, the impressive structure was more a sign of British weakness than strength.

NOTES

1 Clark and Lernoult quoted in James Alton James, ed., *George Rogers Clark Papers, 1771-1781,* 2 vols. (Springfield: Illinois State Historical Library, 1912-26), 1:306-7; 308-9. The letters were written soon after Clark captured Lieutenant Governor Henry Hamilton at Vincennes in February 1779.

2 Numerous historical works document Clark's successes, but they rarely mention Detroit in any detail. See, for example, John D. Barnhart, "A New Evaluation of Henry Hamilton and George Rogers Clark," *Mississippi Valley Historical Review* 37 (1951): 643-52; John Law, *The Colonial History of Vincennes, under the French, British, and American Governments, from Its First Settlement Down to the Territorial Administration of William Henry Harrison* (Vincennes, IN: Harvey, Mason and Co., 1858); and Willis F. Dunbar and George S. May, *Michigan: A History of the Wolverine State,* 3rd rev. ed. (Grand Rapids: Eerdmans, 1995), 81. A notable exception is Philip P. Mason, *Detroit, Fort Lernoult, and the American Revolution* (Detroit: Wayne State University Press, 1964), which briefly but effectively discusses the rivalry between Clark and Lernoult.

3 *City of Detroit,* 2:916; WHC, 18:395.

4 Gideon D. Scull, ed., *The Montresor Journals* (New York: New York Historical Society, 1882), 285. In his journals, Captain Montresor kept a thorough daily account of his time and offered insight about how the British garrison acquired the materials needed for the expansion. He also mentioned a wintering location for ships somewhere along the Rouge River.

5 Henry Hamilton to Earl of Dartmouth, September 2, 1776, in MPHC, 10:264-70; 265 (quote).

6 Hamilton to Dartmouth, September 2, 1776, 10:269.

7 *City of Detroit,* 2:916.

8 George Rogers Clark to [Patrick Henry?], 1777, in James, ed., 1:30-33.

9 Patrick Henry to George Rogers Clark, January 2, 1778, in James, ed., 1:34-36. Henry sent Clark two sets of orders, a secret one that directed him to Kaskaskia and a public decoy that sent him to Kentucky.

10 John D. Barnhart, ed., *Henry Hamilton and George Rogers Clark in the American Revolution: With the Unpublished Journal of Lieut. Gov. Henry Hamilton* (Crawfordsville, IN: R.E. Banta, 1981), 39; Richard Lernoult to Henry Hamilton, February 9, 1779, in James, ed., 1:108-9; Mason. For the circumstances surrounding Hamilton's departure, see also the essay in this volume by Errin T. Stegich.

11 Lernoult to Bolton, March 26, 1779, 1:307-9. The letter is quoted at length in the beginning of the essay.

12 George Rogers Clark to Benjamin Harrison, March 10, 1779, in James, ed., 1:305.

Little Navy on the Great Lakes
Stephen Al-Hakim

The Great Lakes region is seldom included in scholarly analysis of the American Revolutionary War. The handful of existing studies focus almost exclusively on land operations, such as George Rogers Clark's famous exploits within Illinois Country. Meanwhile, naval activity on the Great Lakes during the war is continually overlooked. George Cuthbertson, an influential historian of Great Lakes navigation, even claimed that "the Revolutionary War of the American Colonies had little or no effect on the lakes." His oversight may be forgiven since there was limited knowledge of the topic when he was writing in the early twentieth century. Upon closer inspection, the British Fleet of the Upper Great Lakes was crucial to securing control over the region. With a monopoly over ship traffic, Britain succeeded in keeping American forces out of the upper Great Lakes and American traders away from the economically and diplomatically vital fur trade.[1]

After conquering New France, the British realized they needed armed vessels on the lakes to protect their new territory. Thus began their pioneering endeavor to establish a sailing fleet on the lakes. In 1762, the schooner *Huron* and the sloop *Michigan* were built at Navy Island on the Niagara River. These two vessels played an indispensable role in aiding Detroit when it was under siege by Pontiac and his forces in 1763. Following the uprising, the British consolidated their hold on the region by building or conscripting a number of vessels to navigate the lakes. The Provincial Marine, headed by the governor of Quebec and comprised of members of the Royal Navy and colonial officials, controlled the fleet. In response to difficulties administering such a large unit during the Revolutionary War, the Royal Navy divided its Great Lakes forces into three geographical locales: one for Lake Champlain and Lake George, one for Lake Ontario, and the last for Lake Erie and the three northern lakes. Each fleet was commanded by the senior naval officer in its respective district. In the case of the Upper Great Lakes Fleet based in Detroit, the job went to Captain Alexander Grant. He commanded the fleet from his home in Grosse Pointe until 1813.[2]

The Revolution not only sparked a reorganization of Britain's navy on the Great Lakes, but also ushered in an era of British naval dominance. Shortly after fighting broke out in the east, the sailing of private vessels on the lakes was intensely regulated by British authorities. No vessel was allowed to be built or to navigate the region without the appropriate documentation from commanding military personnel. Britain's chief concern was the secure shipment of military supplies, troops, and official correspondence. In May 1777, Quebec Governor Guy Carleton ordered that "no vessels are to navigate those Lakes except such as are armed and manned by the Crown." As a result, all private trade goods were required to be shipped on naval vessels, and then only if they did not disrupt wartime operations; merchant craft sailed, but only as navy ships. In essence, the Royal Navy claimed a monopoly on Great Lakes shipping and made commerce secondary to military concerns.[3]

Such strict regulations were not popular with Great Lakes merchants. The war increased demand for goods, and the Provincial Marine could not meet all the shipping needs of traders. The eleven vessels commissioned to sail the lakes under the Upper Great Lakes Fleet proved to be especially inadequate. Traders often sent petitions to the authorities requesting more attention to the shipment of their goods, which were continuously filling port storehouses. The prominent fur trader John Askin described in one account how he required two vessels dedicated solely to the shipment of his goods. After succeeding Carleton as governor of Quebec in 1778, Frederick Haldimand was sympathetic to the traders but held firm on merchant shipping restrictions. The governor continued to enforce the policy mostly due to fear of rebel attacks on supply lines. Disruptions by American forces would have caused a far greater shock to the region's economy than the navy's tight regulation of commerce, he reasoned.[4]

Despite concerns over the safety of commerce, the British did make some concessions for the fur trade. The trade was crucial economically and for maintaining key alliances with Native American groups. In July 1779, Lieutenant Governor Patrick Sinclair received the order from Governor Haldimand "to pay great attention to the Indians . . . endeavour to preserve them in good Humour, and attach them by every [means] in your Power to the King's Interest."[5] The British needed Indian warriors to provide support for land skirmishes and wanted to avoid a repeat of Pontiac's uprising. Consequently, Indian traders traveling in canoes were exempt from the trade embargo. In addition, the Upper Great Lakes Fleet supported those and other traders with vessels such as the *Felicity*, which became the backbone of the fur trade. By keeping the industry alive, the fleet served Britain's most essential economic and diplomatic interest in the region.[6]

Not content with simply using its navy for defensive purposes, Britain attempted to push toward the Mississippi River in the latter years of the Revolutionary War. As a first step, in mid-1779 the commander of Fort Michilimackinac, Colonel Arent De Peyster, made diplomatic overtures to the Potawatomi and Ottawa Indians along the southern shores of Lake Michigan. De Peyster failed, but his successor, Sinclair, continued the efforts. Rather than follow De Peyster's diplomatic route, Sinclair opted to coerce Indian fealty. Food stores were low at his new post, so he crafted a plan for a vessel to sail to the southern coast of Lake Michigan to confiscate Indian corn and awe the tribes with Britain's naval power. In late October, Captain Samuel Roberts left Michilimackinac aboard the sloop *Felicity* on a two-week mission. He found less corn than expected, which still left food stores at the fort below capacity. Furthermore, talks with Indian leaders went dismally. Sinclair's initiative ended in failure, much like De Peyster's, but the attempt itself was significant because it was the first time the British tried to expand power in Lake Michigan by using the Upper Great Lakes Fleet.[7]

When the Revolutionary War ended, the British had still not succeeded in securing the Mississippi River route. A late-war attack on St. Louis, aided by the *Felicity* and another unnamed vessel, failed. However, the result could have been more disastrous had the two vessels not been available to rescue retreating British soldiers. The Treaty of Paris in 1783 put all dreams of British expansion in North America on hold. Thereafter, until the American takeover of 1796, Britain used its navy in the upper Great Lakes to continue pursuing the same goals as it had during the Revolution: to retain a monopoly on the fur trade, maintain alliances with Indian groups, and keep American settlers out of the region. Although trade restrictions loosened by 1785, the Provincial Marine continued to dispatch navy vessels to prevent American enterprise. Some scholars attribute this policy to the economic incentives of the fur trade, but others refute such arguments by noting that the cost of maintaining forts had risen so high that the fur trade lost its appealing profit margin.[8]

In either case, the navy continued to serve Britain's key economic and diplomatic interests in the Great Lakes. Even though it failed at expanding British territory, the Upper Great Lakes Fleet played a critical and underappreciated role in maintaining Britain's power in the region during the Revolutionary War and beyond. The fleet was vital in preventing rebel movement, maintaining Indian relations, and controlling trade and supplies. Indeed, without the navy, the British could not have held Detroit and its environs until 1783, much less 1796.

NOTES

1 George A. Cuthbertson, *Freshwater: A History and a Narrative of the Great Lakes* (New York: Macmillan, 1931), 119. Few works discuss the British navy on the Great Lakes during the American Revolution. Most are dated and of limited use because they fail to use modern methods of historical referencing. See, for example, Cuthbertson, 122-38, and John B. Mansfield, *History of the Great Lakes*, 2 vols. (Chicago: J.H. Beers, 1899), 1:119-23. More recent works are limited in number. An important exception is Brian Leigh Dunnigan, "British Naval Vessels on the Upper Great Lakes, 1761-1796," *Telescope* 31 (1982): 92-98. Another, David A. Armour and Keith R. Widder, *At the Crossroads: Michilimackinac during the American Revolution* (Mackinac Island: Mackinac Island State Park Commission, 1978), only discusses the navy in brief instances periodically throughout the book. Patrick J. Jung, "A Valuable and Dependable Little Navy: The British Upper Great Lakes Fleet during the American Revolution," *Inland Seas* 53 (1997): 68-75, 142-50, 204-7, provides a thorough description of the Upper Great Lakes Fleet, but neglects its larger strategic importance in securing the Great Lakes region.

2 Cuthbertson, 117-19; Jung, 70; Thomas H. Raddall, *The Path of Destiny: Canada from the British Conquest to Home Rule: 1763-1850* (Toronto: Doubleday, 1957), 90. The term Provincial Marine was not used until the American Revolution. However, during the Seven Years' War and Pontiac's War, the British used armed naval vessels on the lakes manned in the same fashion as the Provincial Marine. Guy Carleton held the position of administrative head of the Provincial Marine until Frederick Haldimand was appointed governor of Quebec in 1778. See "General Orders, and Regulations for the better Government of the Naval Force employed on the different Lakes, July 1778," in *WHC*, 11.194.

3 John Askin to Alexander Grant, April 28, 1778, in *Askin Papers*, 1:76; "To Lt. Govr. Hamilton or Officer Commanding at Detroit" (from E. Fox, undated), in *MPHC*, 9:345; Guy Carleton to Frederick Haldimand, Quebec, May 22, 1777, in *MPHC*, 9:348.

4 Armour and Widder, 66, 73; John Askin to James McGill, Benjamin Frobisher, and Charles Patterson, April 28, 1778, in *Askin Papers*, 1:74-75; Joseph Williams to William Robertson, Detroit, March 30, 1781, in *MPHC*, 19:602-3; D. Brehm to Patrick Sinclair, Quebec, April 17, 1780, in *MPHC*, 9:537.

5 "Instructions for Captain Patrick Sinclair, Lieut. Governor & Superintendent of Indian Affairs at Missilc." (from Frederick Haldimand, July 1779), in *MPHC*, 9:517. For the fur trade's ongoing diplomatic significance, see Frederick Haldimand to Arent De Peyster, Quebec, May 20, 1779, in *MPHC*, 9:359.

6 Arent De Peyster to Frederick Haldimand, Fort Michilimackinac, June, 14, 1779, in *MPHC*, 9:384; "To Lt. Govr. Hamilton or Officer Commanding at Detroit," 9:345; Jung, 148; Melvin E. Banner, "The Riddles of the *Felicity*," *Telescope* 18 (1969): 61-64.

7 Armour and Widder, 109-11, 123; Jung, 204-5; "Remarks on Board his Majesty's Sloop *Felicity* by Samuel Roberts on Piloting her on Lake Mitchigon," Oct. 21, 1779, in *WHC*, 11:203.

8 Jung, 205; Carl E. Krog, "The British Great Lakes Forts," *Inland Seas* 42 (1986): 252-60.

American Sympathy and Resistance in British Detroit

Alexandria Reid

During the American Revolution, Detroit served as a launching point for combined British army and Indian raids against American settlers. There was no "Battle of Detroit," and its residents never raised an armed resistance against the British. From this, it might be assumed that the people of Detroit passively accepted British rule until the Americans arrived in 1796. While it is true that the majority of Detroit's population supported the British, there was a small community that supported the Americans. When discussing these American sympathizers, the trend has been to attribute their actions to their support for the "American cause." However, the sympathizers at Detroit chose to resist the British for reasons that belonged uniquely to the frontier: the economic advantages of an American victory against the British and anger at the British alliance with the Indians. To attribute their actions to American nationalism is an oversimplification, one that conceals the complex nature of the conflict on the frontier.[1]

"The disposition of the people at this place," wrote Henry Hamilton, describing Detroit to one of his superiors in 1778, "requires something more than the shadow of authority to keep them in the Bounds of Duty."[2] Indeed, by the late 1770s, the British at Detroit faced an ever-growing population of discontented subjects who made it their mission to irritate, inconvenience, and hinder the British in any way possible. This group consisted of several segments of Detroit society, predictably the French, but also the Spanish and even some British nationals, of whom Hamilton voiced his suspicions in a 1778 letter to Quebec Governor Frederick Haldimand: "The greatest part of the traders among them who are called English, are rebels in their hearts."[3] The methods of the "rebels" were creative and varied. Many of the traders at the fort, for example, began refusing to fill British orders, one of Hamilton's frustrations in 1778. Additionally, some men chose to taunt the British at every available opportunity. In 1779, James Cassidy and William Boswick were brought up on treason charges after speaking against the British government. They both said that Detroit would soon be in the hands of the Americans and insulted the British army, calling one of its officers a "damn'd coward."[4]

Some men were more blatant in their support for the American cause, and their behavior raises the most questions. Two of the best-documented cases involve Israel Ruland and John Edgar, who were arrested by the British in August 1779. Prisoners John Higgins and William Humphreys gave depositions that stated Edgar and Ruland had helped them to flee Detroit by providing clothes, ammunition, food, guns, and other supplies. Furthermore, the depositions stated that Ruland was working for United States Army Colonel George Rogers Clark. Edgar had reportedly aided other prisoners in a similar manner. In a deposition he wrote to Congress, Edgar stated that the British had previously detained him for providing the U.S. Army with information about the British army's movements. He also said that he helped prisoners escape so that they could deliver intelligence to the Americans regarding Indians who were allied with the British.[5]

These actions had a disastrous affect on the lives of these two men. When the British came to arrest the pair, Ruland abandoned his business in Detroit and fled to the Americans at Vincennes. Edgar, however, was not initially able to make an escape. Instead, the British detained him for eighteen months at Fort Niagara, after which time he fled to Montreal. During Edgar's ordeal, the British seized his home and his stores, which totaled more than £3500. Added to the ill effect that his captivity had on his health, Edgar's economic losses in the war were extensive.[6]

What did Edgar and Ruland hope to gain from their actions? They acted independent of the American military. It was an enormous risk, lacking any institutional support. These men never mentioned the grievances against the British crown most often cited by the thirteen eastern colonies, such as taxation without representation and general British tyranny. They never indicated that they felt the British crown was depriving them of their rights. Still, the fact that they were willing to sacrifice so much indicates a sense of purpose, one that was clearly different from that of the eastern colonists.

After the war, Ruland engaged in land speculation in Quebec, as well as in present-day Ohio and Indiana. A 1795 agreement shows that Ruland had purchased Indian lands at some previous point, suggesting that he likely engaged in land speculation in the west, a practice that was illegal under the Proclamation of 1763. Ruland likely believed that an American victory would lend legitimacy to his land titles; he was dismayed when he found out that would not be the case.[7]

In a letter from 1798, Ruland stated that he would sell land to the children of U.S. Army Major John Buell at the price of $1 an acre, if only Buell acknowledged his right to the land. Ruland probably did not anticipate having his claim to this land questioned. Indeed, as the British had been technically forbidding Americans to settle west of the Appalachian Mountains since 1763, it is not surprising that a settler assumed that a British defeat would mean an end to an irritating policy. Despite Ruland's numerous petitions to the United States government, his land titles were ignored.[8]

Ruland was not the only person hoping to make a profit from the Americans. James Cassidy, one of the men brought up on treason charges in 1779, bragged about how he had a large quantity of leather that he was going to sell to the Americans, and that he hoped to "make a great deal of money by it."[9] Additionally, he expected the United States would open up more territory to settlement; Cassidy told his friend that, when the Americans came, it would be possible to procure a farm for nothing. While these men may seem opportunistic, they were reacting to the circumstances of their particular time and place. Looking for personal advantage in any situation was a common trait among those living on the frontier.[10]

Economics was only part of the picture. Many British resisters took actions that harmed them financially. For example, traders such as Cassidy, who refused to sell his leather to the British, took an economic loss. The British army was more likely to cover its debts than the financially struggling Americans. In his scathing remarks about the British, Cassidy does not condemn them as tyrants who trample on liberties, but rather as cowards. Cassidy found the alliance between the British and Indians to be so noxious that one man claimed that he said, "Colonel Butler [the feared British frontier raider] with his scalping crew would soon meet their deserts . . . and that he [Cassidy] would turn hangman for him [Butler] and the whole [British] Indian Department!" Therefore, while the economic promise of an American victory may have motivated some frontier support, it did not explain all cases.[11]

Edgar was also motivated by the British-Indian alliance, going so far as to risk his life to aid prisoners to escape so that they could deliver intelligence about possible raids. Ruland, meanwhile, worked for George Rogers Clark, whose purpose in the west centered on quelling Indian raids against civilians. Detroiters knew that Hamilton—and through Hamilton, the British—supported and encouraged the Indian raids that killed dozens of Americans. He was known as "Hamilton the Hair-buyer," although he probably never actually paid for scalps. The disgust that some Detroiters felt toward the actions of the British-Indian alliance could easily have driven them to hate the British with the same fervor as their eastern brethren.[12]

John Edgar and Israel Ruland were not Americans fighting against the British in an attempt to save their nation from tyranny. Rather, they acted for reasons exclusive to the frontier: the promise of economic benefits and objections to the British and Indian alliance. The idea of a unified "American" cause, beyond the ultimate goal of winning independence from Britain, is flawed. Americans across the continent resisted the British for reasons particular to their region. Detroit's American sympathizers had more pressing concerns than nationalism motivating their opposition to the British.[13]

NOTES

1 Scholarship on American supporters at Detroit during the American Revolution is sparse. For the Revolution on the northwestern frontier, see David Curtis Skaggs, ed., *The Old Northwest in the American Revolution: An Anthology* (Madison: State Historical Society of Wisconsin, 1977); George M. Waller, *The American Revolution in the West* (Chicago: Nelson-Hall, 1976); and Walter S. Dunn, *Choosing Sides on the Frontier in the American Revolution* (West Port, CT: Praeger, 2007). For American nationalism in the revolutionary era, see John M. Murrin, "A Roof without Walls: The Dilemma of American National Identity," in *Beyond Confederation: Origins of the Constitution and American National Identity*, ed. Richard Beeman et al. (Chapel Hill: University of North Carolina Press, 1987), 333-48, and David Hackett Fischer, *Washington's Crossing* (New York: Oxford University Press, 2004), 7-30.

2 Henry Hamilton to Lieutenant Governor Cramahe, Detroit, August 12, 1778, in *MPHC*, 9:462.

3 Henry Hamilton to Frederick Haldimand, Detroit, August 1778, *MPHC*, 9:465.

4 "Deposition of John Cornwall" (quote) and "Deposition of William Miller," in *MPHC*, 10:344; Hamilton to Haldimand, August 1778, 9:464-73.

5 "Deposition of John Higgins" and "Deposition of William Humphreys," in *MPHC*, 10:355-56; John Edgar to U.S. Congress, 1782 [?], John Edgar Papers, BHC.

6 Deposition of William Stags, 1782, and Edgar to U.S. Congress, 1782 [?], John Edgar Papers, BHC.

7 "Syndicate for Promotion of Cuyahoga Purchase," in *Askin Papers*, 1:545-48. For additional cases of land speculation, see the essays in this volume by Susan Ward, Kimberly Steele, and Douglas D. Fisher.

8 Israel Ruland to John Buell, May 5, 1795, Miscellany by Date, BHC.

9 "Deposition of Henrick Iago," in *MPHC*, 10:343.

10 Dale Van Every, "George Rogers Clark in Kentucky and the Illinois Country, 1772-1778," in Skaggs, ed., 163. The author refers to "the nearly universal frontier inclination, in whatever situation, to look first for personal advantage."

11 Edgar to U.S. Congress, 1782 [?]; "Deposition of John Cornwall," 10:344-45 (quote). For the participation of Butler's Rangers in a frontier Indian raid, see the essay in this volume by John Maisner.

12 Edgar to U.S. Congress, 1782 [?]; Arthur M. Woodford, *This is Detroit, 1701-2001* (Detroit: Wayne State University Press, 2001), 30; "Deposition of John Higgins," 10:355.

13 See Louis Gottschalk, "Causes of Revolution," *American Journal of Sociology* 50 (1944): 1-8, for a classic definition of political revolution as inherently multi-causal. See also Murrin, and Fischer, 7-30, for the broad cultural spectrum and different motivations for revolution along the eastern seaboard of North America.

Crawford's Defeat: Raids and Retaliation on the Frontier

John Maisner

Raids along the frontier during the American Revolutionary War produced terror for both Indians and American settlers, as both groups coveted the same land and resources. The expedition known interchangeably as Crawford's Defeat and the Battle of Sandusky in June 1782 reflected larger patterns of British-Indian frontier raids while at the same time signifying an influential event in the history of Revolutionary Detroit. Crawford's Defeat cemented Detroit's reputation as a central staging ground of the British and Indian frontier alliance. The event also had the unfortunate effect of fueling visions in the early American imagination of remorseless Indian "savagery" in western lands.[1]

Though the war in the east virtually ended with General Charles Cornwallis's surrender at Yorktown the previous year, 1782 was a particularly vicious period in the western theater, known afterward as the "Bloody Year." The British Indian Department, under agents Alexander McKee, Simon Girty, and Matthew Elliott, organized bands of Wyandot, Shawnee, and Delaware warriors from the area surrounding Fort Detroit to attack American settlements and disrupt trade and military exercises in western Pennsylvania and the Ohio River Valley.[2]

American responses usually emanated from Fort Pitt, the base of American power in the west. Separated from Detroit by three hundred miles of wilderness, Americans stationed at Fort Pitt found it nearly impossible to mobilize a comprehensive response to British and Indian attacks, and many expeditions failed in the planning stages. Others quickly got out of control, resulting in the massacre of innocent Indian women and children.[3]

One example was the massacre of Christian Indians at the Moravian missionary village of Gnadenhütten (today Gnadenhutten, Ohio) on March 8, 1782. The British had removed most of the Indians, primarily Delawares and Wyandots, to a new village on the Sandusky River the previous year, and took Moravian leaders to stand trial in Detroit for supplying intelligence to the Americans. In the spring of 1782, the praying Indians returned to Gnadenhütten for food. Colonel David Williamson led

160 Pennsylvania militiamen into the village and slaughtered ninety-six unarmed men, women, and children. The massacre infuriated the Ohio Indians, and convinced many that the Americans meant to exterminate their people.[4]

General William Irvine, the commander at Fort Pitt, and General George Washington believed that the only way to end the war in the west was to destroy the British garrison at Detroit. However, Congress did not have the resources to approve such a major offensive. Rather than wait, Irvine decided to launch his own expedition using militia against a less ambitious target: the Indian towns on the Sandusky River in Ohio Country. Due to ongoing Indian raids, including one that claimed the lives of a local Baptist minister's wife and children on May 12, 1782, there was no shortage of American volunteers.[5]

Irvine's expedition aimed to disrupt British and Indian raids on the American frontier by removing a base of Indian power in the west. He issued these orders to the militia at Fort Pitt: "The object of your command is, to destroy with fire and sword (if practicable) the Indian town and settlement at Sandusky, by which we hope to give ease and safety to the inhabitants of this country; but, if impracticable, then you will doubtless perform such other services in your power as will, in their consequences, have a tendency to answer this great end."[6]

The men elected as their commander Colonel William Crawford of Pennsylvania, a personal friend of Washington's and a veteran of several similar expeditions. Roughly five hundred militiamen mustered at Mingo Bottom (today Mingo Junction, Ohio), on the Ohio River about thirty-five miles west of Fort Pitt, with enough provisions for thirty days. They departed on May 25, 1782, for the Wyandot village of Upper Sandusky (also known as Half King's Town) and encountered few obstacles that were not caused by the militia's inherent lack of discipline. The column got lost and stopped often, occasionally for hours, and some of the volunteers deserted.[7]

The Americans hoped to conceal their operation, but the British at Detroit learned of it even before the militiamen left Mingo Bottom. Girty acquired accurate information through an American prisoner, and reported it to his superiors on April 8, 1782. Major Arent De Peyster, commander of the garrison at Detroit, used Girty, McKee, and other agents to alert Indians along the Sandusky River and to coordinate a response. De Peyster also dispatched Captain William Caldwell with his company of mounted Butler's Rangers and a party of Indians from Detroit led by Elliott to meet the Americans.[8]

Indian scouts had also tracked the American expedition since it entered Ohio Country and sent word back to the Sandusky area. As the militia approached, Wyandot and Delaware women and children hid in ravines near their villages and

British fur traders fled the area. Delawares led by Chief Captain Pipe and Wyandots following Dunquat, the "Half King," joined forces on June 4, 1782, to oppose the American invaders. Along with some Mingo warriors, their force was between two hundred and four hundred men. They expected reinforcements from Detroit and a party of Shawnees from the south to arrive on June 5.[9]

Crawford's militia arrived at the original Wyandot village of Upper Sandusky on June 4, only to find it abandoned. The Half King had recently relocated the town eight miles upriver, closer to Captain Pipe's village. Most of the militia wanted to return to Fort Pitt, some believing that the Indians had vacated the area and others wary of their potential strength in the region. Crawford and his senior officers decided to turn back if they could not locate the enemy that day, and they dispatched Lieutenant John Rose to lead a scouting party northward.[10]

Rose returned at about 2 p.m., pursued by Captain Pipe's Delaware warriors and in danger of being overtaken. The main body of Crawford's force returned fire, and by the afternoon the dismounted Americans captured a key grove of trees on the Sandusky plains, later known as "Battle Island." By about 4 p.m., the Delawares were pushed from the woods onto the surrounding plains and were joined by the Half King's Wyandot followers and the Mingo warriors. With these reinforcements, Captain Pipe successfully outflanked the Americans and attacked their rear with the help of Elliott's party. After about three and a half hours of intense combat, the Indians fell back with darkness descending. Both sides lit large bonfires to limit the threat of an ambush.[11]

Combat resumed early the next morning, but the Indians did not attack Battle Island, preferring to fire shots from about three hundred yards away while waiting for reinforcements. Crawford planned to hold his position in the grove throughout the day and attack the Indians after nightfall.[12]

In the early afternoon, the Americans noticed that Caldwell's one hundred British Rangers had arrived, igniting much fear and dismay among the militiamen.[13] While Crawford and his officers discussed this development, McKee further reinforced the British and Indians with about 140 Shawnees, bringing their numbers in line with those of the militia and effectively completing a circle around the American position. The Shawnees inflated the American perception of their strength by repeatedly firing their muskets into the air, destroying what was left of the militia's morale. As Lieutenant Rose wrote, the arrival of the Shawnees "completed the Business with us."[14]

Crawford reconsidered his earlier plan for an evening attack, and agreed with his advisors that the militia must leave its position on Battle Island since it was surrounded. He mapped a stealthy and highly organized plan of retreat, and the militia began to withdraw in silence. Sensing movement along the American line, the British and Indians fired into the darkness and the militia panicked. The men scrambled away in small groups; Crawford and Dr. John Knight, the regimental surgeon, became separated from the main body.[15]

The majority of the American force reached the abandoned Wyandot town by sunrise on June 6, 1782. With Crawford gone, Colonel David Williamson, who led the massacre at Gnadenhütten, took command. The British and Indian pursuit was hampered by Caldwell's absence; he suffered wounds in both legs the day before. The Americans successfully fended off a number of attacks, and first arrived at Mingo Bottom on June 13, followed by many stragglers. In all, about seventy militiamen never returned from Crawford's Defeat along the Sandusky River.[16]

On June 7, Crawford, Knight, and four other stragglers were captured by members of the Delaware tribe. The Ohio Indians no longer ransomed their prisoners to the British or enslaved them. After the Gnadenhütten Massacre, they reverted to the practice of killing all captives. Knight and Crawford were taken to the Half King's village, where their faces were painted black, the traditional sign of impending execution.[17]

Captain Pipe made a speech in which he declared Crawford responsible for the Gnadenhütten Massacre. After the speech, Crawford was stripped naked, beaten, and tied to a pole near a large bonfire. Indian men fired gunpowder at Crawford's body and cut off his ears while poking him with burning logs. After two hours, Crawford fell unconscious and was revived only to be scalped and have hot coals placed on his wounds. When he finally died, his body was thrown into the bonfire. In other locations, prisoners from Crawford's expedition were also tortured and executed.[18]

News of Crawford's execution and the failure of his expedition shocked both sides of the conflict. Along the American frontier, often-exaggerated reports of merciless torture did much to amplify fear and racism toward Indians. An embellished narrative of Dr. Knight's experiences served as propaganda against the Ohio Indians and their British allies, and the "Ballad of Colonel Crawford" became extremely popular.[19]

The British at Detroit were also horrified at reports of Crawford's fate. De Peyster attempted to justify the circumstances to his superiors by claiming that the execution was in response to the Gnadenhütten Massacre. He also instructed McKee to "tell them [the Indians] I shall be under the necessity of recalling the Troops (who must be tired of such scenes of cruelty) should they persist . . . I am confident, Sir, that you and the officers do all in your power to instill humane Principles into the Indians."[20]

The British spent much of the rest of 1782 waiting for the expected, but never launched, American response to Crawford's Defeat. They eventually dispatched several additional raids on American frontier settlements. Though the war in the west concluded in late 1782, the image and idea of Indian savagery, fueled by depictions of Crawford's torture, long remained both a rallying cry and justification for western expansion and Indian extermination.[21]

NOTES

1 The definitive source on Crawford's Defeat is Consul Wilshire Butterfield, *An Historical Account of the Expedition against Sandusky under Col. William Crawford in 1782* (Cincinnati: Clarke, 1873). Butterfield's narrative remains sound, but he did not have the advantage of using the key firsthand account, John Rosenthal, *Journal of a Volunteer Expedition to Sandusky* (1894; reprint, New York: New York Times, 1969). The author, better known as Baron Gustave Rosenthal, or Lieutenant John Rose, was a Russian nobleman who enlisted in the United States Army after he killed a man in a duel. No American knew of Rose's true identity until several years later. His memoir about the expedition was published after his death in 1829. Few other sources provide a comprehensive examination of the expedition, but some mention it as part of a larger work. See, for example, James H. Anderson, *Colonel William Crawford* (Columbus: Ohio Archaeological and Historical Publications, 1898); Milo Milton Quaife, "The Ohio Campaigns of 1782," *Mississippi Valley Historical Review* 17 (1931): 515-29; Parker B. Brown, "'Crawford's Defeat': A Ballad," *Western Pennsylvania Historical Magazine* 64 (1981): 311–27; and Brown, "Reconstructing Crawford's Army of 1782," *Western Pennsylvania Historical Magazine* 65 (1982): 17–36. H.H. Brackenridge, ed., *Indian Atrocities: Narratives of the Perils and Sufferings of Dr. Knight and John Slover, among the Indians during the Revolutionary War, with Short Memoirs of Col. Crawford & John Slover* (Cincinnati: U.P. James, 1867), gives an in-depth account of the torture and burning of Crawford, but it is heavily edited and cannot be trusted as a reliable source.

2 Quaife, 517. For the British Indian Department and agents McKee, Girty, and Elliott, see Larry L. Nelson, *A Man of Distinction among Them: Alexander McKee and the Ohio Country Frontier, 1754–1799* (Kent, OH: Kent State University Press, 1999); "Life of Simon Girty," in *MPHC*, 7:123-29; Roy Boatman, *Simon Girty, the Man and the Image* (Madison: University of Wisconsin Press, 1954); Reginald Horsman, *Matthew Elliott, British Indian Agent* (Detroit: Wayne State University Press, 1964); and Colin Calloway, "Neither White nor Red: White Renegades on the American Indian Frontier," *Western Historical Quarterly* 17 (1986): 43-66.

3 For frontier raids during the Revolutionary War, see Butterfield, 1-16; Philip P. Mason, *Detroit, Fort Lernoult, and the American Revolution* (Detroit: Wayne State University Press, 1964), 7-8; John Grenier, *The First Way of War: American War Making on the Frontier, 1607–1814* (New York: Cambridge University Press, 2005), 146-62; and Quaife, 515–17.

4 Quaife, 517-18. For the Moravians, see the essay in this volume by Melissa R. Luberti.

5 Butterfield, 50-61.

6 Irvine quoted in Butterfield, 69-70.

7 Butterfield, 77; Rosenthal, 161.

8 Nelson, 124-25; Horsman, 37.

9 Butterfield, 172-75.

10 Butterfield, 169-203; Rosenthal, 149. For Rose, see note 1.

11 Butterfield, 207-13; Rosenthal, 150; Horsman, 37. Though Horsman places Elliott on the scene on June 4, Butterfield does not acknowledge his arrival with the rest of the British force until June 5. Americans responded to the Indian tactic of advancing while hidden in the tall grass by climbing trees to achieve a clearer line of sight and prevent surprise attacks. The smoke from their powder further obscured their view and hindered their accuracy. Butterfield, 207-213, 216; Rosenthal, 150-51.

12 Butterfield, 214-15; Rosenthal, 140; Nelson, 125.

13 There is considerable debate about when the Rangers arrived on the battlefield, though the majority of sources state that it was June 5. For the debate, see C.W. Butterfield to Charles Walker, March 22, 1872, Charles Walker Papers, BHC. See the essay in this volume by Alexandria Reid for Butler's feared reputation among American sympathizers in Detroit.

14 Rosenthal, 151. Rosenthal describes the Shawnees' show of strength as a "Feu de joie," or "Fire of joy."

15 Rosenthal, 152-53; Butterfield, 312-14; H.H. Brackenridge, ed., 14-16.

16 Butterfield, 237-59; Rosenthal, 154-56. Caldwell later declared that his injury was the only reason any Americans escaped the pursuit. Quaife, 519.

17 Butterfield, 331; Gregory Evans Dowd, *A Spirited Resistance: The North American Indian Struggle for Unity, 1745-1815* (Baltimore: Johns Hopkins University Press, 1992), 87-88; Nelson, 113-14. For more on Indian captivity, see Marius Barbeau, "Indian Captivity," *Proceedings of the American Philosophical Society* 94 (1950): 522-48. According to Horsman, on June 11 the prisoners were marched to a Delaware village near the present-day sight of Crawford, Ohio. Four fellow prisoners were tomahawked and scalped along the way, and Indian children slapped the scalps in Crawford and Knight's faces. About one hundred people, including Elliott and Girty, gathered to witness the execution of the American commander. Many sources claim that Crawford called to Girty to intervene or shoot him throughout his torture, but this is much disputed. Horsman, 30. See also Brackenridge, ed., 19.

18 Butterfield, 387-91; Horsman, 39; Brackenridge, ed., 21-29. Dr. Knight managed to escape captivity as he was being moved to a new village. The exact number of Crawford's men killed as prisoners may never be known. Dowd, 14-15.

19 Butterfield, 76; Quaife writes, "The sufferings of Crawford were no worse than those of many a humbler unfortunate, but his rank and prominence naturally centered the attention of the entire border region upon his fate" (519). Butterfield quotes the publisher's note on Knight's narrative, originally published in the mid-nineteenth century: "But as they [the Indians] still continue their murders on our frontier, these Narratives may be serviceable to induce our government to take some effectual steps to chastise and suppress them; as from hence, they will see that the nature of an Indian is fierce and cruel, and that an extirpation of them would be useful to the world, and honorable to those who can effect it" (324).

20 Arent De Peyster to Frederick Haldimand, Detroit, June 23, 1782, in *MPHC,* 10:594; De Peyster to Alexander McKee, Detroit, August 6, 1782, in *MPHC,* 20:38 (quote); McKee to De Peyster, Shawnee Country, August 28, 1782, in *MPHC,* 20:50-51. In this last letter, McKee wrote that the execution occurred before he could interfere and assured De Peyster that he had told the Indians of the British abhorrence of the action.

21 Quaife, 523-29. For the influence of frontier violence in creating racialized views of Native Americans, see Peter Silver, *Our Savage Neighbors: How Indian War Transformed Early America* (New York: Norton, 2007).

SPENCER TAKEN PRISONER

Page 41.

Spencer Taken Prisoner
Etching from *The Indian Captivity of O.M. Spencer* (1834). Print. Courtesy of the Purdy/Kresge Library, Wayne State University.

Unfree Detroit: The Varied Experiences of American Prisoners

Caitlyn A.O. Perry

During the Revolutionary War, the American prisoner experience on the western frontier differed greatly from that on the east coast and in England. Whereas prison ships moored off the American eastern seaboard and onshore prisons in England infamously held enemy sailors and soldiers in cramped, unhealthy conditions, captives in frontier prisons experienced greater freedom of movement. At Fort Detroit, the major holding area for American prisoners of war in the west, they were sometimes not detained at all. Because few military engagements took place in the western Great Lakes region, soldiers and especially Indian raiders sought prisoners to exchange for British goods at the fort. The British treated each new prisoner according to his connections and potential economic value, particularly within the frontier trading economy. Thus, while conditions occasionally matched the cruelty of other British prisons, officials in Detroit developed a case-by-case policy for the fort's prisoners. The detainments of John Dodge, Jean Baptiste Pointe du Sable, and Oliver Spencer demonstrated the varied character of frontier prisoner experiences at Detroit.[1]

Dodge's imprisonment was particularly harsh, and showed that the British were not above exploiting captives for economic gain. In the early winter of 1776, Lieutenant Governor Henry Hamilton issued a warrant for the arrest of Dodge, a small-time trader and translator for Indians surrounding Sandusky on the southern shore of Lake Erie in Ohio Country. He was charged with conspiring against the British crown by encouraging local Indians to sign a treaty with the Americans—a true accusation. In his own words, Dodge was held in a "loathsome dungeon, ironed and thrown in with three criminals." Governor Hamilton kept Dodge in this state for six months, only bringing him out into the open for daily interrogations. The brutal treatment, combined with a harsh winter, made Dodge seriously ill and brought him to the verge of death. By the mercy of the fort's doctor, he was removed from the cell in June 1776 and detained in the barracks to recover from his illness and injuries. Hamilton paroled Dodge after he recovered; the former prisoner returned home to discover that the lieutenant governor had confiscated all his goods and property in Ohio Country.[2]

Upon finding his life in Sandusky destroyed, Dodge decided to remain in the Detroit area to establish a trade network with local Indians. He explained, "I being a master of the different Indian languages, Detroit was also of service to me, so that in a short time I paid off my all my debts, and began to add to my stock." Hamilton saw Dodge's talents as an asset to trade near Detroit. Soon after Dodge established his trading post, he received special permission from Hamilton to conduct trade and buy goods from Fort Michilimackinac. Still, Hamilton prevented Dodge from fully profiting from his trade by "picking" from his cargo.[3]

In January 1778, Dodge was arrested again on suspicion of supplying Americans with goods. His second imprisonment was nearly as cruel as the first, with his property sold again, this time for 1,900 New York dollars. Dodge remained in the prison until May 1, 1778, when he was put on a ship and sent to Quebec. Once he reached his new prison, Dodge escaped to Philadelphia, where he unsuccessfully lobbied General George Washington to invade and capture Detroit.[4]

Dodge's best revenge came from publishing an account of his imprisonment. The book, published for an anti-British audience, captured many of the hardships experienced by frontier prisoners of war. In 1779, the Virginia State Council deliberated on how it should treat its new prisoner: Henry Hamilton. The Council referred to Dodge's narrative of his time at Detroit, published the same year, and moved to treat Hamilton in the same manner. The Council declared, "They find that his [Hamilton's] treatment of our citizens and soldiers to be cruel and inhumane; that in the case of John Dodge, a citizen of these states . . . that he loaded him with irons, threw him into a dungeon, without bedding, without straw, without fire, in the dead of winter and severe climate of Detroit." Virginia, under Governor Thomas Jefferson, kept Hamilton in irons before exchanging him for American prisoners in 1781.[5]

By comparison, Jean Baptiste Pointe du Sable, a prominent trader of mixed African-French ancestry and recognized today as Chicago's founder, received extremely lenient treatment while a prisoner in Detroit. In September 1779, British troops captured du Sable near present-day Chicago on suspicion of spying for the American rebels. The British soldiers did not chain or beat du Sable, and they did not destroy or sell his property. A note by British Lieutenant Thomas Bennet remarked, "Corporal Tascon, who commanded the party, very prudently prevented the Indians from burning his [du Sable's] home, or doing him any injury." Instead, the British made a careful inventory of du Sable's goods, which amounted to 8,705 livres. The cordial treatment he received was no doubt a mark of his wealth and importance to the economy of Illinois Country. Unlike Dodge, the British could not have stolen or destroyed du Sable's goods without upsetting an entire trade network.[6]

Rather than detain him, therefore, British officials paroled du Sable on the official condition that he remain in the Detroit area. Yet, he quickly received special permission to return to his regular business activities, including developing his farm in the area of present-day Peoria, Illinois. Special treatment for frontier notables was not unheard of. The frontiersman Daniel Boone also received generous terms from British officers during his imprisonment in April 1778; after ten days, he was released without condition. The difference in du Sable's case was that the goodwill seemed to pay dividends. Although du Sable spent little time in Detroit, he made a distinct impression on the fort's British officers. Commandant Patrick Sinclair gave him a special assignment to supervise his personal trading post at the "Pinery," in the present-day town of St. Clair, Michigan. In 1790, on a trading voyage to Mackinac Island, du Sable was even saluted by the discharge of friendly cannon. The trader's amiable personality and business acumen led to a most favorable "detainment" in Detroit.[7]

Oliver Spencer's captivity further demonstrated the importance of personal connections for prisoners in Detroit. In 1793, ten years after the official end of the American Revolutionary War, Indian raiders descended on twelve-year-old Oliver and his family near Cincinnati. They kidnapped the boy and brought him to Detroit, where he was handed over to the fort's commandant, Colonel Richard England. It was discovered that Spencer had distant relatives in Detroit, the Andre family, through his mother. He spent his detainment living in the Andres' home. In his famous captivity narrative, first published in 1834, Spencer spoke highly of both England and the Andres: "I had spent almost four weeks very agreeably at Detroit becoming very attached to Colonel England and particularly so to Mr. and Mrs. Andre, who treated me with great kindness." After Spencer's unusual captivity in Detroit, he was sent to Quebec and ransomed.[8]

Spencer contrasted his pleasant memories of British captivity with his traumatic experience of being kidnapped by Indians. The raiding party tied him to a tree and threatened to scalp him. Spencer's description was consistent with other accounts of Indian raiders, including Dodge's. The boy did not expect much better treatment by the British until he learned of his fortunate connection to the Andres. He was pleasantly surprised upon arriving in Detroit to receive tea, bread, a new set of clothing, and medical treatment for a stab wound he received from his Indian captors. Years later, Spencer recalled leaving Detroit "with tears" and "momentary regret that I was so soon to be separated from these kind friends and acquaintances." Spencer's treatment may have been different during the heat of the Revolution or if he was an adult without relatives in Detroit, but his experience followed the pattern established by earlier prisoners: Influence and connections bought goodwill from British officials.[9] Detroit was a northwestern crossroads during the American revolutionary era. In addition to a trading post, British military garrison, and Indian gathering site, the town served as a prison. Third parties looking for desirable British goods created a bustling trade in captives. As the varied experiences of John Dodge, Jean Baptist Pointe du Sable, and Oliver Spencer suggest, the British followed no uniform protocol for their detainees on the frontier. On the eastern seaboard, these American prisoners would have been held and, if they survived, eventually exchanged for British prisoners. In Detroit, each case was assessed according to the prisoner's status or what he could provide for the fort and its leaders. Whether prisoners served sentences in irons or by conditioned parole, they left some mark on the small frontier community. And, invariably, Detroit left its mark on them.

NOTES

1 The existing literature on prisoners of war during the American Revolution focuses mainly on the treatment of prisoners in the eastern states. For traditional prisoner accounts, see Edwin G. Burrows, *Forgotten Patriots: The Untold Story of American Prisoners During the Revolutionary War* (New York: Basic Books, 2008); Francis Cogliano, *American Maritime Prisoners in the American Revolutionary War: The Captivity of William Russell* (Annapolis: Naval Institute Press, 2001); Paul A. Gilje, *Liberty on the Waterfront: American Maritime Culture in the Age of Revolution* (Philadelphia: University of Pennsylvania Press, 2004); Jesse Lemisch, "Listening to the 'Inarticulate': William Widger's Dream and the Loyalties of American Revolutionary Seamen," *Journal of Social History* 3 (1969): 1-29; and Charles Henry Metzger, *The Prisoner in the American Revolution* (Chicago: Loyola University Press, 1971). For prisoners in Detroit, see Brian Leigh Dunnigan, *Frontier Metropolis: Picturing Early Detroit, 1701-1838* (Detroit: Wayne State University Press, 2001), 72-73.

2 John Dodge, *A Narrative of the Capture and Treatment of John Dodge by the English at Detroit* (Philadelphia: T. Bradford, 1779), 8 (quote), 10-12.

3 Dodge, 12.

4 Dodge, 19-22.

5 Virginia Council, *In Council June 16, 1779* (Williamsburg: John Dixon and Thomas Nicolson, 1779).

6 Bennet quoted in Thomas Meehan, "Jean Baptiste Pointe du Sable, the First Chicagoan," *Journal of the Illinois State Historical Society* 56 (1963): 447; Norman McRae, "Early Blacks in Michigan, 1743-1800," *Detroit in Perspective: A Journal of Regional History* 2 (1976): 166-70; *Askin Papers*, 1:356 n28; Milo Milton Quaife, *Chicago and the Old Northwest, 1673-1835* . . . (1913; reprint, Urbana: University of Illinois Press, 2001), 138-42. The inventory showed why du Sable was an important asset to the British troops. P. Durand, who logged the inventory, listed: 1 canoe, 1 iron kettle, 1 large axe, 10 measures of wheat, 10 measures of flour, 15 lbs. of gum, 500 lbs. of flour, 220 lbs. of pork and three barrels, 10 barrels of rum each containing 20 gals., 3 bench lines bundles, 4 bear skins, 2 cotton shirts, 2 pairs French shoes with buckles, 1 barrel of sugar, 1 horn full of powder, and 1 sponge (McRae, 168).

7 Quaife, 141; McRae, 170-71. For Boone's captivity in Detroit, see Philip P. Mason, *Detroit, Fort Lernoult, and the American Revolution* (Detroit: Wayne State University Press, 1964), 6, 12, and Metzger, 193.

8 Oliver Spencer, *The Indian Captivity of O.M. Spencer* (1834; reprint, New York: Carlton and Phillips, 1854), 72-73, 136 (quote).

9 Spencer, 130-31, 137 (quote). See Dodge, 13, for his account of the treatment of women and children during Indian and British frontier raids.

John Leeth: Neutral on the Run
Juliegha Norus

During the American Revolutionary War, an ordinary man found himself in extraordinary circumstances. The more John Leeth tried to avoid trouble, the more it followed him. He spent the vast majority of his life running away, and eventually landed at Fort Detroit. Here he discovered that his linguistic skills made him an extremely desirable ally in a war that he wished to avoid. Leeth's experiences exemplify how neutrals shuffled around North America during the Revolutionary War, in and out of allegiances beyond their control.[1]

John Leeth was born on March 15, 1755, in Hickory Grove, South Carolina, to respectable but poor parents. Orphaned by the age of five, he was apprenticed to a local tailor in the hopes of learning the trade and earning a living. Restless, Leeth left his employer after about two years and journeyed to Pennsylvania, known as "the best poor man's country." Arriving in Little York (today York) at age eight and realizing that he did not have the means to care for himself, Leeth bound himself to a farmer for four years, during which time he served with "fortitude and agility." Once his indenture was up in 1767, Leeth ventured west to Fort Pitt, where he gained employment with an Indian trader. His first assignment took him to New Lancaster (today Lancaster, Ohio), an Indian village in Ohio Country. He remained there for several years managing his employer's affairs. In 1773, at the age of seventeen, Leeth was taken captive by Delaware Indians.[2]

During the first of many captivities, Leeth's allegiances were called into question. His primary captor, a Delaware Indian, immediately demanded to know if Leeth knew anything about the conflict between white settlers and Shawnees—a reference, most likely, to fighting preceding Lord Dunmore's War in 1774. Leeth, fearing for his life, assured his captor that he knew nothing about the conflict and wanted to keep it that way. In his autobiography, Leeth admitted to some trepidation: "With a trembling heart I informed him, I knew not what to think of it; that I had never done them any harm; I had no hand in the matter, and hoped they would take care of me."[3] This became Leeth's usual approach to conflict: He sought protection from the strongest faction, while attempting to stay out of the crossfire at all costs. Leeth soon learned that British army regulars were advancing toward the area where he was being held. Some Delawares wanted to kill Leeth because they saw him as a hindrance, but his captor protected him, causing Leeth to reflect that "he was a father to me indeed."[4]

In 1776, the Delawares freed Leeth and sent him off with a few supplies. He pursued trade in furs and skins until he was taken captive again by another group of Native Americans. After escaping, he encountered some white traders and, enticed by the prospect of a profitable business deal, accompanied them to Fort Detroit. Once at the fort, Leeth met a trader who wanted to hire him to accompany goods by water from Detroit to Sandusky in Ohio Country. Given the timing, the opportunity proved impossible to accept. Leeth arrived in Detroit at the height of the Revolutionary War, when the fort was under martial law. Coming and going required a pass from Lieutenant Governor Henry Hamilton. Leeth was denied a pass; Hamilton wanted him to work for the British army in the Indian Department instead because of his fluency in Indian languages. Leeth made the first excuse that came to mind, claiming that he "was a very unhealthy, weakly youth, and not able to perform such services." Hamilton was not convinced, and told Leeth that if he was too sick to help the British army then he was also too sick to travel to Sandusky.[5]

Leeth lamented his inability to stay neutral, and feared being forced to fight for the British. He strove for neutrality out of a natural sense of self-preservation. When Leeth fell ill after a mandatory military training exercise at the fort, he avoided serving in the British army. Thereafter, he feigned illness for the next several weeks. Hamilton was so desperate to have Leeth's services that his name remained first on the muster list. Leeth considered himself a prisoner in Detroit, later writing, "I was then detained, though on wages, against my will."[6] He still recognized that his plight could have been worse after observing prisoners brought to the fort by the British army. Among them were eighteen women and children, whom Leeth described as "poor creatures, dreadfully mangled and emaciated; with their clothes tattered and torn to pieces."[7]

Leeth's time in Detroit presented several difficult choices. He was cornered into choosing to support the British in the war, effectively becoming a loyalist, or to support the Americans and more than likely be put to death. The war put thousands of neutrals and loyalists in a similar situation by pushing them to outposts like Detroit. In Leeth's case, he also contributed to the process by searching for a profitable business. With each indenture and captivity, he gained skills, particularly in Indian languages, that made him more desirable to the British and Americans. Rather than freedom, therefore, the western frontier signified bondage for Leeth. The world created by the American Revolution was not safe for neutrals.[8]

In 1777, Leeth was at last allowed to leave Detroit for Sandusky when his employer's partner posted the large sum of £500 in bail money. The transaction indicated that British officers had given up on securing Leeth's full cooperation. He was determined never to set foot in Detroit again, but returned later so that his benefactor would not lose the bail money. After the visit, Leeth promised his employer, "I will never again plunge myself into such difficulties, or attempt to get another pass, or give bail in this place." He later continued to work as a trader in Sandusky for some time, when his original captors, the Delaware Indians, arrived and asked Leeth to leave with them. He freely consented. The decision led to a series of additional captivities by Indian groups until the war ended, but Leeth made good on his promise to never again visit Detroit. Eventually, he lived peacefully with his family on a farm in Bud's Ferry, Maryland (today Doncaster), until his death in 1832.[9]

Leeth's hardships were shared by many neutrals during the American Revolution. In trying to avoid political allegiances, they were alienated from all sides and became an enemy to many. Detroit was a way station for the powerless during the war. For Leeth, the fort provided both desirable financial opportunities and unwanted political pressures. A true neutral, he ultimately favored waiting out the war among Indian groups, free from the demands of either the British or the Americans. Leeth's original captors proved to be his safest haven from the conflict all around him.

NOTES

1 Leeth left an account of his life for future generations that is rich in detail, yet lacks precision regarding specific dates and times. His autobiography can be found in two formats. The first is a handwritten copy in the Silas Farmer Papers, BHC. The second is a printed version that was first published in 1831 and then reprinted in 1883 and 1904. The manuscript and printed versions are identical as far as the manuscript is complete. However, the manuscript ends after Leeth leaves Detroit for the second time in the late 1770s, whereas the printed version continues to describe Leeth's further captivities with Indian groups and eventual settlement on a farm with his wife and children. For the sake of consistency and ease of citation, all page numbers in this essay are from the 1904 printed version of the autobiography: Reuben Gold Thwaites, ed., *A Short Biography of John Leeth, with an Account of His Life among the Indians* (1831; reprint, Cleveland: Burrows Brothers, 1904).

2 Thwaites, ed., 25. For Pennsylvania, see James T. Lemon, *The Best Poor Man's Country: A Geographical Study of Early Southeastern Pennsylvania* (Baltimore: Johns Hopkins University Press, 1972).

3 Thwaites, ed., 26. For Lord Dunmore's War, see Gregory Evans Dowd, *A Spirited Resistance: The North American Indian Struggle for Unity, 1745-1815* (Baltimore: Johns Hopkins University Press, 1992), 40-46.

4 Thwaites, ed., 27.

5 Thwaites, ed., 30, 31 (quote). In his autobiography, Leeth neglected to provide the names of his associates. Hamilton was an exception. For Hamilton's tenure in Detroit, see Philip P. Mason, *Detroit, Fort Lernoult, and the American Revolution* (Detroit: Wayne State University Press, 1964).

6 Thwaites, ed., 32. For an example of other neutrals from Ohio Country, see the essay in this volume on the Moravians by Melissa R. Luberti.

7 Thwaites, ed., 33.

8 Alan Taylor, "The Late Loyalists: Northern Reflections of the Early American Republic," *Journal of the Early Republic* 27 (2007): 1-34.

9 Thwaites, ed., 37 (quote); 38-67.

Caught in the Revolution: The Moravians in Detroit
Melissa R. Luberti

Nothing still exists of the Moravian settlement in present-day Clinton Township and Mount Clemens, Michigan. The only traces of the settlement are the letters and books left by the community, and a few streets created by or named after them. These German missionaries and the Indians they worked with were caught in an impossible situation. They were pacifists originally living in western Pennsylvania and Ohio Country, trapped between warring armies. Their unwillingness to take sides in the Revolutionary War angered both the British and the Americans. The Moravians were victims of the American Revolution, unwilling participants caught in a whirlwind of bloodshed and forced migration.[1]

The Moravians, officially known as the United Brethren, Germany's first Protestant denomination, came to Britain's American colonies in the 1740s in search of religious freedom and a chance to spread their faith. They soon moved into the Ohio River Valley and established missions with a number of their Delaware Indian converts. The Moravians were among the most successful Protestant missionaries during the colonial era, but the American Revolutionary War posed unprecedented challenges. As pacifists, they tried to maintain a neutral status for themselves and their converts. The British in Detroit grew increasingly suspicious of the Moravians near Fort Pitt, determining that if the missionaries did not actively support the king's side in the war effort, then they supported the Americans. Some scholars have speculated that a few Moravian leaders, especially John Heckewelder, spied for the Americans, but little evidence exists to support the claim; moreover, such actions would have violated the pacifist beliefs of the Moravian religious community.[2]

Still, some British leaders never fully trusted the Moravians. In April 1782, Major Arent De Peyster, commandant of Fort Detroit, ordered David Zeisberger, John Heckewelder, and other Moravian leaders to stand trial at the fort for aiding the Americans. Abducted from their homes and marched to Detroit, the missionaries were acquitted and allowed to return to their mission in Ohio Country. The Moravians cultivated a friendship with De Peyster, but were still looked upon suspiciously by others in the fort.[3]

When they returned home, the Moravians found that ninety-six of their Delaware converts had been massacred at the village of Gnadenhütten (today Gnadenhutten, Ohio) by American militiamen from nearby Fort Pitt. The massacre was one of the most appalling events of the American Revolution. The militiamen entered the village on March 7, 1782, and killed a group of mostly unarmed Indians the next morning. The Americans robbed the Indians and separated the men from the women before they slit the men's throats and tomahawked the women, all while the victims prayed for help. Zeisberger wrote, "This news sank deep in our hearts, so that these our brethren, who, as martyrs, had all at once gone to our Saviour, were always, day and night, before our eyes, and in our thoughts." The sole comfort for the Moravians was that their slain Indian converts were now safe from harm in eternal salvation.[4]

The Moravians were terrified. Put on trial by the British and killed by the Americans, they had few options. Where could they go? The question was answered for them by British officials who still did not trust the Moravians. In July 1782, the British ordered the missionaries and their converts to return to Detroit.[5]

The Moravians and their Indian followers were relatively safe as quasi-prisoners in Detroit. De Peyster remained sympathetic toward them, and negotiated with Ojibwa Indians to loan the Moravians and Delawares use of a large parcel of land located on the Huron River (today Clinton River) within a day's journey of the fort. The Ojibwas understood that the Moravians were to use the land only until the end of the war, and then it would revert back to them. According to Zeisberger, the land was not well-suited for agriculture, and even if they wanted to plant anything, it was too late in the year. Again, De Peyster came to the aid of the missionaries. He gave them rations from the storehouses of Fort Detroit, enough to see the struggling community through the winter. With that, the Moravians cleared land, constructed houses and other buildings, and tried to forge a new community. They called their home New Gnadenhütten, after their previous mission.[6]

The Moravians spent four years there. They succeeded in building a small settlement that was admired by visitors. The Moravians held religious ceremonies that sometimes served Protestant visitors from the surrounding area. The group carried on its mission amidst constant uncertainty. With the war's end in 1783, the Moravians technically lost the lease on their land. They held many discussions about what course to take, and prayed for an answer. Many Detroit residents, including De Peyster, wanted them to stay in the area. Others wished they would leave.[7]

One of the latter groups was the Ojibwa. As owners of the land on loan to the Moravians, they expected that their tenants would depart after the war. As time wore on, the Moravians made no visible effort to move. The Ojibwas repeatedly sent emissaries to pressure them to leave. Zeisberger, in his diary, reported that there were fears within New Gnadenhütten that the Ojibwas would resort to violence and force the Moravians from the land.[8]

The Ojibwas were not the Moravians' only concern. The missionaries were generally liked by the inhabitants of Detroit, for they were industrious and paid their debts on time. Yet, some French and British settlers desired the Moravians' structures and other improvements at no cost. Heckewelder informed the group's agent, John Askin, that several people had told him that they would take the land once the missionaries left the Huron River. Heckewelder instructed Askin to sell the improvements on the land, not to give them away or let people squat in them: "We are told that there are both French and English watching for us to leave the place, who immediately intend to go to our houses and make themselves master of our labor, without the smallest reward." The Moravians did not want to see their years of work amount to nothing.[9]

The Moravians' final motivation to leave the Huron River was their lack of success in farming. Many entries in Zeisberger's diary addressed the issue. The group found the weather unbearably cold, with winters often lasting too long for them to plant viable crops. De Peyster's generosity ended after the missionaries' first winter in the area. The Moravians and their converts resorted to making and selling canoes to the inhabitants of the Detroit River region, and then using their profits to buy food and other necessities. By early 1786, they were resigned to seeking better farming conditions in other places. In the spring, the missionaries and 117 of their Indian converts packed up their belongings and left their home of four years.[10]

The Moravians contributed to the patchwork quality of the Detroit region during the revolutionary era. As victims of both sides of the war, the missionaries arrived on the Huron River as refugees. After four years of uncertainty about their future, some Moravians and their Indian converts settled in present-day Canada while others went to Pennsylvania. They had several reasons to leave Detroit: frustrated landlords, impatient neighbors, and poor farming conditions.

Today nothing remains of the Moravians' settlement, except the recollections of those who lived in the community. There is a park in Clinton Township where New Gnadenhütten was located, with only a sign in remembrance of the Moravians' Delaware converts. Children run and jump on the playground equipment with little knowledge that the site of their beloved park has a connection to one of the great tragedies of the American Revolution. A community nearly shattered by the war, the Moravians disappeared—almost without a trace.

NOTES

1 There are few secondary sources that focus on the Moravians' experience in Detroit. See John P. Bowes, "The Gnadenhutten Effect: Moravian Converts and the Search for Safety in the Canadian Borderlands," *Michigan Historical Review* 34 (2008): 101-18; Clarence M. Burton, "The Moravians at Detroit," in *MPHC*, 30:51-65; John E. Day, "The Moravians in Michigan," in *MPHC*, 30:41-51; and Geoffrey Hoerhauf, "American Spies and Sympathizers at Fort Detroit," Archiving Early America, www.earlyamerica.com (accessed May 5, 2009). For the experience of John Leeth, another neutral in Ohio Country, see the essay in this volume by Juliegha Norus.

For general histories of the Moravians, see Edmund De Schweinitz, *The Life and Times of David Zeisberger* (Philadelphia: J.B. Lippencott, 1870); Aaron Fogelman, *Jesus was Female: Moravians and the Challenge of Radical Religion in Early America* (Philadelphia: University of Pennsylvania Press, 2007); Earl Olmstead, *Blackcoats among the Delaware: David Zeisberger on the Ohio Frontier* (Kent, OH: Kent State University Press, 1991); Olmstead, *David Zeisberger: A Life among the Indians* (Kent, OH: Kent State University Press, 1997); Jacob John Sessler, *Communal Pietism among Early American Moravians* (New York: H. Holt, 1933); and John Heckewelder, *Thirty Thousand Miles with John Heckewelder*, ed. Paul A.W. Wallace (Pittsburgh: University of Pittsburgh Press, 1958).

2 Joan Gundersen, *To Be Useful to the World: Women in Revolutionary America, 1740-1790* (Chapel Hill: University of North Carolina Press, 2006), 19; Fogelman, 159; Hoerauf.

3 John Heckewelder's last name has been spelled a number of ways, including Heckenwelder and Hecksewelder, but they all refer to the same person. This paper uses the spelling favored by his co-missionary David Zeisberger in his diary, Heckewelder.

4 Eugene F. Bliss, ed., *Diary of David Zeisberger, a Moravian Missionary among the Indians of Ohio*, 2 vols. (Cincinnati: R. Clarke, 1885), 1:79-82; 81 (quote); Peter Silver, *Our Savage Neighbors: How Indian War Transformed Early America* (New York: Norton, 2007), 266-74. For the Gnadenhütten Massacre, see also the essay in this volume by John Maisner.

5 Silver, 265-75; Bliss, ed., 1:78-82; De Schweinitz, 549-51.

6 Bliss, ed., 1:106.

7 Bliss, ed., 1:258-59.

8 Bliss, ed., 1:204, 258.

9 John Heckewelder to John Askin, 1786, John Askin Papers, BHC; John Heckewelder to John Askin, February 27, 1786, in *MPHC*, 30:59 (quote).

10 Heckewelder to Askin, 1786, John Askin Papers, BHC; Bliss, ed., 1:181, 196, 253.

PART THREE

LATE BRITISH TO EARLY AMERICAN DETROIT: GRADUAL TRANSITION

The Revolutionary War ended and nation building began for Americans in 1783. The newly victorious United States scrambled to create functional state and national governments from provincial assemblies. To the north, the British reformed administrative districts in their Canadian provinces.

Detroit's de facto inclusion in the new British government was welcomed by most residents, but presented unique legal conundrums. Officially, the territory on the north side of the Detroit River was U.S. real estate. Yet an American governmental presence did not arrive for thirteen years. In the interim, Detroit's residents accepted Britain's quasi-legal control, particularly to keep commerce flowing. The region's Indians remained allied with the British against advancing Americans until being defeated at the Battle of Fallen Timbers in 1794.

Adding to the confusion was a provision of Jay's Treaty in the same year. Negotiated by John Jay to address lingering issues from the American Revolutionary War, the citizenship provision had particular repercussions for Detroit when Americans took control in 1796. Inhabitants were given a year to declare allegiance to either Britain or the U.S. Those pledging to Britain could remain residents of American Detroit indefinitely. Many moved across the river to the newly formed Upper Canada (today Ontario), but the majority remained.

In 1801, the people of Detroit petitioned the legislative assembly of the Northwest Territory to be incorporated as a town, and by January 1802, Detroit had its first American civil administration. In 1805, Congress recognized Michigan Territory, the first step to statehood. Across the river, several settlements welcomed loyalists and other migrants to the familiar security of British rule.

In two generations, Detroit matured from a French fur-trading post to a British command center to the capital of an American territory. The final period of this transition was gradual, reflecting cooperation based on survival and self-interest, between diverse groups of friends, former enemies, and newcomers.

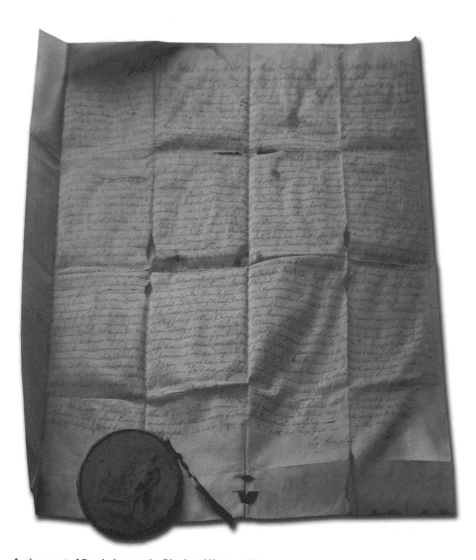

Assignment of first judges to the District of Hesse, 1788
Photograph by Sharon Tevis Finch. Ink on parchment. Courtesy of the Burton Historical Collection, Detroit Public Library.

The Courts of Hesse as a Middle Ground

Sharon Tevis Finch

> On the middle ground diverse peoples adjust their differences through what
> amounts to a process of creative, and often expedient, misunderstandings
> . . . from these misunderstandings arise new meanings and through them
> new practices—the shared meanings and practices of the middle ground.
>
> Richard White, *The Middle Ground*[1]

When the French explorers of the seventeenth century came to the Great Lakes
region and met the indigenous inhabitants, the two groups were able to build a
thriving and successful fur trade despite their wildly different cultures, experiences,
languages, and world views. In the early days, Michigan and southwest Ontario were
not in separate countries, but lay in a single region called by the French the *pays d'en
haut*, or the "upper country"—so named because the French had to go up river from
Quebec, their first enclave in North America, to reach this area with its natural wealth
of animals, the basis of the fur trade.

Richard White calls this area, both the physical and the metaphysical, "the
middle ground," in his seminal study of the same name, in which he develops the
theory that the Indians and the French mediated a metaphorical middle ground on
which to stand when their two cultures, with differing priorities and customs, met and
needed one another.[2] The concept also applies to the same region under later British
rule in the courts of Hesse. The courts demonstrate that the British, despite their
historic aversion to the French and to any accommodation of Indians, maintained the
middle ground in their administration of the Great Lakes region.[3]

At the close of the Revolution, the Americans had won the thirteen colonies
and what was soon to be called the Northwest Territory, which included the present-
day states of Michigan, Ohio, Indiana, Illinois, Wisconsin, and parts of Minnesota.
However, Britain refused to give up possession of its valuable military and fur-trading
posts on the Great Lakes, claiming that the Americans had not compensated the
loyalists for debts. The matter was eventually resolved by Jay's Treaty, which sent

the loyalist debts to arbitration. Finally, in 1796, the posts (including Fort Lernoult, which was located in the heart of what is now downtown Detroit) were relinquished to the United States government, pursuant to the Treaty of Paris of 1783. In the interim limbo period, before the turnover of the ceded lands, the British army continued to occupy the forts, and commanded the entire province of Quebec, which included the Great Lakes region. In Detroit, the fort and surrounding town were mainly on the north side of the Detroit River, while Indian villages surrounded the town and lined both sides of the water. The term "middle ground" seems particularly fitting during this period, when the British government ruled a land that it had legally given up, yet brought order through its court system to a society that sorely needed the rule of law.[4]

The courts of Hesse were created in response to continuing problems with the administration of justice in the region. One problem was the frontier "justice" meted out by Lieutenant Governor Henry Hamilton and his justice of the peace, Philip Dejean, in the mid-1770s.[5] Another was the inability of Detroit merchants to have their frequent legal disputes heard promptly or economically, since they had to file and try their cases in Montreal. In response, Quebec Governor Guy Carleton, Lord Dorchester, in his Proclamation of July 24, 1788, created the District of Hesse, followed by its courts, as a part of the province of Quebec. This new district encompassed what we now know as Michigan and southwest Ontario.[6]

According to Clarence Burton, the British government carefully framed the legal description of the geographical area of the District of Hesse to conceal the fact that it was incorporating a part of the United States into a British province, so as not to raise the level of hostility between Britain and the United States. There was only one lawyer in the region, Walter Roe. Therefore, the first judges appointed by the crown to the Court of Common Pleas were prominent residents with no legal training. They were Jacques Dupéront Baby, Alexander McKee, and William Robertson. Baby and Robertson were prosperous merchants and traders. McKee was an official in the Indian Department. This was awkward because of their lack of legal expertise and a potential for conflicts of interest in commercial lawsuits. They requested to be excused, and in 1789 Dorchester replaced them with William Dummer Powell, a lawyer born in Boston and educated in England. The courthouse itself was located on the south side of the Detroit River, in the Parish of L'Assomption (today a neighborhood in Windsor, Ontario), while Justice Powell lived on the north side of the river (today Detroit), and commuted to court by boat.[7]

The records of the proceedings of the courts of Hesse—the Common Pleas Court (civil cases), the courts of Oyer and Terminer and General Gaol Delivery and the grand jury (criminal cases), and the Prerogative Court (probate or surrogate matters)—demonstrate the cultural diversity of early Detroit and the surrounding region, with its French and métis fur traders, its British merchants and tradesmen, its Indian villagers, its African slaves and freedmen, its Germans, Dutch, Moravians, and other ethnic groups. A visitor in 1793 observed, "The inhabitants of the town are as great a mixture, I think, as ever I knew in any one place. English, Scotch, Irish, Dutch, French, Americans from different states, with black and yellow, and seldom clear of Indians of different tribes in the daytime."[8]

Not only do the court records contain the early French and English names we know so well from both modern Detroit street names and early Detroit history, such as Chene, Dequindre, Campau, Askin, McKee, McDougall, Groesbeck, Visgar, Fraser, Navarre, Meldrum, and Park, but some of the transcripts of court proceedings are in French, some in English. At least one is in both languages. This establishes that the judge and court clerk were bilingual, along with much of the population, and that the judgments were written so that the litigants understood them in their first language. The courts' practices fit the spirit of shared meaning and understanding in White's concept of the middle ground.[9]

Burton, in his *City of Detroit*, mentioned the court records briefly, but in a utilitarian and historical context rather than a cultural one. This approach is illustrated by his straightforward chapter title, "Law and Order in Early Detroit." Only one author, Canadian Justice William Renwick Riddell, discussed these courts at length, and he was more concerned with the history of the court than the cultural nature of the society it served. He touched upon the cultural issues when he praised the British for keeping the peace in view of the complaints of the French, but he did not empower all cultures equally. Certainly, to him, unlike scholars such as White and Gregory Dowd, the Indians were a subaltern group, without agency. More recently, the Canadian historian Sidney Harring has undertaken the history of "Canada's tortured relationship with its First Nations," and in the process, has discussed some of the criminal court records from the King's Bench of the province of Quebec. He is mainly concerned with the question of encroachment upon the legal sovereignty of the Indian nations, in view of their treaty rights.[10]

The fact that the court wrote in two languages (not translating one document, but writing some records in one language and some in another) shows that it accepted the cultures of distinct peoples in the middle ground. Noteworthy also was the adoption of French law in civil cases (until 1792) and British law in criminal cases in the province of Quebec, later including the District of Hesse. The courts of Hesse had but one judge, probably due to the small population, and that judge, with his clerk, bilingually administered both French and English law.[11]

Remarkably, in a third court, the Hesse Prerogative Court, the equivalent of our probate or surrogate courts, there were two practices available, either the French or British style of handling the estates of minors and the deceased. The parties had the option of selecting the one with which they felt most comfortable. Even more remarkable was the enactment of laws that required, in cases between British "Old subjects," British jurors; in cases between French *Canadien* "New subjects," *Canadien* jurors; and in cases between a Briton and a *Canadien*, a jury made up of equal numbers of each group.[12]

These inclusive provisions began with the Quebec Act of 1774, a law which students of the American Revolution usually consider most important for infuriating the colonists along the eastern seaboard. However, the calming effect the act had on the French in the Quebec province, including the upper Great Lakes region, was significant. The Quebec Act, in addition to giving the French recourse to their own accustomed law, codified civil equality between French Catholics and British Protestants. As a result, despite their Catholic religion, the French were recognized as full subjects of the province, and allowed to practice law and to serve as judges, which they could not do under British law outside of Quebec. The British Parliament developed a special oath for French Catholics that did not require swearing allegiance to the Church of England, but only to the king. All this legal maneuvering came about because of the reluctance of the French to give up their religion and familiar law, the *coutume de Paris*, and the similar reluctance of the incoming British loyalists to be governed by the laws of France. An accommodation was made. There was dispute and negotiation, but in the end, the British developed a very unusual, ingenious, and heterogeneous legal system.[13]

A dramatic example of British accommodation of other cultures was in the case of Wawanisse, an Indian who was beaten to death by a mob of French and British civilians and soldiers at Michilimackinac in 1792, after he had "assaulted and wounded several persons," including "Old Bunga a Negro," with a knife. In the initial investigation, no witnesses could be found to the killing, which had taken place in broad daylight and in plain view of many people. The coroner's inquest jury made the absurd finding that "the said Indian Wawanisse's death was occasioned by several stabs in the body and strokes on the head by weapons and persons unknown to them." The commanding officer reproached the coroner for this finding, saying, "There were certainly some [witnesses]." The coroner retorted, "If he [the commander] knew of any, he should have sent them."[14]

The justices of the peace for the District of Hesse did not continue this cover-up, but found and arrested the "missing" witnesses, took their statements, and put them on bond to appear before the court. Though the assailants and some witnesses did not appear as ordered, some witnesses did testify and established the identities of the killers. The grand jury in Detroit, made up of notable persons such as James May, George McDougall, S.F. Girarvin, Charles Moran, J. Schieffelin, and Cassier Campau, found, based on this evidence, and quite contrary to the coroner's jury findings, that Wawanisse was "secured and bound by a multitude of [named] people there present . . . [and] against the King's peace was kicked and stamped upon and with divers weapons beat, cut, stabbed and murdered." The grand jury issued a "Presentment" (an indictment), charging these men with the murder of an Indian. Strikingly, the grand jury went on to specify that its finding in this case was necessary to give due process in the case of murder of Indians, because otherwise they would be likely to seek vengeance for the killing and would keep "alive that spirit of retaliation that marks the savage character."[15]

The grand jury, made up of English, French, Scottish, and German residents, administering British criminal law, feared that the allowance of "loose proceedings," and the failure to enforce the law against those who assaulted and murdered an Indian, would result in brutal revenge and civil disorder. This decision does not mean that Indians were exempt from the law. In another case, two Indians, Chabouguoy and Cawquochish, were indicted for the murder of a European in the Court of Oyer and Terminer and General Gaol Delivery (a lower level criminal court) in 1792. In a third case, Mishinaway was acquitted of murder in 1795. The British government was intent on keeping the peace between its culturally diverse populations through the enlightened approach of the courts of Hesse under Justice Powell and the King's Bench of the province. Even-handed administration of the law kept the Indian population from rebelling, and preserved the middle ground, while at the same time bringing justice to the Europeans who suffered at the hands of Indians.[16]

Some scholars of early Detroit, such as Burton and Willis Dunbar and George May, do not view British conciliations to the cultures of French *Canadiens* and Indians as positive mediation, but rather as merely a selfishly motivated manipulation of subject peoples. These appraisals are perhaps just the opposite sides of a coin, but the distinction is important to the premise of this paper, that White's middle ground, as applied to the British courts of Hesse and the province of Quebec, is a valuable concept demonstrating intercultural negotiation, not just the cynical control of conquered populations. The legal historian Sidney Harring touches on this same vein when he criticizes the British for indicting Indians in the "white man's court," rather than acknowledging their separate sovereignty and sending them to a tribal court. This is certainly a valid point in current legal discourse and regulation. Yet, the British made a protected middle ground of legal safety for both cultures, by treating Indians and Europeans equally under the law, whether victim or defendant. Likewise, the British treated the French as legally equal to Britons in the courts of Hesse. This legal equality was certainly not the same as social equality, but it did allow the region to develop a cultural fluidity and comfort level that would not otherwise have been possible. In this way, the British created their own "new practices," a process White has shown was so important to the original French-Indian middle ground.

NOTES

1 Richard White, *The Middle Ground: Indians, Empires, and Republics in the Great Lakes Region, 1650-1815* (New York: Cambridge University Press, 1991), x.

2 White, *Middle Ground,* esp. 50-70. Following this groundbreaking study of the relationship between the Europeans and the Indians in the Great Lakes area, historians began to use the term "middle ground" in many ways. See Susan Sleeper-Smith, ed., "Forum: The Middle Ground Revisited," *William and Mary Quarterly* 63 (2006): 3-96. Some of the essays in the forum, including Philip DeLoria, "What is the Middle Ground, Anyway?" (15-22), question alternative uses of the term, wondering if it has been bastardized by its popularity among historians. White himself acknowledges that the term "has taken on something of a life of its own," but views its use by other scholars as valid, so long as they are exploring how mediation works in human affairs to create a space in which competing interests can co-exist ("Creative Misunderstandings and New Understandings," 9). It is in this spirit that this essay is written. White's own discussion of a British middle ground after Pontiac's War is limited to trading and diplomatic alliances between the British and Indian groups and does not consider the legal interactions of the European and Indian populations of the District of Hesse (*Middle Ground,* 269-365). For a more recent discussion of linguistic and cultural mixing between the French and Indians, see David Hackett Fischer, *Champlain's Dream* (New York: Simon and Schuster, 2008), 508-11.

3 Our knowledge about the local justice system under Britain during this period comes from only a very few sources. Clarence M. Burton, still the leading authority on early Detroit, gave an overview in three chapters of *City of Detroit,* 1:160-295. Canadian jurist Justice William Renwick Riddell (1852-1945) made a second career on and off the bench as a historian. He was a judge in the Supreme Court and Court of Appeal of Ontario, and published some 1,258 articles, reviews, lectures, pamphlets, and books in the fields of legal, constitutional, medical, and social history, any number of which were on the topic of early Canadian and Michigan history, particularly legal history ("William Renwick Riddell," The Canadian Encyclopedia, www.thecanadianencyclopedia.com [accessed April 5, 2009]). This paper relies heavily upon Riddell, who like Burton frequently transcribed large blocks of original sources in support of his points. I also use manuscripts of original court documents from the Archives of Ontario in Toronto and gratefully acknowledge the invaluable long-distance assistance of the staff, particularly Yuri Shimpo, a reference archivist who, on her own initiative, researched the King's Bench records and found the Wawanisse case that is so important to this paper.

Transcripts of the Court of Common Pleas and Prerogative Court (civil cases) are found in Riddell's *Michigan under British Rule: Law and Law Courts, 1760-1796* (Lansing: Michigan Historical Commission, 1926), and in Alexander Fraser, ed., *Fourteenth Report of the Bureau of Archives for the Province of Ontario* (Toronto: A.T. Wilgress, 1917). Transcripts of some of the King's Bench (criminal cases) are found in Riddell, *The Bar and the Courts of the Province of Upper Canada, or Ontario* (Toronto: Macmillan, 1928). (*The Bar* and *The Courts* are two separate books, with separate pagination, published in one volume under the joint title *The Bar and the Courts.* References in this paper are to *Courts,* which is found in the second half of the volume.) Burton, Riddell, and Fraser all knew one another and worked cooperatively in reconstructing the legal history of early Detroit and Canada. There is a fascinating account by Fraser of how, in 1910, he and Burton discovered by candlelight in the dusty bowels of Osgoode Hall in Toronto, the bulk of the records of the Court of Common Pleas for the District of Hesse "which had long been given up as irrecoverably lost." Fraser then tells us that three years later, Riddell unearthed the equally long-lost first volume of those records, dating from 1789 (*Fourteenth Report*, v-vi). For a succinct analysis of the development of the legal system and the courts of Hesse in early British Canada, from 1759 on, see David B. Read, *The Lives of the Judges of Upper Canada and Ontario, from 1791 to the Present Time* (Toronto: Rowsell and Hutchison, 1888). See Willis F. Dunbar and George S. May, *Michigan: A History of the Wolverine State*, 3rd rev. ed. (Grand Rapids: Eerdmans, 1995), 88-89, for an abbreviated but informative review of the development of the British governmental system in Michigan and Upper Canada (today Ontario). A detailed discussion of the entire development of the court system in early Detroit is found in the introduction to Ernest J. Lajeunesse, ed., *The Windsor Border Region, Canada's Southernmost Frontier; a Collection of Documents* (Toronto: Champlain Society, 1960), lxxx-lxxxix.

4 Dunbar and May, 88-89; Riddell, *Michigan*, 25-26. In 1782, in De Peyster's Census, among the population of 2,191, 248 of 309 family names were French. See William Renwick Riddell, *The Life of John Graves Simcoe: First Lieutenant-Governor of the Province of Upper Canada, 1792-96* (Toronto: McClelland and Stewart, 1926), 73; 197 n1, n3.

5 Dejean's first and last names were also spelled Philippe, Phillippe, Dejeane, and DeJean. For overviews of his career, see "Phillippe Dejean," Dictionary of Canadian Biography Online, University of Toronto, www.biographi.ca (accessed March 22, 2009); *City of Detroit*, 1:167; Riddell, *Michigan*, 49-51, 382; Riddell, *Courts*, 68; Lajeunesse, ed., lxxx-lxxxii; and the essay in this volume by Errin T. Stegich.

6 *City of Detroit*, 1:181, 206-11; Riddell, *Michigan*, 20-22. Burton, relying on British Parliamentary debate, states that before the Quebec Act, there was only military government in Detroit, which had been excluded from the Proclamation of 1763 because of a very small European population. Civil law was established earlier in Quebec, but there were no courts located near Detroit. Seeing a need for more localized administration of justice, the Quebec government, under Lord Dorchester, set up four new court districts, the farthest west being Hesse. The German nomenclature recognized George III's Hanoverian background. See R. Alan Douglas, *Uppermost Canada: The Western District and the Detroit Frontier, 1800-1850* (Detroit: Wayne State University Press, 2001), 4.

7 *City of Detroit*, 1:213; Riddell, *Michigan*, 53-59.

8 Frederick Clever Bald, *Detroit's First American Decade, 1796-1805* (Ann Arbor: University of Michigan Press, 1948), 26-41; 28 (quote).

9 For transcripts of original official records of Court of Common Pleas, Province of Quebec, District of Hesse, see Riddell, *Michigan*, 72-264. An example of a case in two languages is *Schieffeling and Askin vs. Jean Bte. Sancrainte*, September 3, 1792 (292).

10 *City of Detroit*, 1:160-236; Sidney L. Harring, *White Man's Law: Native People in Nineteenth-Century Canadian Jurisprudence* (Toronto: Osgoode Society, 1998), 3 (quote), 109-118. For Riddell, see note 3 above.

11 Riddell, *Michigan*, 34-35.

12 Riddell, *Courts*, 27-76. In particular, see 39-40 and 59-70 for prerogative courts. Riddell transcribes the cases of the Hesse Prerogative Court and discusses, interprets, and, in some cases, translates the proceedings. These cases are probably of primary interest to lawyers, but would also be helpful to historians seeking detailed knowledge of events in the lives of well-known Detroiters. Jury composition is discussed in Riddell's introduction to Fraser, ed., 16.

13 Riddell, *Courts*, 20-26. Dunbar and May discuss this accommodation, but state that the British motive in appeasing the French was to keep them from joining the colonists in revolutionary activity (77).

14 "Re: Wawanisse, an Indian 1792," B248832, MS and Translation, RG-22-138, Western District, Archives of Ontario, Toronto. Wawanisse has varied spellings in historical and court records, including Wawanissé, Wawanesse, and Owaowanise. For a contemporaneous description of Wawanisse's murder, the coroner's inquest, and the initial release upon bail of the defendants, see Captain Charlton to Lieutenant Colonel England, Michilimackinac, July 1, 1792, in *MPHC*, 12:38. Charlton noted that the Indians at the post were satisfied with the proceedings and "behaved in every respect perfectly quiet."

15 "Re: Wawanisse, an Indian 1792." The usually meticulous Justice Riddell, in a lengthy discussion of this case in *Michigan*, does not seem to know of the second verdict, that of the grand jury in Detroit, at least as of the time he published that volume, in 1926. He says that "no Bill (True Bill of Indictment) was found," and recites only the coroner's jury's defective finding. He editorializes about the unfairness of the decision, saying the case proves that the general attitude was, "There is no good Indian but a dead Indian" (336, 454 n5). The best explanation for the discrepancy is that the judge did not have access to records that are now available in the Archives of Ontario, particularly the grand jury Presentment (indictment). The indictment states that the perpetrators were guilty of the crime, but had been set free on bond and had absconded. Further research is needed to find the final disposition of the Wawanisse case. The last reference I could locate in the docket books was to a hearing in the Court of Oyer and Terminer and General Gaol Delivery (apparently a lower level criminal court on the magistrate level), where testimony was taken from witnesses in the matter before the grand jury on September 4, 1792 (Fraser, ed., 180-81). This was before the indictment itself was issued by the grand jury on September 6, 1792. Were the missing defendants ever arrested? Was there a trial? Was there a conviction? Was there an execution of a white man for the murder of an Indian? Answers to these questions may still be buried in an archive somewhere.

16 Riddell, *Michigan*, 356, 462-72.

Blue Jacket: Pan-Indian Leader, Warrior, and Cultural Mediator

Molon Rahman

The Shawnee warrior Blue Jacket secured his status among America's most formidable Indian leaders during the war for the frontier following the American Revolution. His military leadership in the 1791 Battle of the Wabash resulted in the most staggering blow ever delivered against the United States at the hands of Indians, and his recruiting efforts to gather native forces before the next major campaign at the Battle of Fallen Timbers were unparalleled. Beyond this, however, scholars have overlooked Blue Jacket's accomplishments in linking his home region, the Ohio River Valley, with Detroit and the upper Great Lakes. His military successes owed much to his ability to create a strong Indian confederacy throughout the Old Northwest and to forge alliances with European traders and military personnel in outposts such as Detroit. Blue Jacket's familial relations, pan-Indian recruiting efforts, European connections, and eventual cooperation with the American hero of Fallen Timbers, General "Mad" Anthony Wayne, give him a prominent place not only in the annals of the American frontier, but in the rich history of Detroit as well.[1]

Blue Jacket's skill at moving between different worlds has led to confusion about his identity. Early chroniclers of his life even claimed that the Shawnee leader was not a Native American. In 1877, a sensational article penned by Thomas Jefferson Larsh, titled "Very Interesting Facts about a Noted Indian Chief," appeared in the *Daily Ohio State Journal.* The article stated that Blue Jacket was actually a European named Marmaduke Van Swearingen, who rose to the status of Shawnee war chief in 1786. According to this legend, Marmaduke Van Swearingen was captured along with his younger brother Charles by Shawnee Indians during a hunting expedition at the time of the American Revolutionary War. Marmaduke then agreed to join the tribe in return for his younger brother's freedom. The name "Blue Jacket," Larsh claimed, was given to Marmaduke because of the blue hunting shirt he reportedly wore at the time of his capture. Though no written record certifying Blue Jacket's date of birth exists, historians estimate that he was born between 1738 and 1740. In contrast, the surviving Swearingen family Bible traces

Marmaduke's birth to January 2, 1763. Additional verifiable historical records further refute the theory that Blue Jacket was white, and should put Larsh's fantastical story to rest once and for all.[2]

Still, the Shawnee leader's career was not free of contradictions. Blue Jacket seemed to violate his own reputation as a fierce warrior and pan-Indian leader by readily embracing European culture. He was first touched by European influences as a child, with the constant influx of French, British, and Spanish traders carrying loads of merchandise into the Ohio River Valley to exchange for deerskins, beaver pelts, and other furs in Indian villages. The historian John Sugden has argued that the fur trade was "encouraging a new kind of Shawnee, an individualist who accumulated property in the style of the whites and whose home reflected a fatter living." Blue Jacket exemplified this "new kind of Shawnee" in his consumption habits and in fraternizing with and modeling his behavior after whites.[3]

Contemporaries were struck by the depths of Blue Jacket's cultural mixing. After visiting his home in Ohio Country, the white captive Oliver Spencer recounted Blue Jacket's "scarlet frock coat, richly laced with gold, and confined around his waist with a party-colored sash . . . while from his neck hung a massive silver gorget and a large medallion of His Majesty, George III."[4] In 1788, a witness described Blue Jacket as "a Shawnee chief of considerable note and property," and another white prisoner related that his home was "a fine plantation, well stocked with cattle." Blue Jacket lived at the geographic and figurative intersection of Indian and European life.[5]

The Shawnee warrior's close ties to European traders helped him to maintain such lavish style. Some of these connections came by way of his second wife, who was the métis daughter of the French *Canadien* trader Jacques Dupéront Baby of Detroit. The marriage likely opened trading opportunities for Blue Jacket in Montreal and Detroit, as his wife understood French and remained in contact with her father. When Blue Jacket ventured into Miamitown (today in southwestern Ohio) he also mixed with a variety of traders operating out of Detroit, "including the French Laselles, the Adhemars, John Kinzie, the Rivards, George Ironside, and David Gray," according to Sugden.[6]

Blue Jacket's close relationships with Europeans did not make him any less of an Indian. On the contrary, he used his white contacts to help defend Indian land in Ohio Country against American settlers in the 1780s and 1790s. Following the formation of the northwest Indian confederacy in 1786, Blue Jacket was given the honor of serving as a representative on behalf of the Shawnee, Delaware, and Miami Indians to British officials in Detroit and Montreal. The Ohio Indians used British supplies to help fortify their headquarters against the American advancement at the junction between the Auglaize and Maumee rivers. Known as the Glaize, the area quickly developed into a complex multicultural society that included European trading posts and seven Indian villages, comprised mostly of Shawnees, Delawares, and Miamis.[7]

Detroit's Indian population shared a strong interest in the fate of Ohio Country. As the historian Helen Hornbeck Tanner explains, the "principal warpath for Indians from Detroit and the upper Great Lakes led up the Maumee River from Lake Erie," and the number of Indians using the waterways "increased as inter-tribal war parties gathered at the Glaize for attacks on settlers in southern Ohio and Kentucky." Blue Jacket, with help from the brilliant Miami chief Little Turtle, scored his greatest victory by leading an alliance of Ohio and Great Lakes Indians against Arthur St. Clair's American forces at the Battle of the Wabash in November 1791. Shawnees, Miamis, Delawares, Mingoes, Cherokees, Wyandots, Ojibwas, Ottawas, and Potawatomis all combined to exact 948 casualties on St. Clair's army, with no more than thirty-five deaths on the Indian side. In percentage terms, the battle was one of the worst defeats in the history of the United States Army.[8]

After the Battle of the Wabash, Blue Jacket toured Ohio Country and the Great Lakes region promoting his view that a continued united front was the Indians' only hope for defending their land. He also preached the Shawnee belief that the spirit world was on the side of the Indians to triumph over outside forces. In 1792, Blue Jacket visited Detroit on his tour. In addition to recruiting Indian warriors, he sent runners to what was left of the small Moravian mission on the southeastern side of the Huron River (today Clinton River). The pacifist Delaware converts living at the mission had declined to participate in previous military campaigns. Blue Jacket warned that they "should not think that they alone could sit so quiet and see others go to war for them." The strong words demonstrated the Shawnee's relentless efforts to build his alliance.[9]

In August 1794, Blue Jacket prepared his recruits for another showdown with the U.S. Army. Fifteen hundred Indian warriors formed a battle line on the northwestern bank of the Maumee River near the British Fort Miami (today Maumee, Ohio). The composition of the line was diverse and included Wyandots, Ottawas, and Potawatomis from Detroit. A group of about fifty militiamen from the Detroit area, led by William Caldwell, were also dispatched to strengthen Fort Miami but chose instead to join the ranks of the Indians on the frontlines due to close relations between the wives of Blue Jacket and Caldwell. Among the other whites present were captives who had been raised in native villages, and traders who were tied to the Indians by economic interest and kinship.[10]

Despite Blue Jacket's recruiting, General Wayne's larger and more disciplined army overwhelmed the Indians and their allies at Fallen Timbers. After the loss, Blue Jacket initiated a bold meeting with Wayne that risked him losing face with his followers. But the Shawnee leader was simply following his long pattern of using mediation as a means to advance his people's interests. On February 8, 1795, Blue Jacket and Wayne met face-to-face for the first time. Speaking on behalf of the Shawnees, Delawares, and Miamis at the meeting, Blue Jacket agreed to accept rations of meat, flour, and salt as compensation to the tribes for surrendering land in Ohio Country to the Americans. Wayne later reported that Blue Jacket privately requested additional compensation in the form of flattery and a document issued by Wayne declaring his former foe to be a war chief. The general understood Blue Jacket's need for validation, and considered the action a small sacrifice in return for the Indian warrior's cooperation. Later, Wayne trumpeted the submission "of the famous Blue Jacket" in letters to the Department of War.[11]

The loss at Fallen Timbers, followed by the Treaty of Greenville of 1795, resulted in the Indian surrender of Ohio Country and other portions of the Old Northwest to the Americans. Combined with Jay's Treaty of 1794, the battle paved the way for the American takeover of Detroit in 1796. Amidst these defeats, it was easy to lose sight of the accomplishments of Blue Jacket and his pan-Indian alliance. For more than a decade following the Revolutionary War, he brilliantly defended Indian land and other interests in the Ohio River Valley and the Great Lakes region through a combination of war, mediation, and conciliation. His British military and commercial allies in the Detroit area were essential to his success. Indeed, it is fitting that previous generations confused Blue Jacket's close connections to Europeans with him actually being European. His example demonstrated that cultural mixing was one of the few options available to Indians for preserving their way of life.[12]

NOTES

1 John Sugden, *Blue Jacket: Warrior of the Shawnee* (Lincoln: University of Nebraska Press, 2000), is the best existing study on Blue Jacket, particularly his leadership role in the battle for Ohio Country. This essay explores Blue Jacket's connections to Detroit by drawing on Sugden's work and multiple other studies, including Helen Hornbeck Tanner, "The Glaize in 1792: A Composite Indian Community," *Ethnohistory* 25 (1978): 15-39; Paul Lawrence Stevens, "His Majesty's 'Savage' Allies: British Indian Policy during the Revolutionary War: The Carleton Years, 1774-1778" (Ph.D. diss., State University of New York at Buffalo, 1984); and Dan L. Thrapp, *Encyclopedia of Frontier Biography*, 4 vols. (Glendale, CA: Arthur H. Clark, 1988), 1:129-30.

2 For the controversy over Blue Jacket's identity, see Carolyn D. Rowland et al., "Was the Shawnee War Chief Blue Jacket a Caucasian?," *Ohio Journal of Science* 106 (2006): 126-29.

3 Sugden, 11-12, 13 (quote).

4 Spencer quoted in Sugden, 33. For Oliver Spencer's experience as a prisoner, see the essay in this volume by Caitlyn A.O. Perry.

5 Sugden, 80.

6 Sugden, 31-32, 80 (quote).

7 Tanner, 16-18.

8 Tanner, 16; Sugden, 113-27,

9 Blue Jacket quoted in Sugden, 129. For the Moravian mission, see the essay in this volume by Melissa R. Luberti.

10 Sugden, 172-73.

11 Sugden, 189-91.

12 For the Treaty of Greenville, see *American State Papers, Indian Affairs*, 2 vols. (Washington: Gales and Seaton, 1832-34), 1:562-83, and the essays in this volume by Susan Ward, Kimberly Steele, and Douglas D. Fisher.

A View of Detroit July 25th 1794

Signed E.H. (probably Lieutenant Edmund Henn, 1794). Pen, ink, watercolor on paper. Courtesy of the Burton Historical Collection, Detroit Public Library.

Safe at Home: The French in Detroit

Leslie Riehl

The events of the American Revolution brought significant demographic and political changes to Detroit. An influx of loyalists increased the number of British settlers substantially. In addition, the ceding of Detroit to the Americans in 1796 splintered a region that had long represented a single entity—politically, economically, and religiously. The Detroit River, which had served as the main highway for commerce and communication, instead became the dividing line between the United States and Britain's Upper Canada (today Ontario). Even with all these changes, Detroit's French population remained remarkably fixed, both physically and culturally. The identities of French habitants in the Great Lakes region were not altered with America's independence any more than they were with Britain's victory in the Seven Years' War.[1]

Although Detroit's population increased slowly during the early eighteenth century, by the 1750s the French had established a stable and growing settlement surrounding Fort Pontchartrain. The area's earliest French *habitants* settled along the Detroit River's north shore within the fort's protection. Its founder, Antoine Laumet de La Mothe, Sieur de Cadillac, envisioned that these early residents would eventually develop a thriving agricultural settlement.[2] Establishing a farming community in the interior of the vast North American continent proved to be a daunting task for the French. Even with generous land and supply grants by the French crown, the population of Detroit made small gains. Until the early 1720s, it never surpassed two hundred people. Over time, the town spread to both sides of the river, and the 1750 census documented ninety-six families with ninety-five children under the age of fifteen on the north and south shores. The total European population was about 480 people amidst several Indian villages. These numbers paled in comparison to the fifteen thousand people in Boston and the eight thousand in Montreal at the time. Still, Detroit had gradually emerged as one of the leading commercial centers of the northwest frontier. The town's young, family-based settlement had made an unmistakable French imprint on both sides of the

Detroit River.[3]

By the time the British took control of Fort Pontchartrain in 1760, therefore, the area was anything but a blank slate. French settlers had created a political, economic, and ecclesiastical center on the north shore of the river. At the same time, the south shore included sixty-one homesteads. Ste. Anne's on the north side began as the parish church for all French inhabitants of the region, while the Huron Mission of the Assumption at La Pointe de Montréal on the south side was originally intended only for Native Americans. As the number of white settlers increased, though, the French began attending services alongside their Indian neighbors at the Huron Mission. In 1767, the Church of the Assumption at La Pointe de Montréal du Détroit was elevated to the status of an official parish. The formation of two parishes did not signal a break in the unity of the region, but rather the success of the settlement. The population of Detroit was large enough to warrant a parish on each side of the river.[4]

Detroit's population continued to grow under the British administration, particularly during the years of the American Revolutionary War. Lieutenant Governor Henry Hamilton wrote to the Earl of Dartmouth on August 29, 1776, that there were approximately 1,500 white settlers that occupied thirteen miles along the north shore and eight miles along the south. The 1782 census, ordered by Major De Peyster, showed that the settlement had increased to more than two thousand white settlers—a 33 percent increase in less than a decade. The population grew on both sides of the river, but the north remained dominant; 194 of the 321 heads of family counted resided on the north shore. In other words, as Britain was surrendering its thirteen colonies along the eastern North American seaboard, Detroit was becoming larger and more British.[5]

French settlers also continued to thrive in Detroit during the American Revolution. Although a handful of British settlers, including John Askin, Gregor McGregor, and the Macomb brothers, had the town's largest land and livestock holdings, the French still dominated in total numbers. The 1782 census was full of French names like Meloche, Campau, Drouillard, Parent, Beaubien, and Reaume. Many families had members who settled on both shores of the river. Out of the five Meloches listed in the census, for example, three lived on the south shore and two on the north. The most prominent French landholders, such as Antoine Labadie, Alexis Maisonville, and Pierre Reaume, now resided on the south shore. The American Revolution heralded many changes for Detroit, but it did not upend the strong French presence that permeated the region.[6]

French influence in Detroit also did not wane under the American administration. When the United States assumed full control of the town in 1796, a large majority of its French residents stayed. Most of the French names from earlier censuses remained on the north (American) side of the river, including families such as the Meloches that had land on both shores. Moreover, most French setters elected to become American citizens rather than remain British subjects. In 1796, the newly established Wayne County was home to 653 men over the age of sixteen. Only 118, or 18 percent, took advantage of the offer in Jay's Treaty to remain British subjects while residing in the American territory. Of this group, thirty were French. The overwhelming majority of Detroit residents, especially the French, chose to cast their lot with the Americans rather than remain British subjects or uproot their lives and move.[7]

After 1796, French settlers on the south shore of the Detroit River displayed the same pattern of staying home. The British turned the former southern shore of Detroit into the town of Sandwich (today Windsor, Ontario). Most of the initial proprietors of lots in the new town were French and already residents or landholders on the south shore; over time, Sandwich became increasingly Anglicized. The neighboring community of Petite Côte (today parts of Windsor and LaSalle, Ontario), the first European settlement on the south shore in 1749, was also heavily French. The British also founded Fort Malden and its accompanying community of Amherstburg farther downriver. As the new site for Britain's official interest on the Detroit River, the fort and town had the strongest concentration of British inhabitants on the south shore.[8]

Yet, Amherstburg still had a strong French presence, especially on Second Street. Charles Reaume was listed as having 120 French arpents of clear land on the south shore in 1782 and was awarded Lot 10 on Second Street in 1796 (an arpent in North America equaled about 192 English feet). Likewise, Alexis Maisonville had 280 arpents of open land before he was awarded Lot 2 on Second Street. Both Reaume and Maisonville also held lots in Sandwich. Through these communities, the French retained strong cultural influence in what became southwest Ontario well into the nineteenth century.[9]

As the first European settlers in the upper Great Lakes, the French played an integral role in the development of Detroit. They did not disappear when the British took command of the fort in 1760, nor when the Americans took control in 1796. The American Revolution had a dramatic impact on the flow of people in and out of Detroit, with the important exception of the French. Many lived through the Revolutionary War exactly where their ancestors had received their initial land grants on the north or south shore of the Detroit River. The revolution's aftermath also did not lead to mass migrations of French settlers out of Detroit. Few left with the British army or other loyalists in the period after 1796. The majority of French residents in Sandwich and Amherstburg already held land on the south shore. In the Detroit River region, the American Revolution's greatest effect was not the creation of the new American nation, but rather the fracturing of a region that had previously been united.

NOTES

1 Few historical works explore the shared French heritage of both southwestern Ontario and southeastern Michigan. Important exceptions include Richard White, *The Middle Ground: Indians, Empires, and Republics in the Great Lakes Region, 1650-1815* (New York: Cambridge University Press, 1991), and John J. Bukowczyk et al., *Permeable Border: The Great Lakes Basin as a Transnational Region, 1650-1900* (Pittsburgh: University of Pittsburgh Press, 2005). For works detailing the migration of British loyalists, see Maya Jasanoff, "The Other Side of Revolution: Loyalists in the British Empire," *William and Mary Quarterly* 65 (2008): 205-33; Keith Mason, "The American Loyalist Diaspora and the Reconfiguration of the British Atlantic World," in *Empire and Nation: The American Revolution in the Atlantic World*, ed. Eliga H. Gould and Peter S. Onuf (Baltimore: Johns Hopkins University Press, 2005), 239-59; Mary Beth Norton, *The British-Americans: The Loyalist Exiles in England, 1774-1789* (Boston: Little Brown, 1972); and Alan Taylor "The Late Loyalists: Northern Reflections of the Early American Republic," *Journal of the Early Republic* 27 (2007): 1-34.

2 For a description of Cadillac's role in early Detroit history, see *MPHC*, 13:96-100, and Ernest J. Lajeunesse, ed., *The Windsor Border Region, Canada's Southernmost Frontier; a Collection of Documents* (Toronto: Champlain Society, 1960), xxxix-xlvi.

3 In 1708, there were only sixty-three French settlers, including thirty-four traders. The next year the population increased to about two hundred. After Cadillac's departure, many families left, reducing the population. The population again reached two hundred people in 1722. Silas Farmer, *The History of Detroit and Michigan of the Metropolis Illustrated* (Detroit: S. Farmer, 1884), 333. The 1750 census showed ninety-six heads of households, eighty women, forty-nine boys aged fifteen years and over, thirty-three girls aged fifteen years and over, ninety-six boys under fifteen years, ninety-five girls under fifteen, and thirty-three slaves. "Census of the Inhabitants of Detroit on September 1st, 1750," in Lajeunesse, ed., 54-56. For Boston and Montreal, see Edward M. Hartnell, Edward W. McGlenen, and Edward O. Skelton, *Boston and Its Story, 1630-1915* (Boston: Printing Department, 1916), 190, and William H. Atherton, *Montreal, 1535-1914* (Montreal: S.J. Clarke, 1914), 219.

4 "Extract from the Census of All the Inhabitants of Detroit Made By Philip DeJean in the Year 1768 on January 23rd," enclosed in George Turnbull to Thomas Gage, Detroit, February 23, 1768, Thomas Gage Papers, American Series, vol. 74, CL. For the development of the church on the south shore, see E.C. Lebel, "History of Assumption, the First Parish in Upper Canada," *Report of the Canadian Catholic Historical Association* 21 (1954): 23-37.

5 Henry Hamilton to the Earl of Dartmouth, Detroit, August 29, 1776, in *MPHC*, 10:264-67; "A Survey of the Settlement of Detroit Made by Order of Major De Peyster the 16 Day of July 1782," in *MPHC*, 10:601-13. In 1782, seventy-eight male slaves and 101 female slaves also resided on both sides of the river, bringing the total population to 2,191.

6 "Census of 1782," in *Michigan Censuses 1710-1830 under the French, British, and Americans*, ed. Donna Valley Russell (Detroit: Detroit Society for Genealogical Research, 1982), 49-56.

7 "The 1796 Census of Wayne County," in Russell, ed., 59-74. For a list of men who elected to remain British while residing in American Detroit, see Lajeunesse, ed., 189, and *MPHC*, 8:410-11.

8 "Appendix IX: Holders of Farm Lots in Essex County About 1794," in Lajeunesse, ed., 357-60. For the founding of Amherstburg and Fort Malden, see the essay in this volume by Mark A. Mallia. Petite Côte was also known as Turkey Creek and later split into two communities: Ojibway (a town in 1913) and LaSalle (a town in 1924). Ojibway was annexed into Windsor in 1966. LaSalle became the Township of Sandwich West in 1959. Parts were annexed by Windsor in 1966, and the remainder became the Town of LaSalle in 1991. "County History > Early Years," County of Essex, Ontario, www.countyofessex.on.ca (accessed August 11, 2009); "Heritage," City of Windsor, Ontario, www.citywindsor.ca (accessed August 11, 2009).

9 "Census of 1782," 52-56; "Names of Lot Holders in the Town of Amhertsburg 1799," in Lajeunesse, ed., 226. For a map of the original lots in Amherstburg, see Lajeunesse, ed., cxxviii. For Alexis Maisonville, see the essay in this volume by Kimberly Steele.

From Detroit to Fort Malden: The Transfer of Sovereignty and Subjects

Mark A. Mallia

When Britain handed Detroit over to the United States in July 1796, a thirty-six-year period of British control ended on the northwestern shore of the Detroit River. Jay's Treaty accomplished what the American Revolution alone had not, dividing the upper Great Lakes region between the United States and Britain. After 1796, British interests in the region became centered on the new Fort Malden and in the community of Amherstburg. The initial migration of British loyalists across the river was small, numbering no more than a few hundred. It was limited mostly to the soldiers of the 24th Regiment of Foot, agents in the British Indian Department, and a few merchants with government contracts. The transfer of British sovereignty and subjects to Fort Malden, however modest, was significant for maintaining Britain's influence in the upper Great Lakes region. For the first time, the Detroit River was a boundary between separate political entities.[1]

Fort Malden was located near the entrance to Lake Erie at the mouth of the Detroit River for strategic purposes. The fort's canon controlled all ships entering and exiting the upper Great Lakes, including those bound for or stationed at Detroit. The Amherstburg Channel, between Fort Malden and Bois Blanc Island (today Boblo Island), was the only deep portion of the river wide enough for large ship traffic. Fort Malden allowed British officials to closely monitor their neighbors across the river.

The British first discussed building a second fort on the Detroit River in 1792. That year Captain Gother Mann of the Royal Engineers described the need for another military installation on the river's eastern shore (today Ontario). His report to Governor Guy Carleton also provided the geographical rationale for Fort Malden's subsequent location:

> Detroit is the only Military Post here, and stands on the Western Shore,
> where the River is about half a mile wide, and is distant from the entrance
> of the streights from Lake Erie about eighteen miles . . . But a post in this

quarter being essentially necessary, and circumstances not having perhaps yet rendered it expedient to take new ground . . . I think a much preferable position for combining those objects . . . is on the East main shore, near the entrance of the Streights from Lake Erie and opposite the Isle aux Bois Blanc, where there is a good situation for Naval business, and a safe & commodious Harbour; which may be well protected . . . the Ship Channel would at this place be effectually commanded; the ground here has a good elevation, and the place could not be annoyed from any part of the opposite shore, for although the ship Channel is narrow the River is wide. Should therefore a Boundary Line ever be run limiting the British to the Eastern Shore and middle of the Water Communication between the Lakes Erie and Huron, this place will be a resource of some security to our navigation.

Four years later, Mann's prophecy was realized. A "Boundary Line" was indeed "limiting the British to the Eastern Shore," and they needed a post to replace Detroit if they were to retain even partial control of Great Lakes navigation.[2]

The site had the added advantage of already being owned by British subjects; thus, the government avoided negotiating with nearby Wyandot Indians for the land. The British Army Ordinance purchased much of the site from Captain Henry Bird, who had already built two houses and cleared nearly twenty acres for a garden and orchard. Indian agents William Caldwell, Matthew Elliott, and Alexander McKee owned land south of the fort. An important function for the garrison was to staff and supply a storehouse for Indians. The storehouse, completed in 1798, stood only yards from the end of the Great Sauk Trail—a river trading network that extended to Illinois Country.[3]

Colonel Richard England, the last British commandant of Detroit, supervised the transfer of Britain's official interest to Amherstburg in July 1796. Since taking command of Detroit in 1792, England maintained a strong British presence in the region despite the ongoing diplomatic dispute between his government and the United States over portions of the Old Northwest. Without a large army garrison, he secured the native alliances necessary to slow the advance of the U.S. Army and American settlers into the Ohio River Valley and upper Great Lakes in the early 1790s. In the spring of 1794, England oversaw the construction of Fort Miami (today Maumee, Ohio). In August 1794, whatever aspirations Britain had for Ohio Country ended with the American victory at Fallen Timbers. When British soldiers locked the gates of Fort Miami to keep out their Indian allies retreating from the battle, it signified the end of Britain's dominant influence in the region.[4]

Jay's Treaty, signed in late 1794, created a timeline for Detroit to be formally turned over to the United States, but the British government considered the area much too valuable to abandon it completely. When news of the treaty arrived in North America in 1795, England received orders to begin the process of relocating all British military personnel across the Detroit River to the previously scouted area opposite Bois Blanc Island. The colonel oversaw the construction of several buildings that became the nucleus of the fort and new town of Amherstburg. England's leadership also helped to guarantee that the handover of Detroit to the Americans went smoothly. In an important but largely forgotten act, he put down an attempt by resentful British soldiers to destroy public and private property in Detroit prior to the final evacuation. On July 11, 1796, the British left Detroit, one month behind schedule but without incident. With the construction of Fort Malden ongoing, England soon left with his family for Quebec, and then returned home to Britain.[5]

Matthew Elliott, the assistant Indian superintendent at Detroit, also relocated his administrative post to Fort Malden. In the years following the American Revolutionary War, Elliott added to his vast estate along the Detroit River as he organized Ohio Indians against advancing Americans. By 1796, his holdings totaled more than four thousand acres and about fifty slaves. That year, the traveler Isaac Weld came upon Elliott's farm while sightseeing along the Detroit River. He described it as "cultivated in a style that would not be thought meanly of even in England." Much of Elliott's estate later became part of Amherstburg and Malden Township.[6]

After the handover of Detroit to the United States, Elliott became superintendent of Indian Affairs at Fort Malden. He succeeded in establishing a network to distribute goods from the Indian commissary, but in the process was accused of corrupt dealings and insubordination and was removed. Elliott and others fought to rescue his reputation. In 1808, he was reappointed superintendent of Indian Affairs due to his experience and knowledge of Indian groups amidst renewed frontier tensions with the United States.[7]

Thomas Reynolds was deputy commissary for Fort Lernoult in Detroit and then held a similar position at Fort Malden until his death in 1811. Under his guidance, all materials and supplies needed to build Fort Malden came from barges floated downriver from Detroit. Once the new fort was constructed, Reynolds had the equally difficult task of provisioning British soldiers and sailors. A hard winter during the first year at Malden damaged the region's wheat crop. Meanwhile, the local grain supply was strained by the new American garrison in Detroit. Reynolds remained in close contact with other British officials and merchants in Upper Canada to secure the necessary wheat to make flour for Britain's new settlement on the Detroit River.[8]

The partnership of Leith, Shepherd & Duff, made up of loyalists James Leith, William Shepherd, and Alexander Duff, followed the British from Detroit to Amherstburg to keep its contracts. The firm claimed Lot 17 on First Street in

Amherstburg, where it supplied the British army and Indian Department. The commercial and government spheres of the new settlement were highly integrated. Duff married Phyllis Grant, a daughter of British Commodore Alexander Grant, commander of the Royal Navy's fleet on the upper Great Lakes, and the couple bought a slave from Matthew Elliott. At the same time, Commodore Grant remained a loyal British subject without crossing the Detroit River. He commanded the British navy from his home in Grosse Pointe on American soil until his death in 1813. The Detroit River was established as an international boundary in 1796, but it remained a porous crossing for at least another generation.[9]

Early migrants to Fort Malden and Amherstburg shared a deep connection to the British government. Whether employed in the army, the Indian Department, the civil service, or in private business, their jobs and fortunes were vested in Britain's continued presence in the upper Great Lakes. British military and government officials did not sever thirty-six years of cultural ties when they relocated from Detroit in 1796, but the move filled three major needs: a new home for the British army to garrison its troops; a point for the British navy to command the waterways of the upper Great Lakes; and a site for British Indian agents and traders to access the region's Indian groups. In Fort Malden and Amherstburg, the British established an ideal home to pursue these interests.

NOTES
1 For early migration to Upper Canada (today Ontario), see Alan Taylor "The Late Loyalists: Northern Reflections of the Early American Republic," *Journal of the Early Republic* 27 (2007): 1-34; Ernest J. Lajeunesse, ed., *The Windsor Border Region, Canada's Southernmost Frontier; a Collection of Documents* (Toronto: Champlain Society, 1960); *Amherstburg 1796-1996: The New Town on the Garrison Grounds* (Amherstburg, ON: Amherstburg Bicentennial Book Committee, 1996); and Gerald Craig, *Upper Canada: The Formative Years, 1784-1841* (New York: Oxford University Press 1963). I am also indebted to John MacLeod, the cultural resources specialist at the Fort Malden National Historic Site of Canada, Amherstburg, and Jennifer MacLeod, the resource manager at the Marsh Collection Society, Amherstburg, for their assistance.

2 Gother Mann, "A general view of the situation and Importance of the several Military Posts in Upper Canada" (to Lord Dorchester, Oct 29, 1792), in *MPHC*, 24:502-9; 505 (quote). In 1788, Carleton sent Mann to survey and assess all British land and sea defenses from the St. Lawrence River to Michilimackinac. Mann recommended improvements to Fort Lernoult, Detroit, in addition to a new fort to secure the waterway between the mouth of Lake Erie and the entrance to the St. Clair River.

3 Historic Landscape Conservation Study, Fort Malden National Historic Site (Canada Public Works and Government Services, 1997), Marsh Collection Society. Today the old Indian Commissary Building and storehouse are no more than fifty yards from the Great Sauk Trail historical marker on Dalhousie Street in Amherstburg.

4 *City of Detroit*, 1:135-36, 152-54.

5 "Richard England," Dictionary of Canadian Biography Online, University of Toronto, www. biographi.ca (accessed May 5, 2009).

6 Weld quoted in "Matthew Elliott," Dictionary of Canadian Biography Online (accessed May 5, 2009). See also *Amherstburg 1796-1996*, 10-12, and Reginald Horsman, *Matthew Elliott, British Indian Agent* (Detroit: Wayne State University Press, 1964).

7 "Matthew Elliott."

8 *Amherstburg 1796-1996*, 131-32; Thomas Reynolds to John McGill, Amherstburg, May 30, 1797, in *MPHC*, 23:185-86.

9 *Amherstburg 1796-1996*, 173; "Cares of Mrs. Grant" (Alexander Grant to John Askin, Amherstburg, May 17, 1803), in *Askin Papers*, 2:388-90; Frederick Clever Bald, *Detroit's First American Decade, 1796-1805* (Ann Arbor: University of Michigan Press, 1948), 32.

Meldrum & Park: Commerce, Society, and Loyalty in Frontier Detroit

Charles Wilson Goode

The United States assumed power in Detroit on July 11, 1796. While the transfer of authority from British to American hands was peaceful, the transition from a well-known institution to one that was virtually unknown posed serious questions for the British residents of the region. What factors warranted consideration when deciding one's loyalty? How would the exchange affect the entrenched commercial relationships of the merchant class? Would the American governmental or legal systems create significant shifts in balances of power and influence? The political geography of the region changed significantly—what had been a single community was divided into two sovereign bodies.

George Meldrum and William Park, partners in the successful frontier trading firm Meldrum & Park, illustrated the personal nature of citizenship choices made by Detroiters during the early years of American rule. Jay's Treaty of 1794 stipulated that declarations of citizenship had to be made within one year of the changeover in authority. Once ratified, the treaty gave residents on the American side of the border until July 1797 to become United States citizens or continue as British subjects. Those who indicated continued allegiance to Britain could stay in the United States indefinitely, although expectations later arose in Detroit that they should cross the border to Upper Canada (today Ontario). Meldrum and Park each chose initially to remain loyal British subjects, but the business partners ultimately went separate ways: Park moved across the Detroit River to Petite Côte (today parts of Windsor and LaSalle, Ontario) in the spring of 1798; Meldrum never left the United States, and died an American citizen in 1817. Their different choices reflected larger migration patterns from the era, but mostly came down to personal preference.[1]

When the Americans arrived in July 1796, Meldrum & Park was thriving, with multiple ventures on both sides of the Detroit River. By the late eighteenth century, the fur trade in the upper Great Lakes had faded considerably. Trading firms such as Meldrum & Park survived by gradually expanding their operations to take advantage of settlement expansion and the region's other natural resources.[2] In the 1780s, the firm diversified into such ventures as a pinery (commercial forest) and lumber yard, grain mill, distillery, shipbuilding, ranching, and real estate.[3] Meldrum & Park had to consider which government would implement policies more conducive to these enterprises. The British record for supporting commercial interests had been wanting, but American financial policies were unknown.[4]

The summer of 1796 was a period of scrutiny for the new American regime in Detroit. Park offered an assessment to Meldrum just days after the Americans' arrival: "Nothing is changed in business, but the New Appearance is not very agreeable to Many who has long breathed under the British Government." The mixed reaction showed that for Park, especially, cultural factors weighed as heavily as commercial concerns. Financially, the transfer of power disrupted Meldrum & Park's business supplying British military, engineering, and Indian departments at Detroit. The firm faced a number of other challenges, including the decline of the fur trade, scarce specie, and questions over the legitimacy of existing land holdings and deals. Despite the uncertainty, the partnership completed its first major deal under the new government by selling the sloop *Detroit* to the United States Army in July 1796. Meldrum & Park also secured army contracts for timber and lumber, and for transporting supplies aboard their sloop *Saguinah*.[5]

British merchants in Detroit certainly welcomed new economic opportunities under the Americans, but several other factors played into their decisions about citizenship. Dr. Charles Brown, who arrived in Detroit with the first wave of Americans in 1796, observed that the merchants were "all Scotch & as great torys as ever you knew." Park was one of those tories who had prospered under British rule and was now skeptical of the Americans and his own future. His decision to migrate across the river in March 1798 was not borne simply from loyalty to the crown; that better describes the official British government interest that left for the new Fort Malden and Amherstburg immediately after the American takeover. The Surveyor General's Office in Upper Canada enticed prospective emigrants with an offer of twenty-four acres for those who built a "good dwelling house" for themselves or tenants. Park was one of the first to receive the land bounty.[6]

Another glaring incident may have finalized Park's decision to resettle. On July 12, 1797, one year and one day after control of Detroit passed to the Americans, Brigadier General James Wilkinson declared martial law in the town. The proclamation was ostensibly to keep local merchants from selling alcohol to U.S. soldiers, which posed a potential threat to social order. However, Wilkinson's declaration was likely timed to remind equivocating loyalists that the citizenship provision of Jay's Treaty had expired. Park and other Detroit tories knew very little about the Americans before their arrival, and looked for signs of the newcomers' true colors. Wilkinson delivered. Community leader John Askin drafted a petition, signed by Meldrum, Park, and others, claiming that the proclamation violated Jay's Treaty and that the merchants had not intended to undermine American interests.[7]

Park moved out of Detroit less than eight months after the controversy over Wilkinson's proclamation. The affair may have expedited Park's move, but no single factor caused his relocation. He fit several characteristics of the late British loyalist migrant described by contemporaries of the period and current scholars. Upper Canada offered free or nearly free tracts of land, more assurances for existing land claims, opportunity to live under British rule, and the security that came from dealing with a known governmental quantity. Moreover, in the case of Park and other elites, crossing the Detroit River often meant the chance to maintain or expand one's social and political status. Once settled in Upper Canada, Park served as a justice of the peace and as a prominent militia member. All these considerations factored into a highly personal decision to leave Detroit. Migrants are naturally viewed as people seeking change, but just as often, they move to keep other aspects of their lives constant. By migrating, Park was able to remain a prominent figure in a British settler society.[8]

Meldrum accomplished many of the same ends by staying in the United States. After Jay's Treaty, he also made clear his intention to remain a British subject. Meldrum's personal correspondence provides no exact reason why he stayed in Detroit, but his circumstances and activities demonstrate that his commitment to his family and community outweighed his tory tendencies. In 1796, Meldrum was sixty years old and had seven children. His older children lived and worked in Detroit, and his younger ones were school-aged. Meldrum's commitment to education is well documented. He helped to found and finance the town's first Protestant schools, hiring Peter Joseph Dillon and David Bacon to teach his children and other well-to-do families. Meldrum's property was mentioned as a possible site in Father Gabriel Richard's 1808 petition to the Michigan territorial legislature advocating Detroit's first public school. In addition, his property on Woodbridge Street in Detroit was used for classes by John Monteith, one of the co-founders of the University of Michigania (a precursor of the University of Michigan), during construction of the university's first building in 1817.[9]

Meldrum participated in numerous other forms of community service, including civil government, public safety, and church affairs. His signature on the 1768 petition making Justice of the Peace Philip Dejean a judge is the first record of Meldrum in Detroit. Subsequently, he served as a commissioner and coroner for the District of Hesse, was active in attempting to implement fire codes in 1791 and 1792, and served as a lieutenant to John Askin in the militia. Both Meldrum and Park made donations to Reverend George Mitchell's Anglican Church, where Meldrum served as a vestryman. His commitment to public service did not stop when the Americans arrived. He served as a jury foreman for the Court of Common Pleas in 1798, and sat on the Board of Trustees for the newly incorporated Town of Detroit in 1802. Whereas Park had left Detroit before having a chance to become a member of the new ruling elite, Meldrum became increasingly invested in the town's emerging political and social structure. Meldrum's choices suggest that his loyalty to Detroit trumped his affection for either Britain or the United States.[10]

The firm Meldrum & Park survived Park's emigration in 1798, but the political reconfiguration of the Detroit River region affected the commercial venture. In March 1799, Matthew Ernest, U.S. inspector of revenue for the port of Detroit, began enforcing tariff laws on imported spirits, wines, and teas. British merchants in Detroit balked at paying duties, claiming exemption pursuant to Jay's Treaty. Their protest was rejected by U.S. Secretary of the Treasury Albert Gallatin. These duties helped to gradually supplant the old Detroit-Montreal commercial connection with new trading networks between Detroit and Albany, Buffalo, New York City, and Pittsburgh. In May 1800, Park informed an old trading partner in Montreal that the American duties would limit his firm's imports. Amherstburg increasingly replaced Detroit as a center of trade with business outfits in the St. Lawrence River Valley.[11]

These changes might have been a geographic blessing, as the two-to-three year turnaround time for profits in the Detroit/Montreal/London/Paris trading network had always hindered Meldrum & Park's cash flow. A single shipment of alcohol from Montreal could produce a long series of correspondences concerning scheduling, damage, quantity, reshipping, and receipt. The problem was that the firm's business connections were nearly exclusively with large Montreal mercantile houses. The river between Park and Meldrum made the situation worse. After Park's move, the pair exchanged accusations about lost letters, accounting errors, and ledger discrepancies. By the early nineteenth century, the men had been working together for more than twenty years, and both were beyond the mean life expectancy for the era. Their correspondence indicated growing infirmity and impatience with the business and one another.[12]

The firm had other problems as well. Difficulties with collections plagued Meldrum & Park, and the proprietors were no strangers to the Wayne County Court of Common Pleas, appearing regularly as plaintiffs and occasionally as defendants. Litigation often ended with settlements, but sometimes the partners left the courthouse with no more than a lien or a warrant to claim their debts. In 1805, the Miamis Company, in which Meldrum & Park had a stake, was still tracking debt that was more than a decade old. In a January 1809 letter to Meldrum, Park described chasing debt as "throwing good money away."[13]

A third party, John Askin, provided some of the clearest signs that the geographic separation between Park and Meldrum was bad for business. In February 1802, Askin wrote to the partners, "Our scattered situation [is] making it impossible to hold a joint share in the *Saguinah*." The matter was settled by August, with the sale of the sloop and Meldrum and Park telling Askin, "We are equally happy as you are in bringing this Business to a Conclusion."[14] In April and June 1802, Meldrum complained to Park about the firm's ledgers, rancid grain stores, and his partner's "trifling" behavior. Park responded that September with countercharges of missing correspondence, accounting errors, and dodged queries. He threatened "extremities" if affairs were not put in order.[15] The following year, it became clear that Park desired further divestiture, ruing time spent on "Our long and intricate connections." He deplored the appearance of "quarrelling partners" and requested division of all Meldrum & Park properties.[16] In notes to Meldrum in March and April 1805, Park again pressed for a division or sale of all joint holdings. But the division never took place.[17]

The firm survived Detroit's devastating fire of June 11, 1805, yet continued to face multiple obstacles. A difficult business climate existed in early national Detroit, particularly because of a lack of specie. On top of their cash flow problems, Meldrum and Park each suffered from failing health. In November 1806, Meldrum complained to Park that he could not walk and decried, "No good paper to be gotten here." In May 1808, Park described his condition as "very weak." By January 1809, he lamented, "I cannot command a dollar on this side," and insisted that the firm had to sell what it could.[18] Park died in 1811, but even his death could not extricate Meldrum from the partnership. In March 1814, as Meldrum continued to suffer physically and financially, he complained to Askin that "Mrs. Park [is] keeping back the papers of the Co[mpany]."[19]

Despite all their difficulties, Meldrum and Park contributed greatly to the economic development of the Detroit River region. They prospered during British rule, helped to create a business infrastructure in early American Detroit, and enjoyed unusual longevity. Their respective decisions made upon the Americans' arrival were born of sincere personal convictions—Meldrum's to family and community, Park's to British society and culture. Neither man expressed regret with his decision, even though physical separation plagued their firm in its final years. The partners might have realized a better financial outcome only by agreeing to stay on the same side of the Detroit River—each close to the ledger.

NOTES

1 The stories of Meldrum and Park and their partnership have not been a distinct focus of historical scholarship. This essay attempts to synthesize references to the partners' personal and commercial experiences available in primary and secondary sources, including *City of Detroit*; Frederick Clever Bald, *Detroit's First American Decade, 1796-1805* (Ann Arbor: University of Michigan Press, 1948); George B. Catlin, *The Story of Detroit* (Detroit: The Detroit News, 1923); John Clarke, "Geographic Aspects of Land Speculation in Essex County to 1825: The Strategy of Particular Individuals," in *The Western District: Papers from the Western District Conference*, ed. K.G. Pryke and L.L. Kulisek (Windsor, ON: Essex County Historical Society, 1983); Brian Lee Dunnigan, *Frontier Metropolis: Picturing Early Detroit, 1701-1838* (Detroit: Wayne State University Press, 2001); *Askin Papers*; Alexander Fraser Papers, BHC [hereafter Fraser Papers]; Jacob Merritt Howard Papers, BHC; George Meldrum Papers, BHC; and Meldrum & Park Papers, BHC. For population figures and migration patterns from Detroit to Upper Canada, see Bald, 27; Catlin, 104; Willis F. Dunbar, *Michigan through the Centuries: Michigan in the Making and at Mid-Century*, 4 vols. (New York: Lewis Historical, 1952-55), 1:119; Nick Mika and Helma Mika, *United Empire Loyalists: Pioneers of Upper Canada* (Belleville, ON: Mika, 1976), 196; and Neil F. Morrison, "Windsor—Its Early History," in Essex County Tourist Association, *Essex County Sketches* (Windsor, ON: Herald Press, 1974), 7.

2 Ronald G. Hoskins describes a dampening of the fur trade in Ohio Country after the American Revolutionary War, citing disruptions caused by conflicts with Indians. Meldrum & Park's partnership in the Miamis Company with John Askin and several other Detroit area moguls in the late 1780s is a good example. The company's activities in the Maumee and Wabash River valleys were "abandoned after a few years as an unprofitable enterprise." Hoskins, "Angus Mackintosh: The Baron of Moy Hall," in *Western District*, 148.

3 The diverse commercial operations of Meldrum & Park are described in the letters and business records of the partners. Secondary sources emphasize the importance of mills in attracting settlers and fostering economic growth. Dunnigan includes a 1793 Charles Smythe map that labels the Rouge River mill owned by Askin, Meldrum, and Park as "Askins Mill for grinding dollars" (99). See also Essex County Tourist Association, 8, and Ontario Heritage Administration Branch, *Historical Sketches of Ontario* (1977; reprint, Toronto: Ontario Heritage Conservation Division, 1979), 23.

4 Clarke cites a 1791 District of Hesse Land Board assessment that "many people are leaving the area" and attributes the desertions to perceived governmental discouragement regarding development, including nullification of some previously purchased lands. Park was denied a claim along the Thames River. Nonetheless, the firm of Meldrum & Park owned 1,599 acres in Essex County. The scattered configuration of those holdings, as opposed to the more geographically concentrated properties of Askin, resulted from acquisition of lands as debt payments in lieu of cash. Clarke, 81-82, 96-100. Hoskins cites limitations imposed on Great Lakes shipping by the British during the Revolutionary War as a disincentive for commerce. Hoskins, 148. Edwin C. Guillet also mentions "continual complaints" against governmental dominance of shipping. Guillet, *Pioneer Travel in Upper Canada* (1933; reprint, Toronto: University of Toronto Press, 1963), 76. For government restrictions on Great Lakes shipping, see also the essay in this volume by Stephen Al-Hakim.

5 William Park to George Meldrum, Detroit, July 15, 1796, Jacob Merritt Howard Papers (quote); Bald, 73, 133, 167.

6 Brown quoted in Bald, 29. For the land bounty, see Ernest J. Lajuenesse, ed., *The Windsor Border Region, Canada's Southernmost Frontier; a Collection of Documents* (Toronto: Champlain Society, 1960), 194-95. For the migration to Fort Malden and Amherstburg, see the essay in this volume by Mark A. Mallia.

7 *City of Detroit*, 1:247-48; Clarke, 98.

8 Clarke, 71; Frederick H. Armstrong, "The Oligarchy of the Western District," in *Historical Essays on Upper Canada: New Perspectives*, ed. J.K. Johnson and Bruce G. Wilson (Ottawa: Carleton University Press, 1989), 518-19, 526; Norman Knowles, *Inventing the Loyalists: The Ontario Loyalist Tradition and the Creation of Usable Pasts* (Toronto: University of Toronto Press, 1997), 15; William McCormick, *A Sketch of the Western District of Upper Canada: Being the Southern Extremity of that Interesting Province*, ed. R. Alan Douglas (Windsor, ON: Essex County Historical Association, 1980), 39, 40; J.J. Talman, "The United Empire Loyalists," in *Profiles of a Province: Studies in the History of Ontario*, ed. Edith G. Firth (Toronto: Ontario Historical Society, 1967), 3. For the influence of political ideology on loyalist migration to Upper Canada, see Bruce W. Hodgins, "Democracy and the Ontario Fathers of Confederation," in *Profiles of a Province*, 85-86.

9 *City of Detroit*, 1:710-14, 726, 757. For David Bacon's school in Detroit, see the essay in this volume by Joshua Shelly.

10 *City of Detroit*, 1:170, 209, 218-19, 303; *Askin Papers*, 1:303, 311, 366; Eric Freedman, *Pioneering Michigan* (Franklin, MI: Altwerger and Mandel, 1992), 88; Bald, 133, 197.

11 Bald, 165, 197, 214; Clarence M. Burton, *When Detroit Was Young: Historical Studies*, ed. Milo Milton Quaife (Detroit: Burton Abstract and Title, 1951), 22; Dunbar, 126.

12 Bald describes the turnaround time for Detroit/Montreal/London profits as two years (78); Burton includes Paris in the equation and counts a three-year turnaround (*City of Detroit*, 1:497). For the potential problems with alcohol shipments, see the six letters exchanged between Meldrum & Park and James Caldwell between May 1, 1799, and February 7, 1800. For disagreements between Park and Meldrum, see their correspondence between April 20, 1805, and January 18, 1809. Both series of letters are in Folder ZM 48, Fraser Papers.

13 William Park to George Meldrum, Petite Côte, January 18, 1809, Meldrum and Park File, 1806-1825, Folder ZM 48, Fraser Papers. Records from the Court of Common Pleas for early national Detroit list many cases with Meldrum & Park, including suits involving Joseph Campau, Eleazor Moore, Paul Bellair, John Jason, Messieurs Anderson, Lee, and Pelletier, and the U.S. government. See the Court of Common Pleas File, Wayne County Northwest Territory Papers, BHC; Folder ZM 48, Fraser Papers; and *Askin Papers*, 2:114 n31.

14 "Sale of the *Saguinah*" (John Askin to George Meldrum and William Park, Detroit, February, 23, 1802; William Park and George Meldrum to John Askin, Sandwich, August 17, 1802), in *Askin Papers*, 2:370-71; 2:380.

15 George Meldrum to William Park, April 6, 1802 ("trifling"), and June 29, 1802, Meldrum and Park File, 1782-1805, Folder ZM 48, Fraser Papers; William Park to George Meldrum, September 7, 1802, Campau Family Papers, BHC.

16 William Park to George Meldrum, December 15, 1803 ("intricate connections"), and December 27, 1803 ("quarreling partners"), Meldrum and Park File, 1782-1805, Folder ZM 48, Fraser Papers.

17 William Park to George Meldrum, March 1, 1805, and April 5, 1805, Meldrum and Park File, 1782-1805, Folder ZM 48, Fraser Papers.

18 George Meldrum to William Park, Detroit, November 2, 1806, and William Park to George Meldrum, January 18, 1809, Meldrum and Park File, 1806-1825, Folder ZM 48, Fraser Papers; William Park to George Meldrum, May 2, 1808, Meldrum & Park Papers. For the Detroit fire, see John Askin to Arent De Peyster, Near Sandwich, August 30, 1805, in Askin Papers, 2:479, and Bald, 239-41.

19 "Troubles of George Meldrum" (George Meldrum to John Askin, Detroit, March 29, 1814), in *Askin Papers*, 2:778.

Silhouette of John Askin
Artist unknown (n.d.). Paper. Courtesy of the Burton Historical Collection, Detroit Public Library.

"Will Diligently and Faithfully Serve": Mr. Askin's Indentured Servants

Kimberly Steele

On nearly a daily basis in August 1794, John Askwith stopped by James Donaldson's tavern to imbibe in some liquid refreshments. Askwith regularly ordered anywhere from one to three "boles of punch" and a glass or two of brandy, on occasion asking instead for a bowl of sangria, or a pint of rum to share with a couple of soldiers who were with him. Upon placing his order, Donaldson "ladled these expensive drinks from pure silver," as may have been expected at a tavern that catered to "lucrative, gentlemanly drinking parties." What seems surprising is that Askwith was barely a month out of a three-year indenture to John Askin, one of British Detroit's most successful merchants and traders. How could an indentured servant have been rubbing elbows at such an establishment, let alone running up a bar tab that totaled nearly £14 in New York currency by mid-April 1795? Askwith also ran up a tab at Thomas Smith's establishment for more than £11 between April 1794 (four months before his indenture would be complete) and June 1795. Apparently, indentured servitude worked differently in Detroit than it had earlier in the American colonies.[1]

The concept of indentured servitude was nothing new in the 1790s. The practice of contracting labor had been around since the beginning of England's colonial enterprise. James Ballagh, one of the institution's earliest historians, wrote, "The main ideas on which servitude was based originated in the early history of Virginia as a purely English colonial development before the other colonies were formed."[2] Indentured servitude spread throughout colonial America, and it procured much needed labor. The most common stipulation of early indentures was for servants to work for a determined period of time, usually four to seven years, in exchange for their cost of living—food, clothing, shelter—and the expense of transportation across the ocean to the colonies. Yet, indentured servants under the charge of John Askin had a different experience. Detroit frontier settlers modified the institution to fit their particular needs.[3]

Born in 1739 in Aughnacloy, County Tyrone, Ireland, Askin settled in the

Great Lakes region after serving in the British army during the French and Indian War. Askin held much sway in Detroit; he had connections with many Indian groups, and did business with most settlers, whether British, French, or American. In addition, he was a justice of the peace, and lieutenant-colonel of the local militia. A merchant, fur trader, land speculator, and farmer, Askin needed labor to run his multiple enterprises in Detroit and Upper Canada (today Ontario). He held slaves and a number of indentures, both male and female. Paying for transportation from Europe was not a factor for Askin's indentured servants—John Askwith, Robert Nichol, Alexis Maisonville, and Charlotte Moses—but they did need his maintenance and support.[4]

Askin's earliest known indenture was for the services of John Askwith. Although there is no known copy of the contract between the men, a letter sent from Askwith to his mistress, Margaret Jervis, offers proof of the indenture. In November 1793, Askwith wrote to Jervis, who was in Montreal with their daughter Fanny: "I shall do every thing in my power to assist you and her, and perhaps wou'd do more than you imagine wou'd circumstances admit; but I cannot do impossibilities. I am in a state of servitude at present and cannot be at liberty untill Next July."[5]

Little is known about Askwith's life prior to his indenture other than that he was an Englishman who came to Detroit by way of Montreal. He was educated, at least enough to keep Askin's ledgers, and was later appointed notary and clerk of the district court where Askin served as justice of the peace. Even while fulfilling his indenture, Askwith was "engaged actively in extensive land speculations," according to historian Milo Quaife. Askwith was either given a salary or a line of credit while serving his indenture, unusual since most servants were given only food, clothing, and shelter.[6]

Askwith told his mistress that he was not happy in Detroit: "I wish my time was out tomorrow I wou'd immediately go on board the last Vessel that sails, as this is at present perhaps the most miserable place in all Canada."[7] Yet, he did not leave the area when his service was up in July 1795. Multiple sources place Askwith at negotiations for the Treaty of Greenville in July and August 1795. Along with other speculators, including John Askin Jr., Patrick McNiff, Israel Ruland, and Alexander Henry acting as power of attorney, Askwith set out to purchase a large tract of land from Indians in northern Ohio Country and have it validated by General Anthony Wayne. Per the "Cuyahoga Grant to Askin and Associates," the former servant would have received one tract of land outright and shared a second with McNiff, but the deal fell through at an estimated loss of one million dollars to the partners. Askwith did not live long enough to see this failure. He died on the western frontier, possibly in northern Ohio Country, in the fall of 1795. Leaving no will, his old master, John

Askin, was appointed to dispose of his estate. Along with the two tavern bills previously mentioned, Askwith left behind outstanding debt that came to a total of more than £600. His assets included two town lots and a schooner in the town of William Henry and an improved farm nearby (all in the vicinity of present-day Sorel-Tracy, Quebec), as well as a house and lot in Detroit. Indentured servitude had not kept Askwith from accumulating debt or property.[8]

Shortly after Askwith's service ended, Askin purchased the indenture of another young man to serve as his clerk. On September 18, 1795, Robert Nichol entered into a contract to "diligently and faithfully serve" for a period of three years. Nichol's indenture stated that he was to keep the "Books of accompts" and follow all "lawful and reasonable commands . . . without disclosing the same or the secrets of his employment, business, or dealings, to any person or persons, whatsoever." Should Robert comply, Askin promised "the sum of Fifty pounds, New york Curency, for each years of service, and shall and will during the said term, find and provide . . . good and sufficient diet, washing, and lodging."[9]

There were similarities between Nichol's indenture and contracts elsewhere in the colonial period, including service for a specified term while receiving support from the master. Nichol's indenture differed in its requirement that he be sworn to secrecy about his master's business and he was to receive £50 for each year of service. Nichol was born in Dumfriesshire, Scotland, around 1774, and he went to sea at an early age. It was rumored that he jumped ship in 1792 because of abuse by the ship's captain. After serving Robert Hamilton, a shipping magnate in Upper Canada, for a couple of years, Nichol signed his indenture with Askin. Like Askwith, Nichol managed the day-to-day accounts of Askin's business and notarized numerous legal documents, including several made by John Askwith. One such document witnessed by Nichol was the "Syndicate for Promotion of Cuyahoga Purchase."[10]

Upon completing his term of service with Askin, Nichol settled in Queenston, Upper Canada. He began a trade similar to that of Askin's Detroit operation, and often wrote to his former master about the state of his business. Nichol served on the British side during the War of 1812, eventually rising to the rank of lieutenant-colonel of the Second Norfolk Militia, and subsequently quartermaster general. He married a granddaughter of Commodore Alexander Grant, the British naval commander who lived on the American side of the Detroit River and one of Askin's closest friends. Nichol died in a freak accident in 1824, when his horse and carriage went over the side of a cliff near Queenston. Prior to his death, Nichol's term of servitude did not hinder his opportunities. Indeed, his connection to the Askin family spurred his eventual successes.[11]

Alexis Maisonville, a long time resident of Detroit, also began serving a three-year indenture to Askin in 1795. Though apparently much older than Nichol, he too was bound as a clerk and served as witness for numerous legal documents, including the indenture between Nichol and Askin. Maisonville was also a co-witness with Nichol on the "Syndication for Promotion of Cuyahoga Purchase" and a sale of Indian land near Lake St. Clair on April 3, 1797. On the same day, Askin mentioned that his servant wanted to sell land, possibly referring to Maisonville's holdings on Peche Island in Lake St. Clair or a lot on the riverfront in the vicinity of present-day Walkerville, Ontario.[12]

Like Askwith and Nichol, Maisonville's land dealings in the region only increased after completing his indenture. He maintained a business relationship with Nichol, and Askin continued to help Maisonville. In September 1800, Askin mentioned that "my Recommendation got Mr. Maisonville 3000 Acres of Land that had been refused him in every Quarter in lower and upper Canada." By 1805, Maisonville was not faring well. Askin wrote to Colonel Arent De Peyster that the "poor fellow [Maisonville] is something reduced in Circumstances. though [he] still has his Farm yet [he] is much cast down. he who never has had Education cant support Misfortunes."[13]

In December 1807, Maisonville served as captain in the Northern Regiment of Essex Militia, and wrote to Askin, the colonel in command of the regiment, to request that he and his troops not be punished for arriving late for muster. Maisonville explained that his men had been delayed due to weather and it was his "hope that from our having done our utmost to arrive in time, You will not put us on a footing with deliquents, and exempt us from the Fine." Thereafter, Maisonville disappeared from the historical record until his death and burial in Sandwich (today Windsor, Ontario) in September 1814.[14]

Detroit's 1782 census included four young or hired men next to Askin's name. It is likely that James McClintock, who clerked for Askin during the disposal of Askwith's property, was an indentured servant.[15] The only other known indenture between John Askin and a servant was dated July 25, 1808, for a term of three years. This indenture, however, was with a young mulatto or Panis Indian from Detroit named Charlotte Moses, who served Askin after his move across the river to Sandwich in 1802. According to her contract, Moses was to "bind herself . . . as his Covenant servant . . . [and] shall behav herself as a good and faithfull servant ought and is obliged to do." In return, Askin would provide her "with good and sufficient diet and cloathing during the continuance of her Servitude." Moses was only able to sign her contract with an X, indicating a lack of education, unlike the men Askin had earlier contracted with. Most likely a house servant, she left no other records.[16]

Although each of the indentures held by John Askin resembled earlier versions of servitude established in Virginia and elsewhere in colonial America, there were also marked differences. The goal of indentured servitude in the colonial era was to secure the most labor for the cheapest cost; the main expense was transporting laborers. Askin's servants had already arrived by their own means, or were born in North America, as in the case of Charlotte Moses, and served for relatively short periods by colonial standards. Moreover, most servants were not able to pursue their own business opportunities such as buying and selling land while still under indenture, as John Askwith and Alexis Maisonville had. By the late eighteenth and early nineteenth centuries, indentured servitude had all but disappeared in the eastern states. The experience of early Detroit showed that a modified version, suited to the particular labor needs of masters such as Askin, was alive and well on the frontier.[17]

NOTES
1 "Tavern Bill of John Askwith," in Askin Papers, 1:598-603; Frederick Clever Bald, Detroit's First American Decade, 1796-1805 (Ann Arbor: University of Michigan Press, 1948), 96. For Donaldson's tavern, see Julia Roberts, In Mixed Company: Taverns and Public Life in Upper Canada (Vancouver: University of British Columbia Press, 2009), 11-12. For an explanation of New York currency, see Askin Papers, 1:74 n18.

2 James Curtis Ballagh, White Servitude in the Colony of Virginia: A Study of the System of Indentured Labor in the American Colonies (Baltimore: Johns Hopkins Press, 1895), 9.

3 For the development of indentured servitude in colonial America, see Abbot Emerson Smith, Colonists in Bondage: White Servitude and Convict Labor in America, 1607-1776 (New York: Norton, 1947), and Aaron S. Fogelman, "From Slaves, Convicts, and Servants to Free Passengers: The Transformation of Immigration in the Era of the American Revolution," Journal of American History 85 (1998): 43-76. For comparative studies of slavery and indentured servitude, see Marcus Wilson Jernegan, Laboring and Dependent Classes in Colonial America, 1607-1783 (Chicago: University of Chicago Press, 1931); David W. Galenson, White Servitude in Colonial America: An Economic Analysis (Cambridge: Cambridge University Press, 1981); Daniel Meaders, Eighteenth-Century White Slaves: Fugitive Notices, Volume 1, Pennsylvania, 1729-1760 (New York: Garland, 1993); and Don Jordan and Michael Walsh, White Cargo: The Forgotten History of Britain's White Slaves in America (New York: New York University Press, 2007). For servitude in individual colonies, see Jerry M. Hynson, Cecil County Maryland Indentures, 1777-1814 (Westminster, MD: Heritage Books, 2007); Eugene Irving McCormack, White Servitude in Maryland, 1634-1820 (Baltimore: Johns Hopkins Press, 1904); Sharon V. Salinger, "To serve well and faithfully": Labour and Indentured Servants in Pennsylvania, 1682-1800 (New York: Cambridge University Press, 1987); Lawrence William Towner, A Good Master Well Served: Masters and Servants in Colonial Massachusetts, 1620-1750 (New York: Garland, 1998); and Karin L. Zipf, Labor of Innocents: Forced Apprenticeship in North Carolina, 1715-1919 (Baton Rouge: Louisiana State University Press, 2005).

4 For Askin's biography, see Askin Papers, 1:4-17. For Askin's role in early Detroit, see Nelson Vance Russell, The British Régime in Michigan and the Old Northwest, 1760-1796 (1939; reprint, Philadelphia: Porcupine Press, 1978), 128-33; Arthur M. Woodford, This is Detroit, 1701-2001 (Detroit: Wayne State University Press, 2001), 36, 38; and Bald, 73-78, 152-59, 220-25.

5 "Estate of John Askwith" (Margaret Jervis to John Askin, Montreal, November 1795; John Askwith to Margaret Jervis, Detroit, November 7, 1793), in *Askin Papers*, 1:592-93.

6 For Askwith's biography and examples of his land deals, see *Askin Papers*, 1:448-49 (quote), 556-60, 580-83.

7 "Estate of John Askwith," 592.

8 For Askwith's debts and business dealings, see *Askin Papers*, 1:597-615; 2:14-16, and Milo Milton Quaife, ed., *Burton Historical Collection Leaflets*, 10 vols. (Detroit: Detroit Public Library), 8:49-64. At the time of his death, Askwith's debts totaled more than £600; the auction of his belongings and a house and lot in Detroit brought in less than £400, leaving a deficit of at least £200. For land speculators and the Treaty of Greenville, see the essays in this volume by Susan Ward and Douglas D. Fisher.

9 "Indenture of Robert Nichol to John Askin," in *Askin Papers*, 1:567-68.

10 "Syndicate for Promotion of Cuyahoga Purchase," in *Askin Papers*, 1:545-48. For Nichol's life, see *Askin Papers*, 1:324, 461; 2:75.

11 For Nichol's career and relationship with Askin after completing his indenture, see *Askin Papers*, 2:187, 214, 227-28, 324, 354, 385-87, 403, 429-31, 434-38, and 507-8. See John Van der Zee, *Bound Over: Indentured Servitude and American Conscience* (New York: Simon and Schuster, 1985), for examples of successful outcomes by indentured servants.

12 "Indenture of Robert Nichol to John Askin," 567-68; "Syndicate for Promotion of Cuyahoga Purchase," 1:545-48; "Grants of Land in Sandwich," and "Grant of Land Near Lake St. Clair," in *Askin Papers*, 2:100-102; 2:102-4. For additional references to Maisonville, see *Askin Papers*, 1:325, 548, 568; 2:7, 40, 48-49, 122-24, 193, 207, 237, 314, 337, 350, 479, 586.

13 "Difficulties Affecting Land Titles" (John Askin to Isaac Todd Esquire, September 18, 1800), and "From John Askin to Colonel De Peyster" (August 30, 1805), in *Askin Papers*, 2:314; 2:479.

14 "Absence from Militia Muster" (Alexis Maisonville to John Askin, December 14, 1807), in *Askin Papers*, 2:586.

15 Donna Valley Russell, ed., *Michigan Censuses 1710-1830 under the French, British, and Americans* (Detroit: Detroit Society for Genealogical Research, 1982), 50. For James McClintock, see *Askin Papers*, 1:607; 2:341.

16 "Indenture of Charlotte Moses," in *Askin Papers*, 2:607-8. For the difference between Indian slaves (Panis) and servants in Detroit, see Bald, 40, 96 n9, and Gregory Evans Dowd, *War under Heaven: Pontiac, the Indian Nations, and the British Empire* (Baltimore: Johns Hopkins University Press, 2002), 65. Whether Moses was of Indian or mixed African and European descent, she could not have been a slave by Upper Canada law unless she was already enslaved on May 31, 1793, or born to a slave woman after that date, in which case she could not have been held for longer than twenty-five years.

17 See Fogelman for the decline of indentured servitude in the eastern United States after the American Revolution.

A Dollar Lost, a Life Taken: The Impact of Great Lakes Shipwrecks on Detroit

Jaclyn Kinney

From its founding, Detroit was a maritime town. The remote settlement straddling the Detroit River, with island chains and easy access to the upper Great Lakes, depended on ships for its military and economic viability. British reaction to the American Revolutionary War increased the importance of ships for the movement of supplies, military and other government personnel. In this environment, shipwrecks not only had tragic personal costs but extensive social, political, and economic ramifications. The expansion of shipping on the Great Lakes during and after the war led to an unprecedented number of lost and damaged vessels. The consequences of a single shipwreck were felt by posts throughout the region. The wreck of HMS *Speedy* in 1804 was particularly catastrophic: It demonstrated the interrelated dimensions of Great Lakes shipwrecks during the period.[1]

The total fleet on the Great Lakes at the beginning of the revolutionary era was small. Of the approximately two dozen publicly and privately owned hulls, roughly half were on Lake Ontario and half on Lake Erie and the three northern lakes. With the onset of the war, the Provincial Marine department of the British navy forbade ships to sail under private ownership, taking those vessels into the service and manning them with navy crews. During the period between 1763 and 1783, seven of the estimated twenty-four vessels were wrecked—almost 30 percent. For such a small fleet, the high percentage of wrecks was startling.[2]

A number of factors contributed to wrecks and delays in the region, including extreme weather, hasty ship construction, and a lack of navigational experience. Of these, fickle and cold weather on the Great Lakes had the most influence. Winds and sea conditions changed quickly, with unforgiving shores never far away. The shipping season on the lakes was also short and unreliable; crafts were commonly locked in ice from November to April. For example, on December 5, 1796, the schooner *Nancy* was locked in ice near the mouth of the Detroit River. The schooner became trapped while sailing from Fort Erie (today in Ontario) to Detroit. Of the four men aboard the *Nancy* who attempted to walk the ice back to the British side, two froze to death.[3]

Weather dictated entire shipping schedules. When winds were unfavorable, ships stayed in port. John Askin, a prominent Detroit merchant, often speculated about the timing of his shipments based on the weather. For instance, in May 1778 he waited several days at Michilimackinac for favorable winds to bring a ship into port. Shipping delays due to ice and wind had an economic ripple effect in a region stretching south to Detroit and east to Montreal, causing both merchants and their customers to wait in uncertainty before completing business transactions.[4]

Poorly constructed ships were another frequent cause of shipwrecks. Rushed construction of Great Lakes hulls resulted in vessels made from unseasoned, soft timber such as pine or spruce rather than oak. Many vessels were also designed with drafts too deep for the shallow waters of lakes and rivers. In April 1765, General Thomas Gage, commander of British forces in North America, wrote to Captain Joshua Loring, commander of the British fleet on the Great Lakes, to inform him that a vessel was stuck in Lake Huron due to its deep draft. Gage suggested that the ship would have had less trouble with a flatter bottom; later ship designs proved him right.[5]

A related challenge was limited navigational knowledge of the Great Lakes. Pilots made their own crude charts, and relied on experience and instinct. The waters were filled with unknown hazards, and the problem was exacerbated during the British period by the influx of newcomers to the region. In Detroit, ship captains struggled in particular with changing water depths and proper places to winter ships. In September 1764, Loring explained to Gage his difficulty finding a safe location to anchor his ships: "I likewise search every place at and near Detroit in order to find a proper place for securing the vessels." A wharf to protect vessels from ice had yet to be constructed at the town. In an industry as vital as shipping, navigational trial and error proved costly and dangerous.[6]

A shipwreck had the potential to impact the supply of materials and foodstuffs for the entire region. As a frontier outpost, Detroit relied on maritime transit for necessary goods, and often faced a scarcity of supplies. Askin's merchant logs and correspondence reveal a constant need for corn, flour, and rum in Detroit. Corn and flour were staples for people and livestock, and rum was essential for trade with Indians and others. The limited number of vessels on the Great Lakes meant that ships traveling west were often crammed with supplies that Detroit residents needed. For example, logs of the British naval vessel *Gage* from 1783 recorded that prisoners, private passengers, military personnel, foodstuffs, and other cargo all shared space on voyages. In December that year, British army officers salvaged as much as possible from the ships *Faith*, *Hope*, and *Angelica*, all recently wrecked on Lake Erie. In wartime, the wreck or delay of such vessels had the potential to leave Detroit undermanned, undersupplied, and vulnerable to attack.[7]

Ship captains and merchants also endured economic hardships due to wrecks. In 1798, Askin had a particularly ruinous year; he lost two of his three ships, the *Weazell* and *Annette*, and the third, the *Saguinah*, underwent repairs for the first half of the season. The *Weazell* wrecked in Lake Huron near the coast while sailing for Saginaw Bay. The damages included a total loss of both rigging and cargo. The sloop *Annette* was lost during a storm on Lake Erie. The sloop's commander, Captain Timothy Grummond, was rumored to have been intoxicated when the ship was lost. After the wreck, he was said to have sold what he could salvage for profit. Askin bore the full loss for the cargo and the ship carrying it. Late in the year, Askin despaired that he had "no Spare money nor likely I ever will, as *madame bad luck* took a passage in all my small vessells this fall."[8]

The greatest costs of shipwrecks were human lives. The case of the *Harlequin* on Lake Erie in the late summer of 1801 was representative of the toll that wrecks took on victims, their loved ones, and communities. In August, residents of Detroit worried about the fate of the *Harlequin* when it did not arrive from Presque Isle (today Erie, Pennsylvania) as scheduled, with its small cargo of government goods for the American army quartermaster. Fears increased in September when another ship sailing from Presque Isle, the sloop *Good Intent*, had no information about the missing ship. In October, wreckage from the *Harlequin* washed ashore near Fort Erie. Three crew members and three passengers perished.[9]

The tragedy most affected Detroit merchant and political leader James May. May's brother, Captain Joseph May, died while commanding the ship. James May also lost a slave. Of the accident, he wrote, "The stroke is a very severe one for me, the effects of which I shall feel for a long time; perhaps the rest of my days."[10] May was not the only person affected by the wreck. He described his female slave as "delirious" and "very Ill" from grief after losing her husband. In total numbers, the wreck of the *Harlequin* was small, taking only six lives. Yet, the incident deeply affected a broad cross-section of Detroit's community.[11]

The wreck of HMS *Speedy* was the most catastrophic loss on the Great Lakes during the revolutionary or early national eras. The *Speedy* wrecked in a storm on October 7, 1804, on Lake Ontario, and took nineteen lives. The British naval vessel sailed from York (today Toronto) to Newcastle (today Clarington, Ontario), and carried an Ojibwa Indian on trial for the murder of a white man. Among the passengers were prominent governmental officials of Upper Canada (today Ontario), including a judge, a member of the general assembly, and the solicitor general. The *Upper Canadian Gazette* reported that nine women became widows from the wreck.[12]

The *Speedy* tragedy demonstrated that a major shipwreck on the Great Lakes was a region-wide event with consequences far beyond the ports directly involved. The accident did not claim the lives of any Detroit residents, but its impact was felt on both sides of the Detroit River. News of the wreck reached the area quickly. In November 1804, John Askin, then in Sandwich (today Windsor, Ontario), received a detailed account from a correspondent in Queenston: "[The incident] has filled us with much Greif, & has sent Mourning into every district of the Province." With so many public officials lost, government business was canceled in York during the winter of 1804-1805. Few people in the Great Lakes region at the time would not have known about the *Speedy*.[13]

Detroit's early inhabitants relied on ships for transportation, commerce, and survival. Shipwrecks were a cruel fact of life on the Great Lakes. They became more common during the revolutionary era due to increased ship traffic connected to the Revolutionary War. However frequent, shipwrecks never lost the power to devastate individual lives and shock whole communities. In one year, John Askin's personal wealth was jeopardized by damage to the *Saguinah* and losses of the *Weazell* and *Annette*. James May and his slave were left grief-stricken after the wreck of the *Harlequin*. The entire Great Lakes region was shaken when the *Speedy* went down with a group of prominent officials of Upper Canada. These and other shipwrecks were singular events, but their consequences ran deep for the people of Detroit and the Great Lakes region.

NOTES

1 Although it concentrates on the nineteenth and twentieth centuries, the best overview of shipwrecks in the Great Lakes is Mark L. Thompson, *Graveyard of the Lakes* (Detroit: Wayne State University Press, 2000). Maritime histories that incorporate the eighteenth century focus mostly on naval ships and include little on merchant vessels and shipwrecks. See Robert Malcomson, *Warships of the Great Lakes, 1754-1834* (Annapolis: Naval Institute Press, 2001); Don Bamford, *Freshwater Heritage: A History of Sail on the Great Lakes, 1670-1918* (Toronto: Natural Heritage Books, 2007); and Brian Leigh Dunnigan, "British Naval Vessels on the Upper Great Lakes, 1761-1796," *Telescope* 31 (1982): 92-98.

2 Malcomson, 25-26; David Swayze, "The Great Lakes Shipwreck File: Total Losses of Great Lakes Ships, 1679-2001," http://greatlakeshistory.homestead.com/temp.html (accessed February 25, 2009).

3 Frederick Clever Bald, *Detroit's First American Decade, 1796-1805* (Ann Arbor: University of Michigan Press, 1948), 95, 124.

4 John Askin to Jean Baptiste Barthe, Michilimackinac, May 24 and May 29, 1778, in *Askin Papers*, 1:98-100; 1:102-3.

5 Brendan O'Brien, *Speedy Injustice: The Tragic Last Voyage of His Majesty's Vessel Speedy* (Toronto: University of Toronto Press, 2000), 72; Thomas Gage to Joshua Loring, April 22, 1765, Thomas Gage Papers, American Series, vol. 34, CL.

6 Joshua Loring to Thomas Gage, September 2, 1764, Thomas Gage Papers, American Series, vol. 24.

7 *Askin Papers*, 1:86 n40, 95-108; "Remarks on Board the *Gage*," May 23 and June 15, 1783, Alexander Harrow Papers, BHC.

8 Bald, 134-35, 152-53; "Attitude of Judge Powell Concerning Land Titles" (John Askin to D. William Smith, Detroit, December 4, 1798), in *Askin Papers*, 2:162 (quote).

9 "Wreck of the *Harlequin*" (James May to John Askin, Detroit, September 21, 1801; John Warren to John Askin, Fort Erie, October 20, 1801), in *Askin Papers*, 2:358-60.

10 "Wreck of the *Harlequin*," 2:358.

11 "Wreck of the *Harlequin*," 2:358 (quote); Bald, 187.

12 O'Brien, 3-28.

13 "Wreck of the *Speedy*" (Robert Hamilton to John Askin, Queenston, November 8, 1804), in *Askin Papers,* 2:441-43; 2:441 (quote).

Loyalty for Sale: British Detroiters and the New American Regime

Douglas D. Fisher

In June 1795, John Askin Jr. mounted his horse and took off on an urgent mission from his father in Detroit to southern Ohio Country. In the months since the Battle of Fallen Timbers, the Askin family used its influence with Indians of the Great Lakes region—John's mother was most likely an Ottawa—to acquire millions of acres of land along Lake Erie. The Askins knew that the British government was no longer capable of sustaining its posts in what Jay's Treaty had determined to be American territory, and they wanted United States General Anthony Wayne to certify their land holdings under the new regime. Millions of acres meant millions of dollars in profit, selling land to the expected American migrants or other land speculators.

When George McDougall, a rival Detroit merchant of British heritage, got word of the Askins' plan, he figured it was a splendid opportunity to ingratiate himself with the Americans. He decided to tell General Wayne that the younger Askin had fought against Wayne at Fallen Timbers. McDougall expected to be rewarded for that intelligence with U.S. supply contracts. When John Askin Sr. got word of McDougall's treachery, he sent a letter of warning to his son about "double Friends" betraying him to the Americans. McDougall, whose father withstood Pontiac's siege of Detroit in 1763 and rose to captain of the 84th Regiment of British regulars stationed at Detroit during the American Revolution, won the race to Greenville in Ohio Country. This British loyalist turned American spy told Wayne that Askin was his enemy. The general had young Askin shackled, and his mission failed.[1]

Swearing allegiance to one flag or the other was the most important political issue in Detroit from 1795 to 1802. McDougall, whom a British loyalist Catholic priest once called an "infamous traitor," was not the only turncoat in Detroit.[2] John Askin Sr. lamented those "Poor, Weak, Worthless People" who had so easily shifted their allegiance from the British crown in the mid-to-late 1790s.[3] What made several British residents of the Detroit area seek out the Americans? Some, like John Anderson and much of the French element of town, simply had no desire to move. Detroit was their home, and if they had to accept the American regime to maintain the lives they had built, so be it. After all, many had switched allegiances from France to Britain after 1760. The overriding factor for many of the British residents was greed. McDougall seized the opportunity to hurt the Askins' rival mercantile business and fur-trading outfit. A new government also meant new leadership. Some British Detroiters, like James May, were swayed, in part, by the prospect of political advancement. For still others, new immigrants meant new customers for everything from land to liquor. For these British Detroiters, loyalty was exchanged for financial opportunity.

No historian has fully analyzed the reasons these British subjects stayed in Detroit, and why they so easily transferred their allegiance to the Americans. Milo Quaife's footnotes in both volumes of the *John Askin Papers* detail their biographies, largely compiled from Reverend Father Christian Denissen's genealogies in the Burton Historical Collection of the Detroit Public Library. Neither man, however, explained the reasons for their seemingly treasonous activities. Similarly, Frederick Bald's exceptional work, *Detroit's First American Decade, 1796-1805*, tells the story of the men who stayed, as well as those who left, but he never theorized as to what made them switch sides.[4]

Only one historian has briefly mentioned his theory about why British subjects stayed in Detroit, and it is illogical. Clarence Burton's "Works: Notes from the Sibley Papers" place too much emphasis on the awakening of republican ideals in the former British subjects. Burton surmises: "As soon as the Americans took possession there were a number of the old residents who conceived that a great change had come over their civil rights and they were destined to run the new country."[5] His assertion that freedom was repressed on the Detroit frontier is flawed. Community leaders like McDougall, May, Anderson, William Macomb, James Abbott, and Patrick McNiff, among others, never complained of an oppressive British regime because they were among the residents in charge of it. They experienced no change in their civil rights at all. Most residents of Detroit, which remained 80 percent French, felt elections and a representative form of government were not needed. British men ruled, for the most part, and the French were fine with that as long as they were treated with respect.

Other revolutionary issues, such as new taxes or British military domination, fail to explain the Detroit turncoats' decisions either. The minimal taxes that were collected stayed in the local community to care for the indigent. Residents knew almost nothing of strict martial law until the Americans took over. British troops, in addition to lining the pockets of local businesses like John Dodemead's tavern, safeguarded the community from Indian attack and kept commercial trade on the Great Lakes viable. If anything, residents desired a stronger military presence because, in addition to security, more troops meant more potential for profit.

In the mid-1790s, the Great Lakes fur trade was drying up. Voyageurs had to delve deeper and deeper into the country's midsection to take fewer and smaller hides. At the same time that the quality of the pelts returned to Detroit diminished, expenses rose and the debt load to middlemen at Detroit, Montreal, and London climbed. Some of these British Detroiters hoped to capitalize on the new American regime to sustain them. Still, the loyal faction in town proved a strong influence. The British crown attempted to woo citizens with promises of free land across the Detroit River.

John Anderson, previously an avowed loyalist, reported that British agents "solicited me verey hard," but he was content on the farm he had built. Born in Scotland, Anderson moved to the New York frontier at about age seven, and his father was killed by Mohawk Indians. His mother and his three siblings were taken prisoner, but the family was rescued in Montreal by British agents. In the 1780s, James McGill, the richest man in British North America, sent him to work for Askin Sr. in the fur trade, but even Askin failed to convince him to move into British territory after Jay's Treaty. Some British subjects (Anderson's autobiography does not identify them) told him he would "be sorey for it, and a number of them bore me the gratest ill will so as not to speake." Anderson took a job paying him $1 a day as a United States Indian agent and interpreter. In 1812, after the Americans surrendered Detroit, British troops and Indians destroyed his farm at the River Raisin. Anderson reported that they taunted him, saying "what do you think of your Yankes now."[6]

British troops, Indians, and fur traders were not the only people frustrated by the turncoats. Staunch loyalist Reverend Father Edmund Burke, an Irish-born Catholic missionary to the Detroit River region and vicar-general of Upper Canada (today Ontario), wrote extensively about the problem in the mid-1790s. Burke, who later was named the first vicar apostolic of Nova Scotia and then bishop of Zion, called William Macomb "an absolute pest." Macomb, a member of the assembly of Upper Canada and perhaps the wealthiest man in the Detroit area, became "a most troublesome fellow," "a staunch friend to Congress," and "one of the most dangerous subjects in the Province," in Burke's estimation.[7]

The missionary lamented that money and power were more important to some residents than loyalty to their country. Nonetheless, many families of the Detroit River region accepted that concept. In 1795, some British civil officers and even close personal friends of Colonel Richard England, the British commandant at Fort Detroit, abandoned their allegiance in an effort to add to their wealth. They hoped to get their recent land purchases from the Indians confirmed by General Wayne, or to win military contracts from the new administration.

James May was among the latter. An Englishman, he immigrated to British North America early in the Revolutionary War and moved to Detroit in 1778, where he married well. His first wife was a member of the St. Cosme family, which owned large tracts of land near the Ecorse River that, upon marriage, he obtained. He further capitalized financially as the British prepared to leave Detroit. In June 1796, he leased his ship, the *Swan*, to the United States military, which transported troops and supplies to the fort. May's acceptance of the Americans led them into his mercantile store immediately upon their arrival. A year later, he was appointed an American justice of the peace, and, in 1800, became chief justice of the Court of Common Pleas.

These types of political appointments were typical for the British subjects who changed their allegiance. Many of them had held the exact same office under the British government. In addition to May, Robert Navarre, James Abbott, Louis Beaufait, Joseph Voyer, Francois Navarre, and Nathan Williams became justices of the peace. Of these, Beaufait, Williams, and May had held the same post under British rule, and Robert Navarre had been the notary public. On the Court of Common Pleas, Beaufait, Williams, McNiff, and Charles Girardin were appointed judges alongside May in 1800, and each of them had held the same title before the Americans arrived. George McDougall became sheriff of Wayne County, and McNiff was appointed its surveyor, the same jobs they had held under the British flag. McNiff, a "worthless fellow" according to Colonel England, also earned $40 per month as the Americans' military barrack master and commissary of its supplies. McNiff's transfer of allegiance had paid him well.[8]

Similarly, Jonathan Schieffelin was a devout British resident. In service of the crown during the American Revolution, Lieutenant Schieffelin went on Captain Henry Bird's invasion of Kentucky in 1780. He was among a group of British subjects that tried to secure twenty million acres of land—almost the entire lower peninsula of Michigan—from the Indians in 1796. As late as June 21, 1797, nearly a year after the Americans took over in Detroit, Schieffelin signed a declaration of intention to remain a British subject. Then on August 1, 1797, he accepted a military post from the United States as an Indian interpreter, and became an American citizen. His transfer of allegiance had paid him well, too.

Despite the efforts of British loyalists, including a threat of imprisonment from Colonel England, greed was the primary factor for these former British subjects. Land speculation, which "seems to be the rage at present," a loyalist reported in 1795, allowed some smaller Detroit merchants an opportunity for wealth that was too enticing to pass up.[9] Their shift in loyalty toward the American side had nothing to do with civil rights; their allegiance was for sale. Burke, who spread the Catholic faith among Indians and the French in the Detroit River region from 1794 to 1796, recognized it immediately. The newly converted Americans' "own private interest and profit," he wrote, outweighed their allegiance to the British crown. "They are disaffected, all land-jobbers and rum-venders," Burke said.[10]

In July 1797, about a dozen former British subjects sent a letter to the United States Congress declaring their "attachment to the Government of the United States and most Sincere wishes for the Safety of this Country and its Inhabitants."[11] Men like May, Abbott, Dodemead, and McNiff may have expected that it would bring them additional land, military contracts, or government appointments. These men, who had a great deal of property transferred from the Indians on the line, "showed an unmistakable desire to appease the Americans," as Bald put it.[12] The letter-writers described British loyalists, their former allies still living in Detroit, as a "Menace." The new Americans feared that the Wayne County militia would be overrun by "internal and increasing factions" loyal to the crown, and wanted the U.S. government to protect them from British interlopers and their Indian allies.[13]

Almost fifteen years later, John Askin Sr. was still troubled by the actions and the words of those British traitors. He wrote that he "could not comprehend how a man of honour & honesty can ever change his allegiance."[14] Yet that kind of devotion to the crown was fleeting to some of the lesser traders at Detroit, those that Father Burke had labeled "peddling merchants."[15] These men were simply doing what they thought best for their families to get ahead on the far reaches of the North American frontier. Their motivation was not, as Burton proposed, some wave of republicanism that had washed over them. The Detroiters who took charge of the American government from 1796 to 1802 were, for the most part, the same men running the British government of Detroit in 1795. Their primary motivation was profit, and in this they succeeded.

NOTES

1 "Mission of John Askin Jr. to Greenville" (John Askin Sr. to John Askin Jr., Detroit, July 5, 1795), in *Askin Papers*, 1:551. John Askin Sr. makes no mention of whom the "double Friends" are. That portion of the story is detailed in Frederick Clever Bald, *Detroit's First American Decade, 1796-1805* (Ann Arbor: University of Michigan Press, 1948), 13. For the influence of John Askin Jr.'s métis identity, see the essay in this volume by Nicole Satrun.

2 Edmund Burke to E.B. Littlehales, August 14, 1795, in *The Correspondence of Lieut. Governor John Graves Simcoe*, ed. E.A. Cruikshank, 5 vols. (Toronto: Ontario Historical Society, 1923-31), 4:62.

3 "Mission of John Askin Jr. to Greenville," 1:551.

4 Denissen's genealogies were published after his death. See Christian Denissen, *Genealogy of the French Families of the Detroit River Region 1701-1936*, ed. Harold F. Powell, 2 vols. (1976; reprint, Detroit: Detroit Society for Genealogical Research, 1987).

5 Clarence M. Burton, "Works: Notes from the Sibley Papers, 1798-1808," 53, Clarence M. Burton Works, BHC.

6 John Anderson wrote his life story shortly after the War of 1812. See John Anderson, *A Short History of the Life of John Anderson*, transcribed by Richard C. Knopf (Ann Arbor: University of Michigan Archives, 1956), 9-10.

7 Father Burke wrote at least a pair of letters from the River Raisin detailing the activities of Macomb in regard to the Indians and the Americans on June 17, 1795. Burke considered Macomb a traitor. See Edmund Burke to E.B. Littlehales, and Burke to Alexander McKee in Cruikshank, ed., 4:27-28. Burke was born in Ireland and educated for the priesthood in Paris. He joined the Diocese of Quebec in 1786, and was posted to the seminary where he taught mathematics and philosophy. He grew tired of teaching, however, and longed for missionary work in the Great Lakes region, "as the sacrament of confirmation was never administered to those poor Catholics . . . an hitherto abandoned people." Michael Power, "Father Edmund Burke: Along the Detroit River Frontier, 1794-1797," *Canadian Catholic Historical Association Historical Studies* 51 (1984): 29-46, 32 (quote). For Burke, see also Rev. Brother Alfred, "The Right Reverend Edmund Burke, D.D., 'Apostle of Upper Canada', Bishop of Zion, First Vicar Apostolic of Nova Scotia, 1753-1820," *Canadian Catholic Historical Association Report* 8 (1940-41): 35-76. For Burke's work at the River Raisin settlement (today Monroe, Michigan), see Ghislaine Pieters Bartolo and Lynn Waybright Reaume, eds., *The Cross Leads Generations On: A Bicentennial Retrospect, St. Mary of the Immaculate Conception Formerly Known as St. Antoine at the River Raisin, Monroe, Michigan, 1788-1988* (Tappan, NY: Custombook, 1988).

8 The political appointments from Winthrop Sargent, acting governor of the Northwest Territory, are listed in several scattered sources. For a compilation, see Bald, 55-57. The "worthless fellow" remark stems from R.G. England to J.G. Simcoe, August 20, 1795, in Cruikshank, ed., 4:72.

9 R.G. England to J.G. Simcoe, July 14, 1795, in Cruikshank, ed., 4:44.

10 Edmund Burke to E.B. Littlehales, August 14, 1795, in Cruikshank, ed., 4:62. As newly appointed vicar-general of Upper Canada, Burke received financial backing from the British government for his Catholic missionary work in the Detroit area. John Graves Simcoe, lieutenant-governor of Upper Canada, hoped Burke would strengthen British loyalty among the wavering French and Indian Catholics, who were also being recruited by the Americans. Burke initially saw the mission differently: "Government here is more zealous in the support and extension of the Catholic religion than in any other country on earth; in sound policy they act judiciously; but 'tis yet astonishing that a Protestant Government should pay the expenses of sending Catholic Missionaries, and supporting them, not only amongst the Indian Nations, but even amongst the civilized people; yet 'tis not more surprising than true." Power, 35-36. Due to the relationship between Simcoe and Burke, Detroit area inhabitants perceived Burke as an emissary of the British crown, and his influence was limited. A thorn in the side of U.S. General Anthony Wayne, Burke left Detroit on July 4, 1796, seven days before the British ceded the territory to the Americans. Power, 42.

11 "Machinations Against United States Government," July 12, 1797, in *Askin Papers*, 2:112-14.

12 Bald, 10.

13 "Machinations Against United States Government," 2:112.

14 This famous quote from John Askin Sr. is used in many secondary sources to describe the attitudes of residents of the Detroit River region during the War of 1812. However, it also aptly illustrates his deep-seated mistrust of his former neighbors, those supposedly British patriots who turned against their country fifteen years earlier. See "War Clouds in Detroit" (John Askin Sr. to Charles Askin, April 28, 1812), in *Askin Papers*, 2:707.

15 Edmund Burke to E.B. Littlehales, May 27, 1795, in Cruikshank, ed., 4:22.

David Bacon: Detroit Meets America
Joshua Shelly

In 1798, bound together by a common goal of Christianizing the "Heathen in North America," the congregational peoples of Connecticut formed a missionary society to turn the promise of America as a "city upon a hill" into reality. Two years later, their inaugural mission took shape with an advertisement in the society's first magazine for "a discreet man, animated by the love of God and souls . . . to travel among the Indian Tribes South and West of Lake Erie." The trustees of the society chose David Bacon, a twenty-nine-year-old school teacher without any formal religious training, and announced his departure among a list of others called to bring the gospel to the hinterlands of North America—Vermont, the Ohio River Valley, and the Northwest Territory.[1]

Bacon's interactions with the peoples of Detroit represented a meeting between eastern America and its northwestern frontier. The expectations of the Connecticut Missionary Society (CMS) expressed larger hopes for what the west could become. For the United States, the activities of societies such as the CMS signified one more way that the new nation could exert control over its vast territories, particularly those in the Great Lakes region. British religious organizations such as the London Missionary Society had long taken the lead in evangelizing the American backcountry. By 1800, Congregationalists in Connecticut felt, as the CMS Constitution stated, "impressed with the obligation . . . to propagate a knowledge of its [Christianity's] gracious and holy doctrines." To them, the frontier "long presented a widely extended field" with "many tribes of savages . . . enveloped in the grossest darkness with regard to religion." Americans were eager to care for the souls on their vast continent.[2]

With this mission in mind, David Bacon set out in the late summer of 1800. He first wrote to the trustees of the CMS in September from Buffalo Creek (today Buffalo, New York). Here, "in sight of Lake Erie," Bacon waited for passage to Detroit, in search of an interpreter.[3] By September 11, Bacon landed in Detroit, a settlement that a fellow visitor at the time described as "English, Scotch, Irish and

French, all of whom hated the Yankees most cordially."[4] The foreign peoples and environment of the upper Great Lakes became a recurring theme in Bacon's correspondence. He took some comfort that a handful of American officials occupied the fort at Detroit. He also received help from the British subject John Askin and Jonathan Schieffelin, an "Indian agent . . . well informed with respect to the western tribes." Bacon recognized the challenge that awaited him in converting Detroit's Indian population to Protestantism after generations of French influence and British indifference. He described the "Hurons, or Wyandots" as "Roman Catholics, and very much given to intoxication." After his introduction to Detroit, Bacon decided to begin his mission in the north, where he found the Indian groups of the Mackinac region more open to conversion.[5]

Major Thomas Hunt carried Bacon by boat to Mackinac Island, where the natural beauty of the upper Great Lakes dominated his reports back to the CMS. Bacon noted, "I know of no place in the State of New York so healthy as this. I believe the water and the air as pure here, as in any part of New-England. And I have never been before, where venison, and wild geese and ducks were so plenty; or where there was such a rich variety of fresh water fish."[6] The missionary encountered a few other visitors to the region. Bernardus Harfon, a twenty-six-year-old Dutchman, joined Bacon as an interpreter and taught him local Algonquian Indian languages. Bacon also met other American missionaries, including two ministers from Pennsylvania who belonged to the Ohio Presbytery. The challenge of evangelizing in the wilderness environment reminded him of the success the Moravians had years earlier in "making the Delawares sober, industrious, and happy, like the white people."[7]

Bacon stayed in the Mackinac area until returning home to Hartford in mid-December 1800 to be married. He left elated by the "encouraging prospect" that a "number of sober, likely young Indians" wished for a "good English education."[8] The trustees of the CMS were also pleased with Bacon's progress and concluded that the Great Lakes Indians "appeared disposed to receive Missionaries among them."[9] After he married Alice Parks, the society ordained him officially to the ministry and highlighted his work "laboring as an Evangelist among the Indian tribes of North America," according to the *American Mercury* newspaper.[10]

In February 1801, Bacon returned to Detroit with his wife and her younger brother Beaumont Parks. Parks left a record of the journey that captured the novelty of three young people traveling so far west at the turn of the nineteenth century. Crossing New York, they encountered people who questioned why individuals "so young, should be willing to forsake home and friends and good old Connecticut, and go among the wild sons of the forest." Parks also had doubts. Along the trail to

Detroit, with no wagon road and only trees to mark the way, he and Alice encountered "wild Indians" for the first time; he described them as a "miserably degraded specimen of human nature." Part of Bacon's missionary work would be to convince his own party that Indians were worthy of Christian conversion.[11]

The eastern travelers arrived in Detroit in early May. For Bacon, his second trip to the Great Lakes region proved more challenging than the first. Although the CMS supported him spiritually, they had given him very little financial support, just $400 to cover expenses for both of his journeys and mission work. Bacon opened a school to make ends meet, and he continued to learn local Indian languages. He also preached on the Sabbath to larger congregations than he expected.[12]

Over time, though, conflicting paradigms of faith undermined Bacon's efforts. For many Detroiters, his purpose as a religious figure was to administer baptisms and other sacraments. Bacon was influenced by the traditional Congregational practice of requiring a conversion experience prior to baptism for adults. The minister's school, attended by the children of elites in the community, including some of Askin's sons, soon began to suffer. Parks attributed Bacon's difficulty to him being a *"Yankee."* The four or five Catholic priests in the area still held sway, even among non-Catholics, in part because they did not have such rigorous requirements for baptism. Detroit, though American in name, still retained a strong French identity.[13]

In early 1802, Bacon closed his school and returned to his main purpose of building an Indian mission for the CMS. Discouraged by the continued resistance of Detroit Indians and some Europeans to his message, he turned to the last remaining native settlements on the Maumee River in Ohio Territory. Bacon spent weeks trying to convince Indian leaders to accept a mission. They resisted fiercely, particularly to the missionary's expectation that conversion meant more than ascribing to certain doctrines. For Bacon and other Congregationalists, conversion meant Indians lived "together in permanent settlements," gave up alcohol and other "wild" pursuits, and sacrificed their culture for European ways. In May, Bacon decided to return to Mackinac Island—the site of his only success in evangelizing to Indians. For the next two years, however, he confronted similar cultural objections, ongoing difficulties learning Indian languages, and the strong influence of Catholicism on the island. By January 1804, the trustees of the CMS recalled Bacon, unwilling to fund his mission beyond their original commitment of $400. The society never again launched a major effort to convert Native Americans, choosing instead to focus on evangelizing white settlers.[14]

Bacon's experiences demonstrated that eastern America and the western frontier—particularly the Great Lakes region—were separated by more than distance in the early nineteenth century. Detroit's long history under first French and then

British colonial control had a lasting influence. When Bacon encountered Detroit, the untrained American Protestant ministry and its emphasis on individual conversion collided with the classically trained European Catholic priesthood and communal tradition. Bacon's journey was motivated by dreams and expectations of eastern America for civilizing the "wild sons of the forest." His failures showed that erasing generations of cultural difference was not easy. On his way out of Detroit in the spring of 1804, Bacon met with the Reverend Nathan Bangs, one of the first Methodist circuit riders to visit the town. He told Bangs of his many difficulties and parted by saying, "If you can succeed, which I very much doubt, I shall rejoice."[15]

NOTES

1 Connecticut Missionary Society, *The Constitution of the Missionary Society of Connecticut* (Hartford: Hudson and Goodwin, 1800), 4; *Connecticut Evangelical Magazine and Religious Intelligencer*, July 1800, 14 (quote), and September 1800, 118. Literature on David Bacon is minimal. The most complete source is the biography by his son Leonard, a New Haven minister and anti-slavery advocate: Leonard Bacon, *Sketch of the Rev. David Bacon* (Boston: Congregational Publishing Society, 1876). *City of Detroit*, 1:714-19, summarizes Bacon's time in Detroit. Monthly issues of the *Connecticut Evangelical Magazine and Religious Intelligencer* from late 1800 to 1803 include updates on Bacon and his letters to the trustees of the Connecticut Missionary Society.

2 Connecticut Missionary Society, 3, 7; L. Bacon, 7-8.

3 *Connecticut Evangelical Magazine*, November 1800, 198.

4 L. Bacon, 27. The description of Detroit was made by Beaumont Parks, Bacon's brother-in-law, during the missionary's second trip to the Great Lakes in 1801.

5 *Connecticut Evangelical Magazine*, December 1800, 234. For Schieffelin, see *City of Detroit*, 1:274-75, 714, and the essay in this volume by Douglas D. Fisher.

6 *Connecticut Evangelical Magazine*, December 1800, 236.

7 L. Bacon, 18, 19 (quote). For the Moravians, see the essay in this volume by Melissa R. Luberti.

8 D. Bacon quoted in L. Bacon, 19.

9 *Connecticut Evangelical Magazine,* January 1801, 280.

10 *American Mercury* quoted in L. Bacon, 21.

11 Parks quoted in L. Bacon, 23.

12 L. Bacon, 25-26.

13 L. Bacon, 26-28; 27 (quote). For the development of Congregational (originally Puritan) views on conversion and baptism, see Edmund S. Morgan, *Visible Saints: The History of Puritan Idea* (New York: New York University Press, 1963). For the French influence in Detroit, see the essay in this volume by Leslie Riehl.

14 L. Bacon, 29-68; 40 (quote); Rohrer, 121. For the final two years of Bacon's mission on Mackinac Island, see Brian Leigh Dunnigan, *A Picturesque Situation: Mackinac before Photography, 1615-1860* (Detroit: Wayne State University Press, 2008), 78, 98-99.

15 D. Bacon quoted in Carlisle G. Davidson, "Detroit's Protestant Heritage," in *Heritage of Faith, Detroit's Religious Communities, 1701-1976*, ed. Davidson (Detroit: Detroit's Religious Bicentennial Task Force, 1976), 39. Bacon continued to minister to whites and Indians for the Congregational Church in areas of Ohio that had been part of the Connecticut Western Reserve. In 1807, he became one of the founders of Tallmadge, Ohio, before being evicted from his land in 1812 for not paying his debts. Bacon spent the rest of his life in his native Connecticut pursuing various odd jobs, including selling religious texts; he died in 1817 (L. Bacon, 76-104).

SELECTED BIBLIOGRAPHY

MANUSCRIPTS

Archives of Michigan, Lansing
Edwin James Benson Papers
Map Collection
University of Wisconsin Collection on the Detroit Fur Trade

Archives of Ontario, Toronto
Court of Common Pleas of Hesse Records
Court of King's Bench Records
Western District Records

Bentley Historical Library, University of Michigan, Ann Arbor
Pattengill Family Papers
Sault Sainte Marie Collection
St. Anne's Church Register
United States Bureau of Customs, District of Michilimackinac Impost Book

Burton Historical Collection, Detroit Public Library

James Abbott Papers
Julia Larned Allen Papers
Fanny Johnston Anderson Papers
John Anderson Papers
George Christian Anthon Papers
John Askin Papers
Jacques Baby Papers
Henry Bird Papers
Lewis Bond Papers
Henry Bouquet Papers
William Burnett Papers
Clarence M. Burton Papers
Clarence M. Burton Works
Richard Butler Papers
Campau Family Papers
Jacques Campau Papers
John Campbell Papers
Canadian Archives
Lewis Cass Papers
George Byron Catlin Papers
Chêne Family Papers

Edward V. Cicotte Papers
Christian Clemens Papers
Leonard Covington Papers
Jean Baptiste Crête Papers
William Legge Dartmouth Papers
Philip Dejean Papers
Christian Denissen Papers
Detroit Historical Society Papers
Detroit Notarial Records
John Edgar Papers
William Edgar Papers
Matthew Ernest Papers
John Farmer Papers
Silas Farmer Papers
Otto O. Fisher Papers
Alexander Fraser Papers
Thomas Gage Papers
Aaron Greeley Papers
Gabriel Godfroy Papers
Alexander Grant Papers
Henry Hamilton Papers

John Francis Hamtramck Papers
Alexander Harrow Papers
Harrow Family Papers
James Henry Papers
Patrick Henry Papers
Jacob Merritt Howard Papers
William Hull Papers
Indians of North America
Thomas Jefferson Papers
Sir William Johnson Papers
Jacob Kingsbury Papers
Labadie Family Papers
Laferté Family Papers
Charles Larned Papers
Benson John Lossing Papers
George Fortune MacDonald Papers
Alexander Macomb Papers
Alexander/William Macomb Papers
Macomb, Edgar & Macomb Papers
Macomb Family Papers
Maps of the Great Lakes Collection
John Mason Papers
George McDougall Papers
John McGregor Papers
Alexander McKee Papers
George Meldrum Papers
Meldrum & Park Papers
Michigan Territory Papers
Miscellany by Date
Charles Moran Papers
Moran Family Papers
J. Bell Moran Papers
Moravian Papers
George Morgan Papers
Daniel Morison Papers

Francis (Francois) Navarre Papers
Robert Navarre Papers
George Paré Papers
William Park Papers
Jean Baptiste Pointe du Sable Papers
Ottawa Chief Pontiac Papers
John Porteous Papers
Pierre Potier Papers
Gabriel Richard Papers
Rivard Family Papers
William Robertson Papers
Robert Rogers Papers
Winthrop Sargent Papers
Solomon Sibley Papers
John Graves Simcoe Papers
Thomas Smith Papers
Arthur St. Clair Papers
James Sterling Papers
Harold E. Stoll Papers
Stuart Family Papers
Charles C. Trowbridge Papers
United States Archives
Jeremiah Van Rensselaer Papers
Charles Walker Papers
George Washington Papers
Anthony Wayne Papers
Wayne County NW Territory Papers
John Wilkins Papers
James Wilkinson Papers
John R. Williams Papers
Thomas Williams Papers
Benjamin F. H. Witherell Papers
Lucile Oughtred Woltz Papers
William Woodbridge Papers
Augustus B. Woodward Papers

William L. Clements Library, University of Michigan, Ann Arbor
Montesquiou Abbé Journal, American Travel Collection
Randolph Adams Papers and "Iconography of Detroit" Notebooks
Jeffrey Amherst Papers
John Anderson Papers
British North America Collection
Lewis Cass Papers
George Clinton Papers

Henry Clinton Papers
Arent S. De Peyster Papers, American Revolution Collection
Detroit Iconography Files
Thomas Duggan Papers
Thomas Gage Papers
Henry Glen Papers
Josiah Harmar Papers
Jehu Hay Journal
William Knox Papers
William Henry Lyttelton Papers
Macomb-Rucker Papers
Map Collection
Michigan Papers
Native American History Collection
James Patten Papers
John Porteous Letterbook
Print Division
Quaker Collection
Robert Rogers Papers
Rogers-Roche Papers
William Petty Shelburne Papers
John Graves Simcoe Papers
James Sterling Letterbook
Thompson Family Papers
Anthony Wayne Papers
Wilson Family Papers

Detroit Archdiocesan Archives
Parish Records

Fort Malden National Historic Site of Canada, Amherstburg, Ontario
Alexander McKee Family Genealogical File

Marsh Collection Society, Amherstburg, Ontario
Historic Landscape Conservation Study, Fort Malden
Gregor McGregor Papers

Ohio Historical Society, Columbus
Winthrop Sargent Papers

Pennsylvania Historical Society, Philadelphia
Anthony Wayne Papers

Alvord, Clarence W., and Clarence E. Carter, eds. *The Critical Period, 1763-1765.* Collections of the Illinois State Historical Library 1. Springfield: Illinois State Historical Library, 1915.

American State Papers, Indian Affairs. 2 vols. Washington: Gales and Seaton, 1832-34.

Amherst, Jeffery. *The Journal of Jeffery Amherst: Recording the Military Career of General Amherst in America from 1758-1763.* Edited by J. Clarence Webster. Chicago: University of Chicago Press, 1931.

Anderson, John. *A Short History of the Life of John Anderson.* Transcribed by Richard C. Knopf. Ann Arbor: University of Michigan Archives, 1956.

Armour, David A., ed. *Treason? at Michilimackinac: The Proceedings of a General Court Martial Held at Montreal in October 1768 for the Trial of Major Robert Rogers.* Mackinac Island: Mackinac Island State Park Commission, 1967.

Bacon, Leonard. *Sketch of Rev. David Bacon.* Boston: Congregational Publishing Society, 1876.

Barnhart, John D., ed. *Henry Hamilton and George Rogers Clark in the American Revolution, with the Unpublished Journal of Lieut. Gov. Henry Hamilton.* Crawfordsville, IN: R.E. Banta, 1951.

Bibeau, Claudette P. et al., eds. *Mariages St-Jean-Baptiste d'Amherstburg, 1802-1985* Ottawa: Société Franco-Ontarienne d'Histoire et de Généalogie, 1987.

Brackenridge, H.H., ed. *Indian Atrocities: Narratives of the Perils and Sufferings of Dr. Knight and John Slover, among the Indians during the Revolutionary War, with Short Memoirs of Col. Crawford & John Slover.* Cincinnati: U.P. James, 1867.

Bliss, Eugene F., ed. *Diary of David Zeisberger, a Moravian Missionary among the Indians of Ohio.* 2 vols. 1885. Reprint, Cincinnati: R. Clarke, 1972.

Blume, William W., ed. *Transactions of the Supreme Court of the Territory of Michigan.* 6 vols. Ann Arbor: University of Michigan Press, 1935-40.

Burton, M. Anges, ed. *Journal of Pontiac's Conspiracy, 1763.* Detroit: Clarence M. Burton and the Michigan Society of Colonial Wars, 1912.

————, ed. *Manuscripts from the Burton Historical Collection*. 8 vols. Detroit: Clarence M. Burton, 1916-18.

Burton, M. Agnes, and Clarence M. Burton, eds. *Governor and Judges Journal: Proceedings of the Land Board of Detroit*. Detroit: Michigan Territory Commission on Land Titles, 1915.

Burton, Clarence M., ed. *Ephraim Douglass and His Time, a Fragment of History, with the Journal of George McCully and Various Letters of the Period*. New York: William Abbatt, 1910.

————, ed. *Corporation of the Town of Detroit. Act of Incorporation and Journal of the Board of Trustees, 1802-1805*. Detroit: Detroit Public Library, 1922.

Carter, Clarence E., ed. *The Correspondence of General Thomas Gage*. 2 vols. New Haven: Yale University Press, 1931-33.

Carter, Clarence E., and John Porter Bloom, eds. *The Territorial Papers of the United States*. 27 vols. Washington: Department of State and National Archives and Records Service, 1934-69.

Carver, Jonathon. *Three Years Travels through the Interior Parts of North-America, for More Than Five Thousand Miles . . . 1778*. Reprint, Philadelphia: Key and Simpson, 1796.

Clark, George Rogers. *The Conquest of the Illinois*. Edited by Milo Milton Quaife. Chicago: R.R. Donnelley, 1920.

Cruikshank, E.A., ed. *The Correspondence of Lieut. Governor John Graves Simcoe*. 5 vols. Toronto: Ontario Historical Society, 1923-31.

Cunningham, Wilbur M., ed. *Letter Book of William Burnett: Early Fur Trader in the Land of Four Flags*. St. Joseph: Fort Miami Heritage Society of Michigan, 1967.

Denissen, Christian. *Genealogy of the French Families of the Detroit River Region 1701-1936*. 2 vols. Edited by Harold F. Powell. 1976. Reprint, Detroit: Detroit Society for Genealogy Research, 1987.

Dodge, John. *A Narrative of the Capture and Treatment of John Dodge by the English at Detroit*. Philadelphia: T. Bradford, 1779.

————. *Narrative of Mr. John Dodge during His Captivity at Detroit*. 1780. A facsimile of the second edition with an introduction by Clarence M. Burton. Cedar Rapids, IA: Torch Press, 1909.

Evans, William A., and Elizabeth S. Sklar, eds. *Detroit to Fort Sackville, 1778-1779: The Journal of Normand MacLeod.* Detroit: Wayne State University Press, 1978.

Fliegel, Carl et al., eds. *Moravian Mission Records among the North American Indians from the Archives of the Moravian Church, Bethlehem, Pennsylvania.* New Haven: Research Publications, 1970.

Fraser, Alexander, ed. *Fourteenth Report of the Bureau of Archives for the Province of Ontario.* Toronto: A.T. Wilgress, 1917.

Great Britain Parliament. *A Collection of the Acts Passed in the Parliament of Great Britain and of Other Public Acts Relative to Canada.* Quebec: P.E. Desbarats, 1824.

Haldimand, Frederick. *Sir Frederick Haldimand: Unpublished Papers and Correspondence, 1758-84.* London: World Microfilms Publications, 1977.

Hay, Henry. *Narrative of Life on the Old Frontier: Henry Hay's Journal from Detroit to the Miami River.* Edited by Milo Milton Quaife. Madison: Wisconsin State Historical Society, 1915.

Heckewelder, John G.E. *History, Manners and Customs of the Indian Nations Who Once Inhabited Pennsylvania and the Neighboring States.* 1819. Reprint, New York: Arno Press, 1971.

———. *A Narrative of the Mission of the United Brethren among the Delaware and Mohegan Indians . . .* 1820. Reprint, New York: Arno Press, 1971.

———. *Thirty Thousand Miles with John Heckewelder.* Edited by Paul A.W. Wallace. Pittsburgh: University of Pittsburgh Press, 1958.

———. *The Travels of John Heckewelder in Frontier America.* Edited by Paul A.W. Wallace. Pittsburgh: University of Pittsburgh Press, 1985.

Henry, Alexander. *Travels and Adventures in Canada and the Indian Territories, 1760-1776.* 1809. Reprint, New York: Garland, 1976.

———. *Alexander Henry's Travels and Adventures in the Years 1760-1776.* Edited by Milo Milton Quaife. Chicago: R.R. Donnelley, 1921.

James, James Alton, ed. *George Rogers Clark Papers, 1771-1781.* 2 vols. Springfield: Illinois State Historical Library, 1912-26.

Kappler, Charles J., ed. *Indian Affairs. Laws and Treaties.* 7 vols. Washington: Government Printing Office, 1904-79.

Kelly, Sharon A. et al., eds. *Marriage Records, Ste. Anne Church, Detroit, 1701-1850.* Detroit: Detroit Society for Genealogical Research, 2001.

Kershaw, Kenneth A., ed. *Early Printed Maps of Canada.* 4 vols. Ancaster, ON: Kershaw, 1993-98.

Lajeunesse, Ernest J., ed. *The Windsor Border Region, Canada's Southernmost Frontier; a Collection of Documents.* Toronto: Champlain Society, 1960.

Lees, John. *Journal of J.L., of Quebec, Merchant.* Edited by M. Agnes Burton. Detroit: Speaker-Hines, 1911.

Long, John. *John Long's Voyages and Travels in the Years 1768-1788.* Edited by Milo Milton Quaife. Chicago: R.R. Donnelley, 1922.

Lucier, Armand F., ed. *Pontiac's Conspiracy & Other Indian Affairs: Notices Abstracted from Colonial Newspapers, 1763-1765.* Bowie, MD: Heritage, 2000.

McCormick, William. *A Sketch of the Western District of Upper Canada: Being the Southern Extremity of that Interesting Province.* Edited by R.A. Douglas. Windsor, ON: University of Windsor Press, 1980.

Michigan Pioneer and Historical Society. *Michigan Pioneer and Historical Collection.* 40 vols. Lansing: Michigan Historical Commission, 1877-1929.

Michigan Works Progress Administration. *Early Land Transfers, Detroit and Wayne County, Michigan.* 54 vols. Detroit: Louisa St. Clair Chapter, Daughters of the American Revolution, 1936-40.

Middleton, Richard, ed. *Amherst and the Conquest of Canada: Selected Papers from the Correspondence of Major-General Jeffrey Amherst While Commander-in-Chief in North America from September 1758 to December 1760.* Stroud, Gloucestershire: Sutton, 2003.

Moore, Charles, ed. *The Gladwin Manuscripts; with an Introduction and a Sketch of the Conspiracy of Pontiac.* Lansing: Robert Smith, 1897.

Morris, Thomas. *Journal of Captain Thomas Morris, from Miscellanies in Prose and Verse.* London: James Ridgway, 1791.

Palmer, Friend, Harry P. Hunt, and Charles M. June. *Early Days in Detroit.* 1906. Reprint, Detroit: Omnigraphics, 1996.

Peckham, Howard H., ed. *George Croghan's Journal of His Trip to Detroit in 1767* . . . Ann Arbor: University of Michigan Press, 1939.

————, ed. *Narratives of Colonial America, 1704-1765.* Chicago: R.R. Donnelley, 1971.

Pineau, Dora, ed. *Marriage Register of the Western District, 1796-1856.* Windsor, ON: Essex County Branch, Ontario Genealogical Society, 1993.

Quaife, Milo Milton, ed. *Burton Historical Collection Leaflets.* 10 vols. Detroit: Detroit Public Library, 1922.

————, ed. *The Capture of Old Vincennes: The Original Narratives of George Rogers Clark and of His Opponent, Gov. Henry Hamilton.* Indianapolis: Bobbs-Merrill, 1927.

————, ed. *The John Askin Papers.* 2 vols. Detroit: Detroit Library Commission, 1928-31.

————, ed. *The Siege of Detroit in 1763: The Journal of Pontiac's Conspiracy, and John Rutherford's Narrative of a Captivity.* Chicago: R.R. Donnelley, 1958.

Rogers, Robert. *A Concise Account of North America: Containing a Description of the Several British Colonies on That Continent . . .* London: Printed for the author, and sold by J. Millan, 1765.

————. *Journals, an Account of the Several Excursions He Made under the Generals Who Commanded upon the Continent of North America during the Late War . . .* Edited by Franklin B. Hough. Albany: Munsell, 1883.

————. *Journal of Major Robert Rogers.* Edited by William L. Clements. Worcester, MA: The Society, 1918.

————. *Journals of Major Robert Rogers.* Introduction by Howard H. Peckham. New York: Corinth, 1961.

Rosenthal, John. *Journal of a Volunteer Expedition to Sandusky.* 1894. Reprint, New York: New York Times, 1969.

Russell, Donna Valley, ed. *Michigan Censuses, 1710-1830, under the French, British, and Americans.* Detroit: Detroit Society for Genealogical Research, 1982.

Sagard, Gabriel. *The Long Journey to the Country of the Hurons.* Edited by George M. Wrong. Translated by H.H. Langton. Toronto: Champlain Society, 1939.

Schoolcraft, Henry R. *Information Respecting the History, Condition, and Prospects of the Indian Tribes of the United States of America.* 6 vols. Philadelphia: Lippincott, Grambo, 1851-57.

Scull, Gideon, ed. *The Montresor Journals*. New York: New York Historical Society, 1882.

Shortt, Adam et al., eds. *Documents Relating to the Constitutional History of Canada*. 4 vols. Ottawa: King's Printer, 1914-35.

Simcoe, John Graves. *Simcoe's Military Journal*. 1784. Reprint, Toronto: Baxter, 1962.

————. *A Journal of the Operations of the Queen's Rangers*. 1787. Reprint, New York: New York Times, 1968.

Simmons, R.C., and Peter David Garner Thomas, eds. *Proceedings and Debates of the British Parliament Respecting North America, 1754-1783*. 5 vols. Millwood and White Plains, NY: Kraus, 1982-86.

Smith, James. *An Account of the Remarkable Occurrences in the Life and Travels of Col James Smith During His Captivity with the Indians . . .* Lexington, KY: John Bradford, 1799.

Spencer, Oliver. *The Indian Captivity of O.M. Spencer*. 1834. Reprint, New York: Carlton and Phillips, 1854.

State Historical Society of Wisconsin. *Collections of the State Historical Society of Wisconsin*. 31 vols. Madison: State Historical Society of Wisconsin, 1854-1931.

————. *Joseph Brant Papers*. Madison: State Historical Society of Wisconsin Division of Archives and Manuscripts, 1959.

————. *Calendar of the George Rogers Clark Papers, Series J in the Draper Manuscripts*. Madison: Archives Division, State Historical Society of Wisconsin, 1979.

Stevens, S.K. et al., eds. *The Papers of Henry Bouquet*. 6 vols. Harrisburg: Pennsylvania Historical and Museum Commission, 1972-94.

Sullivan, James et al., eds. *The Papers of Sir William Johnson*. 14 vols. Albany: University of the State of New York Division of Archives and History, 1921-65.

Talman, James John, ed. *Loyalist Narratives from Upper Canada*. Toronto: Champlain Society, 1946.

Thwaites, Reuben Gold, ed. *The Jesuit Relations and Allied Documents*. 73 vols. Cleveland: Burrows Brothers, 1896-1901.

————, ed. *A Short Biography of John Leeth, with an Account of His Life among the Indians*. 1831. Reprint, Cleveland: Burrows Brothers, 1904.

———, ed. *Early Western Travels, 1748-1846.* 32 vols. Cleveland: A.H. Clark, 1904-7.

Thwaites, Reuben Gold and Louise Phelps Kellogg, eds. *The Revolution on the Upper Ohio, 1775-1777.* 1908. Reprint, Port Washington, NY: Kennikat, 1970.

Vexler, Robert I., ed. *Detroit: A Chronological and Documentary History, 1701-1976.* Dobbs Ferry, NY: Oceana, 1977.

Washburn, Wilcomb E. et al., eds. *The Garland Library of Narratives of North American Indian Captivities.* 111 vols. New York: Garland, 1973-83.

Weld, Isaac, Jr. *Travels through the States of North America, and the Provinces of Upper & Lower Canada, during the Years 1795, 1796 and 1797.* 2 vols. 1807. 4th edition, New York: A.M. Kelly, 1970.

SECONDARY SOURCES

Adelman, Jeremy, and Stephen Aron. "From Borderlands to Borders: Empires, Nation-States and the Peoples in Between in North American History." *American Historical Review* 104 (1999): 814-41.

Allen, Robert S. *Loyalist Literature: An Annotated Bibliographic Guide to the Writings on the Loyalists of the American Revolution.* Toronto: Dundurn, 1982.

Amherstburg Bicentennial Book Committee. *Amherstburg, 1796-1996: The New Town on the Garrison Grounds.* Amherstburg, ON: Amherstburg Bicentennial Book Committee, 1996.

Anderson, Frank W. *Hanging in Canada: Concise History of a Controversial Topic.* Surrey, BC: Frontier, 1982.

Anderson, Fred. *The Crucible of War: The Seven Years' War and the Fate of Empire in British North America, 1754-1766.* New York: Alfred A. Knopf, 2000.

———. *The War That Made America: A Short History of the French and Indian War.* New York: Viking, 2005.

Anderson, James H. *Colonel William Crawford.* Columbus: Ohio Archaeological and Historical Publications, 1898.

Armour, David A., and Keith R. Widder. *At the Crossroads: Michilimackinac during the American Revolution.* Mackinac Island: Mackinac Island State Park Commission, 1978.

Axtell, James. *The European and the Indian: Essays in the Ethnohistory of Colonial North America.* New York: Oxford University Press, 1981.

———. *The Invasion Within: The Contest of Cultures in Colonial North America.* New York: Oxford University Press, 1985.

Bak, Richard. *Detroit across Three Centuries.* Chelsea, MI: Sleeping Bear Press, 2001.

Bakeless, John E. *Turncoats, Traitors, and Heroes.* 1959. Reprint, New York: Da Capo, 1998.

Bald, Frederick Clever. *Detroit's First American Decade, 1796-1805.* Ann Arbor: University of Michigan Press, 1948.

———. *Michigan in Four Centuries: Line Drawings by William Thomas Woodward.* New York: Harper, 1954.

Bamford, Don. *Freshwater Heritage: A History of Sail on the Great Lakes, 1670-1918.* Toronto: Natural Heritage Books, 2007.

Banner, Melvin E. "The Riddle of the *Felicity*." *Telescope* 18 (1969): 61-64.

Barbeau, Marius. "Indian Captivity." *Proceedings of the American Philosophical Society* 94 (1950): 522-48.

Barnett, LeRoy, and Roger Rosentreter. *Michigan's Early Military Forces: A Roster and History of Troops Activated Prior to the American Civil War.* Detroit: Wayne State University Press, 2003.

Barnhart, John D. "A New Evaluation of Henry Hamilton and George Rogers Clark." *Mississippi Valley Historical Review* 37 (1951): 643-52.

Barr, Daniel P., ed. *The Boundaries Between Us: Natives and Newcomers along the Frontiers of the Old Northwest Territory, 1750-1850.* Kent, OH: Kent State University Press, 2006.

Bartolo, Ghislaine Pieters, and Lynn Waybright Reaume, eds. *The Cross Leads Generations On: A Bicentennial Retrospect, St. Mary of the Immaculate Conception Formerly Known as St. Antoine at the River Raisin, Monroe, Michigan, 1788-1988.* Tappan, NY: Custombook, 1988.

Beers, Henry P. *The French and British in the Old Northwest: A Bibliographical Guide to Archive and Manuscript Sources.* Detroit: Wayne State University Press, 1964.

Boatman, Roy. *Simon Girty, the Man and the Image.* Madison: University of Wisconsin Press, 1954.

Bodley, Temple. "The National Significance of George Rogers Clark." *Mississippi Valley Historical Review* 11 (1924): 165-89.

Bond, Beverley W. Jr. *The Foundations of Ohio.* Columbus: Ohio State Archaeological and Historical Society, 1941.

Borneman, Walter. *The French and Indian War: Deciding the Fate of North America.* New York: HarperCollins, 2006.

Bowes, John P. "The Gnadenhutten Effect: Moravian Converts and the Search for Safety in the Canadian Borderlands." *Michigan Historical Review* 34 (Spring 2008): 101-17.

Boyea, Earl. *Gabriel Richard: Servant of God.* Ann Arbor: University Litho, 2001.

Brown, George W. et al., eds. *Dictionary of Canadian Biography.* 15 vols. Toronto: University of Toronto Press, 1965-2005.

Brown, Jennifer S.H. et al., eds. *The Fur Trade Revisited: Selected Papers of the Sixth North American Fur Trade Conference, Mackinac Island, MI, 1991.* East Lansing: Michigan State University Press, 1994.

Brown, Wallace. *The Good Americans: The Loyalists in the American Revolution.* New York: Morrow, 1969.

Bukowczyk, John J. et al. *Permeable Border: The Great Lakes Basin as Transnational Region, 1650-1990.* Pittsburgh: University of Pittsburgh Press, 2005.

Bumsted, J.M. *A History of the Canadian Peoples.* 2nd ed. New York: Oxford University Press, 2003.

———. *The Peoples of Canada: A Pre-Confederation History.* New York: Oxford University Press, 2003.

Burton, Clarence M. "Henry ('Hair-Buyer') Hamilton." *Magazine of History with Notes and Queries* 1 (1905): 176-81.

———. *Historical Papers Delivered Before the Society of Colonial Wars of the State of Michigan.* Detroit: Winn and Hammond, 1908.

———. *Early Detroit: A Sketch of Some of the Interesting Affairs of the Olden Time.* Detroit: Speaker-Hines, 1909.

———. *John Connolly: A Tory of the Revolution.* Worcester, MA: Davis Press, 1909.

———. *The City of Detroit Michigan, 1701-1922.* 5 vols. Detroit and Chicago: S.J. Clarke, 1922.

————. *When Detroit Was Young: Historical Studies.* Edited by Milo Milton Quaife. Detroit: Burton Abstract and Title, 1951.

Burton, Clarence M., ed. *The Paul Revere of the West.* Detroit: Speaker-Hines, 1909.

Butterfield, Consul Wilshire. *An Historical Account of the Expedition against Sandusky under Col. William Crawford in 1782.* Cincinnati: Clarke, 1873.

Calhoon, Robert M., Timothy M. Barnes, and George A. Rawlyk, eds. *Loyalists and Community in North America.* Westport, CT: Greenwood, 1994.

Calloway, Colin G. "Neither White nor Red: White Renegades on the American Indian Frontier." *Western Historical Quarterly* 17 (1986): 43-66.

————. "'We Have Always Been the Frontier': The American Revolution in Shawnee Country." *American Indian Quarterly* 16 (Winter 1992): 39-52.

————. *The American Revolution in Indian Country: Crisis and Diversity in Native American Communities.* New York: Cambridge University Press, 1995.

————. *The Scratch of a Pen: 1763 and the Transformation of North America.* New York: Oxford University Press, 2006.

Carstens, Kenneth C., and Nancy Son Carstens, eds. *The Life of George Rogers Clark, 1752-1818: Triumphs and Tragedies.* Westport, CT: Praeger, 2004.

Carter, Harvey L. *The Life and Times of Little Turtle: First Sagamore of the Wabash.* Urbana: University of Illinois Press, 1987.

Catlin, George B. *The Story of Detroit.* Detroit: The Detroit News, 1923.

————. *The Siege of Detroit.* Detroit: The Detroit News, 1926.

Catlin, George B., ed. *Local History of Detroit and Wayne County.* Dayton: National Historical Association, 1928.

Catlin, George B., and Robert B. Ross. *Landmarks of Detroit: A History of the City.* Detroit: Evening News Association, 1898.

Cayton, Andrew R.L., and Fredrika J. Teute, eds. *Contact Points: American Frontiers from the Mohawk Valley to the Mississippi, 1750-1830.* Chapel Hill: University of North Carolina Press, 1998.

Chiasson, Germaine, Carmen MacLeod et al., eds. *Mariages, Paroisse L'Assomption de Windsor, Ontario, 1700-1985.* 2 vols. Ottawa: Société Franco-Ontarienne d'Histoire et de Généalogie, 1985.

Clarke, Peter D. *The Origin and Traditional History of the Wyandotte, and Sketches of Other Indian Tribes of North America.* Toronto: Hunter, Rose, 1870.

Cleland, Charles E. *Rites of Conquest: The History and Culture of Michigan's Native Americans.* Ann Arbor: University of Michigan Press, 1992.

Clifton, James A. *Personal and Ethnic Identity on the Great Lakes Frontier: The Case of Billy Caldwell, Anglo-Canadian.* Window Rock, AZ: American Indian Ethnohistoric Conference, 1978.

Cowan, William, ed. *Papers of the Sixth Algonquian Conference, 1974.* Ottawa: National Museums of Canada, 1975.

Craig, Gerald M. *Upper Canada: The Formative Years, 1784-1841.* New York: Oxford University Press, 1963.

Cuneo, John R. *Robert Rogers of the Rangers.* Ticonderoga, NY: Fort Ticonderoga Museum, 1988.

Cuthbertson, George A. *Freshwater: A History and a Narrative of the Great Lakes.* New York: Macmillan, 1931.

Dalton, M. Arthemise. "The History and Development of the Catholic Secondary School System in the Archdiocese of Detroit, 1701-1961." PhD diss., Wayne State University, 1962.

Danzinger, Edmund J. Jr. *The Chippewas of Lake Superior.* 1978. Reprint, Norman: Oklahoma University Press, 1990.

Darlington, Mary C. *History of Col. Henry Bouquet and the Western Frontiers of Pennsylvania, 1747-1764.* New York: Arno, 1971.

Davidson, Carlisle G., ed. *Heritage of Faith: Detroit's Religious Communities, 1701-1976.* Detroit: Detroit's Religious Bicentennial Task Force, 1976.

Davis, Andrew M. "The Employment of Indian Auxiliaries in the American War." *English Historical Review* 2 (1887): 709-28.

De Schweinitz, Edmund. *The Life and Times of David Zeisberger, the Western Pioneer and Apostle of the Indians.* Philadelphia: J.B. Lippincott, 1871.

Devens, Carol. *Countering Colonization: Native American Women and Great Lakes Missions, 1630-1900.* Berkeley: University of California Press, 1992.

Dippie, Brian W. *The Vanishing American: White Attitudes and U.S. Indian Policy.* 1982. Reprint, Lawrence: University Press of Kansas, 1991.

Dixon, David. *Never Come to Peace Again: Pontiac's Uprising and the Fate of the British Empire in North America*. Norman: University of Oklahoma Press, 2005.

Douglas, R. Alan. *Uppermost Canada: The Western District and the Detroit Frontier, 1800-1850*. Detroit: Wayne State University Press, 2001.

Dowd, Gregory Evans. "The French King Wakes Up in Detroit: Pontiac's War in Rumor and History." *Ethnohistory* 37 (1990): 254-78.

———. *A Spirited Resistance: The North American Indian Struggle for Unity, 1745-1815*. Baltimore: Johns Hopkins University Press, 1992.

———. *War under Heaven: Pontiac, the Indian Nations, and the British Empire*. Baltimore: Johns Hopkins University Press, 2002.

DuLong, John P. *French Canadians in Michigan*. East Lansing: Michigan State University Press, 2001.

Dunbar, Willis F. *Michigan through the Centuries: Michigan in the Making and at Mid-Century*. 4 vols. New York: Lewis Historical, 1952-55.

Dunbar, Willis F., and George S. May. *Michigan: A History of the Wolverine State*. 3rd rev. ed. Grand Rapids: Eerdman, 1995.

Dunn, Walter Scott. *Choosing Sides on the Frontier in the American Revolution*. Westport, CT: Praeger, 2007.

Dunnigan, Brian Leigh. *King's Men at Mackinac: The British Garrisons, 1780-1796*. Lansing: Mackinac Island State Park Commission, 1973.

———. *Milestones of the Past: Military Buttons and Insignia from Mackinac*. Mackinac Island: Mackinac Island State Park Commission, 1975.

———. "Fort Mackinac: A Revolutionary War Post in Michigan." *Military Collector & Historian* 29 (1977): 15-21.

———. "The Post of Mackinac, 1779-1812." M.A. thesis, State University of New York College at Oneonta, 1979.

———. *The British Army at Mackinac, 1812-1815*. Lansing: Mackinac Island State Park Commission, 1980.

———. "British Naval Vessels on the Upper Great Lakes, 1761-1796." *Telescope* 31 (1982): 92-98.

———. *Fort Holmes*. Lansing: Mackinac Island State Park Commission, 1984.

———. *The Necessity of Regularity in Quartering Soldiers: The Organization, Material Culture, and Quartering of the British Soldier at Michilimackinac.* Mackinac Island: Mackinac State Historic Parks, 1999.

———. *Frontier Metropolis: Picturing Early Detroit, 1701-1838.* Detroit: Wayne State University Press, 2001.

———. *Garrison Town: Detroit's Strategic Location Gave Its Early Years a Definitive Military Flavor.* Detroit: Wayne State University Press, 2001.

———. *The Prettiest Settlement in America: A Select Bibliography of Early Detroit through the War of 1812.* Mount Pleasant: Central Michigan University, 2001.

———. *Detroit: Clark's Obsession.* Westport, CT: Praeger, 2004.

———. *Eye of the Beholder: Mackinac Before There Were Photographs.* Mackinac Island: Island Publications, 2005.

———. *A Picturesque Situation: Mackinac before Photography, 1615-1860.* Detroit: Wayne State University Press, 2008.

Eccles, William J. *The Canadian Frontier, 1534-1760.* 1969. Reprint, Albuquerque: University of New Mexico Press, 1983.

———. *The French in North America.* 3rd ed. East Lansing: Michigan State University Press, 1998.

Edmunds, R. David. *The Potawatomis: Keepers of the Fire.* Norman: University of Oklahoma Press, 1978.

———. *Enduring Nations: Native Americans in the Midwest.* Urbana: University of Illinois Press, 2008.

Ellis, David M. et al., eds. *The Frontier in American Development: Essays in Honor of Paul Wallace Gates.* Ithaca: Cornell University Press, 1969.

Englebert, Robert. "Merchant Representatives and the French River World, 1763-1803." *Michigan Historical Review* 34 (Spring 2008): 63-82.

Ens, Gerhard J. *Homeland to Hinterland: The Changing Worlds of the Red River Métis in the Nineteenth Century.* Toronto: University of Toronto Press, 1996.

Essex County Tourist Association. *Essex County Sketches.* Windsor, ON: Herald Press, 1947.

Farmer, Silas. *The History of Detroit and Michigan: Or the Metropolis Illustrated.* Detroit: S. Farmer, 1884.

————. *History of Detroit and Wayne County and Early Michigan: A Chronological Cyclopedia of the Past & Present. 1890.* Reprint, Detroit: Gale Research, 1969.

Farmer, Silas et al., eds. *The Bi-Centenary of the Founding of City of Detroit 1701-1901, Being the Official Report of the Celebration of July 24, 25, 26, 1901.* Detroit: C.M. Rousseau, 1902.

Firth, Edith G., ed. *Profiles of a Province: Studies in the History of Ontario.* Toronto: Ontario Historical Society, 1967.

Fitzgerald, E. Keith, ed. *Ontario People, 1796-1803.* Baltimore: Genealogical, 1993.

Freedman, Eric. *Pioneering Michigan.* Franklin, MI: Altwerger and Mandel, 1992.

Fuller, George N. "Settlement of Michigan Territory." *Mississippi Valley Historical Society* 2 (1915): 25-55.

————. *Economic and Social Beginnings of Michigan: A Study of the Settlement of the Lower Peninsula during the Territorial Period, 1805-1837.* Lansing: Wynkoop Hallenbeck Crawford, 1916.

Fuller, George N. et al., eds. *Michigan: A Centennial History of the State and Its People.* 5 vols. Chicago: Lewis, 1939.

Gaff, Alan D. *Bayonets in the Wilderness: Anthony Wayne's Legion in the Old Northwest.* Norman: University of Oklahoma Press, 2004.

Gavrilovich, Peter, and Bill McGraw, eds. *The Detroit Almanac: 300 Years of Life in the Motor City.* 2000. Reprint, Detroit: Detroit Free Press, 2006.

Genser, Wallace. "'Habitants,' 'Half-breeds,' and Homeless Children: Transformations in Métis and Yankee—Yorker Relations in Early Michigan." *Michigan Historical Review* 24 (Spring 1998): 23-47.

Gilpin, Alec R. *The Territory of Michigan.* East Lansing: Michigan State University Press, 1970.

Glazebrook, George Parkin de Twenebroker. *A History of Transportation in Canada.* 1939. Reprint, New York: Greenwood, 1969.

Goodrich, Calvin. *The First Michigan Frontier.* Ann Arbor: University of Michigan Press, 1940.

Gould, Eliga H., and Peter S. Onuf, eds. *Empire and Nation: The American Revolution in the Atlantic World.* Baltimore: Johns Hopkins University Press, 2005.

Gray, Elma E., and Leslie R. Gray. *Wilderness Christians; the Moravian Mission to the Delaware Indians*. Ithaca: Cornell University Press, 1956.

Greene, George E. *History of Old Vincennes and Knox County, Indiana*. Detroit and Chicago: S.J. Clarke, 1911.

Greenman, Emerson F. *The Indians of Michigan*. Lansing: Michigan Historical Commission, 1961.

Grenier, John. *The First Way of War: American War Making on the Frontier, 1607-1814*. New York: Cambridge University Press, 2005.

Griffin, Patrick. *American Leviathan: Empire, Nation, and Revolutionary Frontier*. New York: Hill and Wang, 2007.

Guillet, Edwin C. *Pioneer Travel in Upper Canada*. Vol. 4 of *Early Life in Upper Canada*. 5 vols. 1933-40. Reprint, Toronto: University of Toronto Press, 1966.

Hamilton, Milton W. *Sir William Johnson Colonial American, 1715-1763*. Port Washington, NY: Kennikat, 1976.

Hamlin, Marie Caroline Watson. *Legends of Le Detroit, Early French Families*. 1884. Reprint, Detroit: Gale Research, 1977.

Haring, Sidney L. *White Man's Law: Native People in Nineteenth-Century Canadian Jurisprudence*. Toronto: University of Toronto Press, 1998.

Harris, Richard C. et al., eds. *Historical Atlas of Canada*. 3 vols. Toronto: University of Toronto Press, 1987-93.

Hatter, Lawrence B.A. "The Transformation of the Detroit Land Market and the Formation of the Anglo-American Border, 1783-1796." *Michigan Historical Review* 34 (Spring 2008): 83-99.

Havighurst, Walter. *Three Flags at the Straits: The Forts of Mackinac*. Englewood Cliffs, NJ: Prentice-Hall, 1966.

Heineman, David E. *Jewish Beginnings in Michigan before 1850*. Baltimore, 1905.

Herstein, H.H., L.J. Hughes, and Ronald Kirbyson. *Challenge and Survival: The History of Canada*. Scarborough, ON: Prentice Hall, 1970.

Horsman, Reginald. "The British Indian Department and the Resistance to General Anthony Wayne, 1793-1795." *Mississippi Valley Historical Review* 49 (1962): 269-90.

———. *Frontier Detroit: 1760-1812*. Detroit: Michigan in Perspective Conference, 1964.

———. *Matthew Elliott, British Indian Agent.* Detroit: Wayne State University Press, 1964.

———. *Expansion and American Indian Policy, 1783-1812.* 1967. Reprint, Norman: University of Oklahoma Press, 1992.

Hudgins, Bert. "Evolution of Metropolitan Detroit." *Economic Geography* 21 (1945): 206-20.

———. "Old Detroit: Drainage and Land Forms." *Michigan Historical Magazine* 30 (1946): 348-68.

Humphreys, Helen F. "Identity of Gladwin's Informant." *Mississippi Valley Historical Review* 21 (1934): 147-62.

Innis, Harold A. *The Fur Trade in Canada: An Introduction to Canadian Economic History.* New Haven: Yale University Press, 1964.

Jacobs, Wilbur R. "Was the Pontiac Uprising a Conspiracy?" *Ohio State Archaeological and Historical Quarterly* 51 (1950). 26-37.

———. *Wilderness Politics and Indian Gifts: The Northern Colonial Frontier, 1748-1763.* 1950. Reprint, Lincoln: University of Nebraska Press, 1966.

———. *Dispossessing the American Indian: Indians and Whites on the Colonial Frontier.* 1972. Reprint, Norman: University of Oklahoma Press, 1985.

Jacobson, Judy. *Detroit River Connections: Historical and Biographical Sketches of the Eastern Great Lakes Border Region.* Baltimore: Clearfield, 1994.

Jaenen, Cornelius J. "'Les Sauvages Ameriquains': Persistence into the 18th Century of Traditional French Concepts and Constructs for Comprehending Amerindians." *Ethnohistory* 29 (1982): 43-56.

James, C.C. *Early History of the Town of Amherstburg: A Short, Concise, and Interesting Sketch, with Explanatory Notes.* Amherstburg, ON: Echo, 1902.

Jasanoff, Maya. "The Other Side of Revolution: Loyalists in the British Empire." *William and Mary Quarterly* 65 (2008): 205-33.

Jenks, William L. *St. Clair County, Michigan, Its History and Its People.* 2 vols. Chicago: Lewis, 1912.

Johnson, J.K., and Bruce G. Wilson, eds. *Historical Essays on Upper Canada: New Perspectives.* Ottawa: Carleton University Press, 1989.

Jung, Patrick J. "A Valuable and Dependable Little Navy: The British Upper Great Lakes Fleet during the American Revolution." *Inland Seas* 53 (1997): 68-75, 142-50, 204-207.

Karamanski, Theodore J. *Schooner Passage: Sailing Ships and the Lake Michigan Frontier.* Detroit: Wayne State University Press, 2000.

Keffer, Marion C. *Migrations to/from Canada.* Ann Arbor: Genealogical Society of Washtenaw County, 1982.

Kent, Timothy J. *Fort Ponchartrain at Detroit: A Guide to the Daily Lives of Fur Trade and Military Personnel, Settlers, and Missionaries at French Posts.* Ossineke, MI: Silver Fox, 2001.

————. *Rendezvous at the Straits: Fur Trade and Military Activity at Fort De Buade and Fort Michilimackinac, 1669-1781.* Ossineke, MI: Silver Fox, 2004.

Kern, John. *A Short History of Michigan.* Lansing: Michigan History Division, Michigan Department of State, 1977.

Knowles, Norman. *Inventing the Loyalists: The Ontario Loyalist Tradition and the Creation of Usable Pasts.* Toronto: University of Toronto Press, 1997.

Krech, Shepard III, ed. *Indians, Animals, and the Fur Trade: A Critique of Keepers of the Game.* Athens: University of Georgia Press, 1981.

Krog, Carl E. "The British Great Lakes Forts." *Inland Seas* 42 (1986): 252-60.

Landon, Fred. *Western Ontario and the American Frontier.* 1941. Reprint, New York: Russell and Russell, 1970.

Lanman, James H. *History of Michigan, from Its Earliest Colonization to the Present Time.* New York: Harper, 1855.

Law, John. *The Colonial History of Vincennes, under the French, British, and American Governments, from Its First Settlement Down to the Territorial Administration of William Henry Harrison.* Vincennes, IN: Harvey, Mason and Co., 1858.

Leach, Hamish A. *The Founding of Fort Amherstburg (Malden) Along the Detroit Frontier, 1796: A Political, Military, and Legal Frontier Study, with Computer Applications.* Houston: Veldt Protea Institute, 1984.

Leake, Paul. *History of Detroit: A Chronicle of Its Progress, Its Industries, Its Institutions, and the People of the Fair City of the Straits.* Chicago: Lewis, 1912.

Leasher, Evelyn M., ed. *Native Americans in Michigan: A Bibliography of the Material in the Clarke Historical Library.* Mount Pleasant: Clarke Historical Library, Central Michigan University, 1996.

Lebel, E.C. "History of Assumption, the First Parish in Upper Canada." *Report of the Canadian Catholic Historical Association* 21 (1954): 23-37.

Leeson, Michael A. et al., eds. *History of Macomb County, Michigan.* Chicago: Leeson, 1882.

Lender, Charles F. *With Wayne at Fallen Timbers.* New York: Cupples and Leon, 1941.

Malcomson, Robert. *Warships of the Great Lakes, 1754-1834.* Annapolis: Naval Institute Press, 2001.

———. "'Not Very Much Celebrated': The Evolution and Nature of the Provincial Marine, 1755-1813." *Northern Mariner/Marin du nord* 11 (2001): 25-37.

Mason, Philip P. *Detroit, Fort Lernoult, and the American Revolution.* Detroit: Wayne State University Press, 1964.

Mast, Dolorita. *Always the Priest: The Life of Gabriel Richard, S.S.* Baltimore: Helicon, 1965.

McConnell, Michael N. *A Country Between: The Upper Ohio Valley and Its Peoples, 1724-1774.* Lincoln: University of Nebraska Press, 1992.

McRae, Norman. "Early Blacks in Michigan, 1743-1800." *Detroit in Perspective: A Journal of Regional History* 2 (1976): 159-75.

Meehan, Thomas. "Jean Baptiste Pointe du Sable, the First Chicagoan." *Journal of the Illinois State Historical Society* 56 (1963): 439-53.

Michigan State Historical Society. *Classified Finding List of the Collections of the Michigan Pioneer and Historical Society.* Detroit: Wayne University Press, 1952.

Middleton, Richard. "Pontiac: Local Warrior or Pan-Indian Leader?" *Michigan Historical Review* 32 (Fall 2006): 1-32.

———. *Pontiac's War: Its Causes, Course, and Consequences.* New York: Routledge, 2007.

Mika, Nick, and Helma Mika. *United Empire Loyalists: Pioneers of Upper Canada.* Belleville, ON: Mika, 1976.

Miles, Richard D. *The Stars and Stripes Come to Detroit*. Detroit: Wayne University Press, 1951.

Moogk, Peter N. *La Nouvelle France: The Making of French Canada—a Cultural History*. East Lansing: Michigan State University Press, 2000.

Moore, Charles. *History of Michigan*. 4 vols. Chicago: Lewis, 1915.

Moran, John Bell. *The Moran Family: 200 Years in Detroit*. 1949. Reprint, Detroit: Higginson, 1991.

Neal, Frederick, ed. *The Township of Sandwich, Past and Present*. 1909. Reprint, Windsor: Essex County Historical Society and Windsor Public Library Board, 1979.

Nelson, Larry L. *A Man of Distinction among Them: Alexander McKee and British-Indian Affairs along the Ohio Country Frontier, 1754-1799*. Kent, OH: Kent State University Press, 1999.

Nester, William R. *Haughty Conquerors: Amherst and the Great Indian Uprising of 1763*. Westport, CT: Praeger, 2000.

———. *The Frontier War for American Independence*. Mechanicsburg, PA: Stackpole, 2004.

O'Brien, Brendan. *Speedy Injustice: The Tragic Last Voyage of His Majesty's Vessel Speedy*. Toronto: University of Toronto Press, 2000.

Olmstead, Earl. *Blackcoats among the Delaware: David Zeisberger on the Ohio Frontier*. Kent, OH: Kent State University Press, 1991.

———. *David Zeisberger: A Life among the Indians*. Kent, OH: Kent State University Press, 1997.

Ontario Heritage Administration Branch. *Historical Sketches of Ontario*. 1977. Reprint, Toronto: Ontario Heritage Conservation Division, 1979.

Otten, William L. Jr. *Colonel J.F. Hamtramck: His Life and Times*. 2 vols. Port Aransas, TX: Otten, 1997-2003.

Paré, George. *The Catholic Church in Detroit, 1701-1888*. 1951. Reprint, Detroit: Wayne State University Press, 1983.

Pargellis, Stanley McCrory. *Father Gabriel Richard*. Detroit: Wayne University Press, 1950.

Parkins, Almon E. *The Historical Geography of Detroit*. 1918. Reprint, Port Washington, NY: Kennikat, 1970.

Parkman, Francis. *The Conspiracy of Pontiac and the Indian War after the Conquest of Canada*. 2 vols. Boston: Little Brown, 1903.

Parmenter, Jon W. "Pontiac's War: Forging New Links in the Anglo-Iroquois Covenant Chain, 1758-1766." *Ethnohistory* 44 (1997): 617-54.

Peckham, Howard H. *Pontiac and the Indian Rising*. 1947. Reprint, Detroit: Wayne State University Press, 1994.

Perkins, James, John Mason Peck, and James R. Albach, eds. *Annals of the West Embracing a Concise Account of Principal Events Which Have Occurred in the Western States and Territories . . . to the Year Eighteen Hundred and Fifty-Six*. Pittsburgh: J.R. Albach, 1858.

Peterson, Jacqueline. "Prelude to Red River: A Social Portrait of the Great Lakes Métis." *Ethnohistory* 25 (1978): 41-67.

———. "The People in Between: Indian-White Marriage and the Genesis of a Métis Society and Culture in the Great Lakes Region, 1680-1830." PhD diss., University of Illinois at Chicago Circle, 1981.

Peterson, Jacqueline, and Jennifer S.H. Brown, eds. *The New Peoples: Being and Becoming Métis in North America*. Winnipeg: University of Manitoba Press, 1985.

Pieczynski, Christopher J. "The First British Naval Vessel on the Upper Great Lakes." *Inland Seas* 61 (2005): 47-49.

———. "Two Little Ships: Naval Action during the Conspiracy of Pontiac." *Inland Seas* 61 (2005): 294-309.

Pflug, Melissa A. "Politics of Great Lakes Indian Religion." *Michigan Historical Review* 18 (Fall 1992): 15-31.

Poremba, David Lee. "British Detroit." *Michigan History* 84, no. 6 (2000): 36-43.

———. *Detroit: A Motor City History*. Charleston, SC: Arcadia, 2001.

Poremba, David Lee, ed. *Detroit in its World Setting: A Three-Hundred Year Chronology, 1701-2001*. Detroit: Wayne State University Press, 2001.

Power, Michael. "Father Edmund Burke: Along the Detroit River Frontier, 1794-1797." *Canadian Catholic Historical Association Historical Studies* 51 (1984): 29-46.

Pratt, G. Michael. "The Battle of Fallen Timbers: An Eyewitness Perspective." *Northwest Ohio Quarterly* 67 (1995): 4-34.

Pryke, K.G., and L.L. Kulisek, eds. *The Western District: Papers from the Western District Conference*. Windsor, ON: Essex County Historical Society, 1983.

Quaife, Milo Milton. *Chicago and the Old Northwest, 1673-1835* . . . 1913. Reprint, Urbana: University of Illinois Press, 2001.

―――. "General James Wilkinson's Narrative of the Fallen Timbers Campaign." *Mississippi Valley Historical Review* 16 (1929): 81-90.

―――. "The Ohio Campaigns of 1782." *Mississippi Valley Historical Review* 17 (1931): 515-29.

―――. *This is Detroit, 1701-1951: Two Hundred and Fifty Years in Pictures*. Edited by William White. Detroit: Wayne University Press, 1951.

Quaife, Milo Milton, and Sidney Glazer. *Michigan: From Primitive Wilderness to Industrial Commonwealth*. New York: Prentice-Hall, 1948.

Raddall, Thomas H. *The Path of Destiny: Canada from the British Conquest to Home Rule: 1763-1850*. Toronto: Doubleday, 1957.

Rau, Louise. "John Askin: Early Detroit Merchant." *Bulletin of the Business Historical Society* 10, no. 6 (1936): 91-94.

Read, David B. *The Lives of the Judges of Upper Canada and Ontario, from 1791 to the Present Time*. 1888. Reprint, Holmes Beach, FL: Gaunt, 1995.

Reibel, Daniel B. "A Kind of Citadel: 1764-1805." *Michigan History* 47 (1963): 47-71.

Rich, E.E. *The Fur Trade and the Northwest to 1857*. Toronto: McClelland and Stewart, 1967.

Richter, Daniel K. *Facing East from Indian Country: A Native History of Early America*. Cambridge: Harvard University Press, 2001.

Riddell, William Renwick. *The First Judge at Detroit and His Court*. Lansing: Michigan State Bar Association, 1915.

―――. *The Legal Profession in Upper Canada in its Early Periods*. Toronto: Law Society of Upper Canada, 1916.

―――. "Criminal Courts and Law in Early (Upper) Canada." *Journal of the American Institute of Criminal Law and Criminology* 9 (1918): 173-86.

―――. "The First British Courts in Canada." *Yale Law Journal* 33 (1924): 571-79.

————. *The Life of William Dummer Powell: First Judge at Detroit and Fifth Chief Justice of Upper Canada.* Lansing: Michigan Historical Commission, 1924.

————. *The Life of John Graves Simcoe: First Lieutenant-Governor of the Province of Upper Canada, 1792-96.* Toronto: McClelland and Stewart, 1926.

————. *Michigan under British Rule: Law and Law Courts, 1760-1796.* Lansing: Michigan Historical Commission, 1926.

————. *The Bar and the Courts of the Province of Upper Canada, or Ontario.* Toronto: Macmillan, 1928.

Roberts, Julia. *In Mixed Company: Taverns and Public Life in Upper Canada.* Vancouver: University of British Columbia Press, 2009.

Rohrer, James Russell. *Keepers of the Covenant: Frontier Missions and the Decline of Congregationalism, 1774-1818.* New York: Oxford University Press, 1995.

Rosalita, Mary. *Education in Detroit Prior to 1850.* Lansing: Michigan Historical Commission, 1928.

Ross, John F. *War on the Run: The Epic Story of Robert Rogers and the Conquest of America's First Frontier.* New York: Bantam Books, 2009.

Ross, Robert Budd. *The Early Bench and Bar of Detroit from 1805 to the End of 1850.* Detroit: Richard P. Joy and Clarence M. Burton, 1907.

Rowland, Carolyn D. et al. "Was the Shawnee War Chief Blue Jacket a Caucasian?" *Ohio Journal of Science* 106 (2006): 126-29.

Russell, Nelson Vance. *The British Régime in Michigan and the Old Northwest, 1760-1796.* 1939. Reprint, Philadelphia: Porcupine Press, 1978.

Sessler, Jacob John. *Communal Pietism among Early American Moravians.* New York: H. Holt, 1933.

Sheehan, Bernard W. *Seeds of Extinction: Jeffersonian Philanthropy and the American Indian.* Chapel Hill: University of North Carolina Press, 1973.

————. "'The Famous Hair Buyer General': Henry Hamilton, George Rogers Clark, and the American Indian." *Indiana Magazine of History* 69 (March 1983): 1-28.

Sheldon, Electra Maria. *Early History of Michigan from the First Settlement to 1815.* New York: A.S. Barnes, 1856.

Shy, John. *Toward Lexington: The Role of the British Army in the Coming of the American Revolution.* Princeton: Princeton University Press, 1965.

Silver, Peter. *Our Savage Neighbors: How Indian War Transformed Early America.* New York: Norton, 2007.

Sioui, Georges E. *Huron-Wendat: The Heritage of the Circle.* Translated by Jane Brierley. East Lansing: Michigan State University Press, 1999.

Skaggs, David Curtis, ed. *The Old Northwest in the American Revolution: An Anthology.* Madison: State Historical Society of Wisconsin, 1977.

Skaggs, David Curtis, and Larry L. Nelson, eds. *The Sixty Years' War for the Great Lakes, 1754-1814.* East Lansing: Michigan State University Press, 2001.

Sleeper-Smith, Susan. "Silent Tongues, Black Robes: Potawatomi, Europeans and Settlers in the Southern Great Lakes, 1640-1850." PhD diss., University of Michigan, 1994.

———. *Indian Women and French Men: Rethinking Cultural Encounter in the Western Great Lakes.* Amherst: University of Massachusetts Press, 2001.

Sleeper-Smith, Susan, ed. "Forum: The Middle Ground Revisited." *William and Mary Quarterly* 63 (2006): 3-96.

Smucker, Isaac. "Rev. John Heckewelder, the Moravian Missionary." *The Historical Magazine* 3 (1875): 287-94.

Stark, George W. *City of Destiny, the Story of Detroit.* Detroit: Arnold-Powers, 1943.

Steckley, John L. *Words of the Huron.* Waterloo, ON: Wilfrid Laurier University Press, 2007.

Stevens, Paul Lawrence. "His Majesty's 'Savage' Allies: British Indian Policy during the Revolutionary War: The Carleton Years, 1774-1778." PhD diss., State University of New York at Buffalo, 1984.

Stevens, Wayne Edson. *The Northwest Fur Trade, 1763-1800.* Urbana: University of Illinois, 1928.

Stewart, Gordon T. *History of Canada before 1867.* 1989. Reprint, East Lansing: Michigan State University Press, 1996.

Sugden, John. *Blue Jacket: Warrior of the Shawnee.* Lincoln: University of Nebraska Press, 2000.

Swan, Isabella E. *The Deep Roots: A History of Grosse Ile, Michigan to July 6, 1876.* Grosse Ile: Swan, 1977.

Sword, Wiley. *President Washington's Indian War: The Struggle for the Old Northwest, 1790-1795.* Norman: University of Oklahoma Press, 1985.

Tanner, Helen Hornbeck. "The Glaize in 1792: A Composite Indian Community." *Ethnohistory* 25 (1978): 15-39.

Tanner, Helen Hornbeck et al., eds. *Atlas of Great Lakes Indian History*. Norman: University of Oklahoma Press, 1986.

Taylor, Alan. *The Divided Ground: Indians, Settlers and the Northern Borderland of the American Revolution*. New York: Alfred A. Knopf, 2006.

———. "The Late Loyalists: Northern Reflections of the Early American Republic." *Journal of the Early Republic* 27 (2007): 1-34.

Tentler, Leslie Woodcock. *Seasons of Grace: A History of the Catholic Archdiocese of Detroit*. Detroit: Wayne State University Press, 1990.

Todish, Timothy J., and Todd E. Harbun. *A Most Troublesome Situation: The British Military and the Pontiac Indian Uprising of 1763-1764*. Fleischmanns, NY: Purple Mountain Press, 2006.

Thrapp, Dan L. *Encyclopedia of Frontier Biography*. 4 vols. Glendale, CA: Arthur H. Clark, 1988-94.

Thwaits, Reuben Gold, ed. *France in America, 1497-1763*. Vol. 5 of *The American Nation: A History*. 28 vols. Edited by Albert Bushnell Hart. New York: Harper, 1905.

Trask, Kerry A. "To Cast Out the Devils: British Ideology and the French Canadians of the Northwest Interior, 1760-1774." *American Review of Canadian Studies* 15 (1985): 249-62.

Tucker, Glenn. *Mad Anthony Wayne and the New Nation: The Story of Washington's Front-Line General*. Harrisburg: Stackpole, 1973.

Utley, Henry Munson, Byron M. Cutcheon, and Clarence M. Burton. *Michigan as a Province, Territory, and a State, the Twenty-Sixth Member of the Federal Union*. 4 vols. New York: Publishing Society of Michigan, 1906.

Van Steen, Marcus. *Governor Simcoe and His Lady*. Toronto: Hodder and Stoughton, 1968.

Wade, Mason. *The French Canadians, 1760-1967*. 2 vols. Toronto: Macmillan, 1968.

Waller, George M. *The American Revolution in the West*. Chicago: Nelson-Hall, 1976.

White, Richard. *The Middle Ground: Indians, Empires, and Republics in the Great Lakes Region, 1650-1815*. New York: Cambridge University Press, 1991.

Widder, Agnes Haigh. "The John Askin Family Library: A Fur-Trading Family's Books." *Michigan Historical Review* 33 (Spring 2007): 27-57.

William L. Clements Library. *Pontiac's War 1763-64: An Exhibition of Source Materials in the William L. Clements Library Two Hundred Years Later.* Ann Arbor: University of Michigan Press, 1963.

Willig, Timothy D. *Restoring the Chain of Friendship: British Policy and the Indians of the Great Lakes, 1783-1815.* Lincoln: University of Nebraska Press, 2008.

Wing, Talcott Enoch. *History of Monroe County, Michigan.* New York: Munsell, 1890.

Wood, Edwin Orin. *Historic Mackinac: The Historical, Picturesque and Legendary Features of the Mackinac Country.* 2 vols. 1918. Reprint, Salem, MA: Higginson, 1999.

Woodford, Arthur M. *This is Detroit, 1701-2001.* Detroit: Wayne State University Press, 2001.

Woodford, Frank B. *Mr. Jefferson's Disciple: A Life of Justice Woodward.* East Lansing: Michigan State College Press, 1953.

————. *Gabriel Richard, Frontier Ambassador.* Detroit: Wayne State University Press, 1958.

Woodford, Frank B., and Arthur M. Woodford. *All Our Yesterdays: A Brief History of Detroit.* Detroit: Wayne State University Press, 1969.

York, Neil Longley. *Turning the World Upside Down: The War of American Independence and the Problem of Empire.* Westport, CT: Praeger, 2003.

WEB SITES

Canadiana.org. "Early Canadiana Online." http://canadiana.org/en/co/eco.

Central Michigan University Library, Mount Pleasant. "I Arrived at Detroit: A Collection of Reminiscences from Letters and Articles." Edited by Evelyn Leasher. http://clarke.cmich.edu/detroit/index.html.

Haldimand Collection. "Haldimand Collection: Contains Over 22,000 Letters and Documents, a Major Source in the Study of the Beginnings of Canada and the United States." Edited by Mario Lamone. www.haldimand-collection.ca.

Indiana University. "Glen A. Black Laboratory of Archaeology." Edited by Glen A. Black. www.gbl.indiana.edu.

Ohio History Central. "Ohio History Central: An Online Encyclopedia of Ohio History." www.ohiohistorycentral.org.

Society of Colonial Wars in the State of Illinois. "Index to the George Rogers Clark Papers at the Virginia State Library and Archives." Edited by Richard Eugene Willson and Donald E. Gradeless. http://my.execpc.com/~sril/grclark.

Solon.org. "The Solon Law Archive." Edited by William F. Maton. www.solon.org.

Swayze, David. "The Great Lakes Shipwreck File: Total Losses of Great Lakes Ships, 1679-2001." http://greatlakeshistory.homestead.com/temp.html.

University of Toronto. "Dictionary of Canadian Biography Online." www.biographi.ca.

Yale Law School. "The Avalon Project: Documents in Law, History, and Diplomacy." http://avalon.law.yale.edu.